A GEORGE ORWELL
COMPANION

Other books by J. R. Hammond

H. G. WELLS: AN ANNOTATED BIBLIOGRAPHY OF HIS WORKS
AN H. G. WELLS COMPANION
H. G. WELLS: INTERVIEWS AND RECOLLECTIONS (*editor*)
AN EDGAR ALLAN POE COMPANION
A ROBERT LOUIS STEVENSON COMPANION

———————

Other Macmillan Literary Companions

A JANE AUSTEN COMPANION	*F. B. Pinion*
A BRONTË COMPANION	*F. B. Pinion*
A COLERIDGE COMPANION	*John Spencer Hill*
A DICKENS COMPANION	*Norman Page*
A GEORGE ELIOT COMPANION	*F. B. Pinion*
A HARDY COMPANION	*F. B. Pinion*
A KIPLING COMPANION	*Norman Page*
A D. H. LAWRENCE COMPANION	*F. B. Pinion*
A WORDSWORTH COMPANION	*F. B. Pinion*

Further titles in preparation

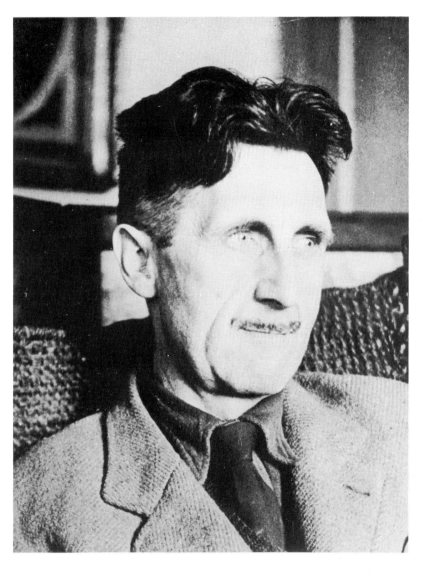

George Orwell, *circa* 1945, at the height of his fame

A GEORGE ORWELL COMPANION

A guide to the novels,
documentaries and essays

J. R. HAMMOND

MACMILLAN PRESS
LONDON   82

First Edition 1982
Reprinted 1984

Published by
THE MACMILLAN PRESS LTD
London and Basingstoke
Companies and representatives
throughout the world

ISBN 0 333 28668 5

Typeset in Great Britain by
PREFACE LTD
Salisbury, Wiltshire

Printed in Hong Kong

He was a tall, lean, scraggy man, a Public House character, with a special gleam in his eye, and a home-made way of arguing from simple premisses, which could sometimes lead him to radiant common sense, sometimes to crankiness.

STEPHEN SPENDER

He had the gift, he had the courage, he had the persistence to go on in spite of failure, sickness, poverty, and opposition, until he became an acknowledged master of English prose.

RUTH PITTER

I was a stage rebel, Orwell a true one.

CYRIL CONNOLLY

Contents

List of Plates

For the provision of illustrations, and permission to reproduce them, grateful acknowledgements are made to: Vernon Richards (frontispiece); Orwell Archive and F. de France (1); Mrs Mabel Fierz (2); Hampstead and Highgate Express (3); British Broadcasting Corporation (4, 5 and 7); BBC Hulton Picture Library (6).

Preface

George Orwell is now acknowledged as one of the most significant literary figures of the twentieth century. As novelist, essayist,
and author of a number of outstanding works of reportage he has
exercised an influence on modern thought which is increasingly
being recognised. Though he died at the age of forty-six he
achieved world-wide fame during his lifetime and since his death
his stature as a writer of prose has grown immeasurably. Today
he belongs to that select company of writers – including Lawrence, Joyce and Kafka – who have made a permanent contribution to modern literature.

The present *Companion* aims to be a guide to the whole range of
his work – novels, documentaries and essays – and to enable the
reader to study and enjoy Orwell with a keener application. I am
indebted in particular to the following critical works: *George
Orwell: A Life* by Bernard Crick, *The Crystal Spirit* by George
Woodcock and *The Unknown Orwell* by Peter Stansky and
William Abrahams. Whilst I have found these works invaluable
as sources of reference and stimulus I have followed my own
judgement in appraising and interpreting Orwell's writings; I
trust that I have succeeded in the pages which follow in communicating to the reader something of my own admiration for
Orwell as both man and writer and my sense of his importance
as a seminal figure in twentieth-century ideas.

As work on the *Companion* has proceeded I have become more
and more impressed both with the complexity of his personality
and the breadth of his achievement. The popular image of him
as the radical author of *Animal Farm* and *Nineteen Eighty-Four*
conceals a much more complex reality: that of a man divided
against himself, a writer who, until 1936, was uncertain of his
basic convictions or role in life and whose moods fluctuated

throughout his career between an engaging happiness and a profound pessimism. This ambiguity at the heart of his make-up will be explored more fully in the succeeding chapters.

The extracts from the works of George Orwell are reproduced by permission of A. M. Heath & Company, the agents for the Orwell Estate. I am indebted to the following publishers for permission to quote copyright material: Hutchinson General Books for the passage from *1985* by Anthony Burgess; Constable & Company for the extract from *The Unknown Orwell* by Peter Stansky and William Abrahams. The quotation from *Tono-Bungay* is reprinted by permission of A. P. Watt Ltd on behalf of the Estate of H. G. Wells. Acknowledgement is made to David Higham Associates for permission to quote an extract from *Four Absentees* by Rayner Heppenstall, published by Barrie & Rockliff.

I wish to express my thanks to the staff of the Orwell Archive, University College Library, and in particular to the Senior Library Assistant, Mr John Allen, for his courtesy and helpfulness. My thanks are also due to Mrs Carol Staves for typing the manuscript with such care, and to Miss Julia Tame and Mr Timothy Fox, on behalf of the publishers, for their encouragement and help at all times.

J. R. HAMMOND

Part I

The Making of George Orwell

In the churchyard of the village of Sutton Courtenay, Oxford-shire, there lies a simple headstone placed near the end of an avenue of yews. Inscribed on the stone are the words:

Here Lies
Eric Arthur Blair
Born June 25th 1903
Died January 21st 1950

There is no indication that this marks the grave of an important literary figure, no clue as to the identity or achievements of Eric Arthur Blair. Many visitors to the churchyard must pass it by unaware that the spot marks the resting place of one of the major twentieth-century English novelists, an essayist of distinction and the author of *Animal Farm* and *Nineteen Eighty-Four*. For the man who is buried in this peaceful spot fashioned a distinctive style of prose writing which carried his name and reputation far beyond the confines of the English-speaking world and earned for his books a readership of millions. He was successively a tramp, a schoolmaster, a village-shopkeeper, a soldier, a radio producer and a sergeant in the Home Guard. He became in the forty-six years of his life a political writer of uncommon ability, a pamphleteer in the tradition of Cobbett and Defoe and an out-spoken commentator on the social and political issues of his time. He was also a man who was 'essentially quixotic',[1] a man who disliked twentieth-century technology and wrote with sim-ple feeling on gardening, wild life and the passing of the seasons. 'The planting of a tree,' he wrote in a characteristic essay, 'especially one of the long-living hardwood trees, is a gift which you can make to posterity at almost no cost and with almost no trouble, and if the tree takes root it will far outlive the visible effect of any of your other actions, good or evil.'[2] This sentence, which might almost serve as his epitaph, so redolent is it of his style and attitude of mind, was the work of a man who wrote under the pseudonym George Orwell: a writer who in his lifetime achieved world-wide fame as the author of satires and who, since his death, has come to be acknowledged as one of the most significant and influential novelists of our times.

How did Eric Blair, an unknown ex-Etonian and teacher in an impoverished private school, become George Orwell, a respected literary figure and author of fables which have been compared with those of Swift? How and why did Blair achieve the transformation from a comfortable, conventional Anglo-Indian background to become one of the most incisive radical journalists of modern times? To answer these questions we will need to trace the life and background of this complex figure and disentangle the forces which helped to shape his mind and outlook.

*   *   *   *   *

Eric Arthur Blair was born at Motihari in Bengal on 25 June 1903. His father, Richard Walmesley Blair, was an official in the Opium Department of the Government of India, and served in that Department from the age of eighteen (1875) until his retirement from the service in 1912. At the age of thirty-nine Richard Blair had married Miss Ida Mabel Limouzin, the daughter of a French father and an English mother, who had lived from an early age in Burma where the Limouzins had extensive business interests. The first child of the marriage was a daughter, Marjorie, born in 1898; then came Eric Arthur; and lastly another daughter, Avril, born in 1908.

This marriage was an unusual one in that it represented a union between two oddly contrasting personalities and attitudes. Richard Blair had been one of twelve children, with no background of wealth or public school; all his life had been spent in humdrum administrative appointments in the colonial service. He embodied many English characteristics which were typical of his class and time: stolidity, perseverance, unimaginitiveness, loyalty and genteelism. He was throughout his life a sincere, well-meaning, hard-working English gentleman who yet displayed little originality or enterprise. Ida Blair was of a very different mould. Eighteen years younger than her husband, all the evidence suggests that she was a much less conventional figure, widely read, imaginative and vivacious. She also possessed qualities of adaptability and resilience which did much to weld the marriage together and to provide a harmonious environment in which to bring up her family.

When Eric was one year old he was brought to England by his mother, her husband remaining behind in Burma to complete his term of service. The family settled at Henley-on-Thames, Oxfordshire, renting an unpretentious house on the Western Road, 'Nutshell'. Henley-on-Thames (and its neighbouring village, Shiplake) was to be the Blair's home from 1904 until 1917: thus, this quiet, respectable Edwardian backwater was Eric's background during the most formative years of his life. At the age of five his mother enrolled him as a day boy in an Anglican convent school, Sunnylands, where his sister Marjorie was also a pupil. Here he remained until he was eight. He seems to have been an intelligent pupil, quick to learn and taking delight in his boyhood reading. During these early school years he was an avid reader, devouring with enthusiasm *Tom Sawyer*, *Coral Island* and *Gulliver's Travels* and also reading widely among Marjorie's books including *Rebecca of Sunnybrook Farm*. Henley and its surrounding countryside made a deep impression upon him, for many years later he drew on his childhood memories of the district in his idyllic description of Lower Binfield in the novel *Coming Up For Air*.

In September 1911, at the impressionable age of eight, he became a pupil at St Cyprian's, a private preparatory boarding school at Eastbourne. His parents, in particular his mother, were determined that he should eventually be awarded a place at one of the great public schools; St Cyprian's had been recommended to them as an establishment with an impressive record of equipping boys for scholarships at Eton and Harrow. Moreover the school made it a practice to accept at reduced fees a small number of pupils of exceptional promise, provided it could be demonstrated that their parents were of limited means. Mr and Mrs Blair, realising that their sole income in the years ahead would be Mr Blair's pension, successfully applied on Eric's behalf for a scholarship at half fees. Eric himself, however, was not advised of this fact at the time: when he did learn of it some years later (he was told by the headmaster) it came to him as a surprise and a humiliation.

The school seems to have been no better and no worse than many other private schools of the time. Cyril Connolly, Cecil Beaton and Gavin Maxwell were also pupils there and have published their reminiscences. The headmaster–proprietor and his wife, Mr and Mrs Vaughan Wilkes, ran St Cyprian's on autocratic lines which were entirely characteristic by the standards of Edwardian England. The emphasis was upon Latin, French, Greek, History, English and Arithmetic; a spirit of emulation was encouraged by a system of weekly placings in all the formal subjects. The values inculcated, both formally and by implication, were those of the English public school tradition: the development of 'character', a spirit of competition, a rigid adherence to discipline, and a total acceptance of the prevailing moral code. Any breach of accepted standards of behaviour – for example, bed wetting – was punishable by the cane. When Eric had been at the school for a few days he found to his horror that he had wet the bed, and did so repeatedly for several nights. This was punished by a savage caning which he never forgave; the disgust and humiliation of this episode rankled in his memory for the remainder of his life. He harboured many other bitter memories: the insipid food, the icy cold water in the swimming pool, the unimaginative teaching, the preferential treatment accorded to boys from wealthy families. Yet there were also happier memories: rambles through the Sussex countryside, wandering round the grounds on summer evenings, cricket, reading and hobbies.

Eric remained at St Cyprian's until December 1916. Throughout that time the school was the focal point of his life, the most important single influence of his boyhood years. He travelled home for the holidays but otherwise St Cyprian's was for five crucial years the centre of his universe. It is difficult to assess the impact this experience had on the young Eric Blair since there are sharp disparities between the contemporary evidence and his own recollections written some thirty years later in the essay 'Such, Such Were the Joys'. In this essay the experience is presented as one of almost unrelieved unhappiness; the school is depicted as an autocratic institution in which sadism, sexual repression and rote learning were rife and where the predominant values and atmosphere were those of Dotheboys Hall in *Nicholas Nickleby*. The evidence of his school friends and the letters he wrote to his mother at the time suggest a rather different picture: the impression one derives from these sources is of a reasonably happy and entirely typical schooling crowded with the enthusiasms of a normal, healthy boy. His letters home are filled with his interests: stamp collecting, football, cigarette cards, pet animals and insects, and his weekly placings in arithmetic, history and languages. It seems safe to assert that the truth lies nearer to that suggested by contemporary testimony than to the picture presented in 'Such, Such Were the Joys'. Orwell's essay (published in 1952 but probably written at least a decade earlier) is a highly selective document: he has deliberately concentrated on the unhappy aspects of the school for polemical effect. In doing so he distorts the truth by presenting an incomplete version of it. This is not to say that his account is exaggerated or fundamentally untrue, but simply that it needs to be treated with caution; his school years contained far more happiness and interest for him than the mature Orwell was willing to admit. There were, in particular, three aspects of these years which were of decisive importance in shaping his personality – his reading, his early literary efforts, and his friendships.

Blair had been a voracious reader long before enrolling at St Cyprian's. At school his reading intensified; the principal memory of those who knew him during these years is of a quiet, bookish, self-contained boy, passionately interested in literature and in curious facts gleaned from his books; even the redoubtable Mrs Vaughan Wilkes had to admit that 'he was a very bright little boy'.[3] Looking back on his school years thirty years later he confessed that one of his brightest recollections was of 'the joy of waking early on summer mornings and getting in an hour's undisturbed reading (Ian Hay, Thackeray, Kipling and H. G. Wells were the favourite authors of my boyhood)'.[4] The list of books which he read between the age of eight and thirteen is impressive and reveals a precocity unusual for one of his background. During these years he read *Vanity Fair*, Wells's *The Country of the Blind* and *A Modern Utopia*, the short stories of Poe and Kipling, and the stories of Conan Doyle, G. K. Chesterton and E. W. Hornung. He was also reading widely in Swift, Dickens, Shakespeare and Charles Reade and dipping into modern works such as Compton Mackenzie's *Sinister Street*. (The latter was

frowned on and his copy was confiscated by the headmaster.)
This extensive reading widened his vocabulary and he became
adept at pencil and paper games which involved a knowledge of
words; this in turn stimulated his interest in writing, particularly
the composition of poetry.

His first piece of work to be published was a patriotic poem,
'Awake! Young Men of England', which was printed in the
Henley and South Oxfordshire Standard on 2 October 1914. He
showed a copy of this to the headmaster's wife who was sufficiently impressed with it to request him to read it aloud to
the assembled school. It is a piece of schoolboy jingoism, concluding with the arresting lines:

> Awake! oh you young men of England,
> For if, when your Country's in need,
> You do not enlist by the thousand,
> You truly are cowards indeed.

The poem is of no literary merit but is of interest if only as an
indication of the impact of the First World War on his consciousness. The war dominated much of his school years; both at
St Cyprian's and at Eton mounting lists of dead and wounded
were read out at morning assembly; former pupils only a few
years older than he were serving in France. Gradually there
dawned on him an awareness that his generation had missed a
traumatic experience of immense significance. It was not until he
had served in the trenches of the Spanish Civil War twenty years
later that he felt he had in some measure exculpated his sense of
guilt at having been too young to serve his country.

A more promising effort was his poem 'Kitchener', published
in the same newspaper on 21 July 1916:

> No stone is set to mark his nation's loss,
> No stately tomb enshrines his noble breast
> Not e'en the tribute of a wooden cross
> Can mark this hero's rest.

> He needs them not, his name ungarnished stands,
> Remindful of the mighty deeds he worked,
> Footprints of one, upon time's changeful sands,
> Who n'er his duty shirked.

Who follows in his steps no danger shuns,
Nor stoops to conquer by a shameful deed,
An honest and unselfish race he runs,
From fear and malice freed.

The significance of these compositions is that they provide the earliest published evidence of his interest in literary effort. In his essay 'Why I Write' he stated: 'From a very early age, perhaps the age of five or six, I knew that when I grew up I should be a writer'. It is known that throughout his preparatory school years he was writing verse, playlets and short stories, some of which were shown to Mrs Vaughan Wilkes and preserved for posterity in her voluminous scrapbooks. Whilst little of this material shows evidence of literary promise it does reveal a growing interest in words and in writing. From the age of eight onwards he was trying his hand at both prose and verse. His literary ambitions, however, were only confided to his very closest friends.

In the autumn of 1914 a new boy entered the school and entered the same class as Eric. This boy, Cyril Connolly, quickly befriended him and the two soon became inseparable companions. They were drawn together by a community of interests and attitudes; they shared a love of reading, an interest in writing, and a cynical, critical attitude towards the school and all it stood for. They also complemented each other – whereas Connolly was romantic, Blair was sceptical; where Connolly's background was wealthy, Blair's was middle class; where Connolly was open, Blair was reticent. They liked one another with an affection which was to outlast their school years and continue throughout their lives. They lent each other books, commented on one another's poetry, and pooled their intellectual and imaginative stock. This was to be the only close friendship Blair made at St Cyprian's and it did much to make the harsh regime more tolerable for him. Now at last he had an ally in whom he could confide. Almost simultaneously Eric was making new friends at home. During the school holidays in the summer of 1914 he had befriended the Buddicom family, two sisters and a brother who lived close to his parents' home at Shiplake. These children, Jacintha (aged 13), Guinever (11) and Prosper (10) became firm friends and continued to share their holidays with him until his departure for Burma in 1922. After his death Jacintha Buddicom published her reminiscences of him in a charming and fascinating memoir, *Eric and Us*.[5] Among the wealth of interesting detail is further confirmation of his ambition to become a writer:

> With Prosper and Guiny, Eric was mostly involved in outdoor or sporting pursuits: with me, he *talked*. We both had independent minds with many ideas in common, and we shared a love for books . . . He was always giving me books, lending me books, borrowing or exchanging books with me. He said that reading was good preparation for writing: *any* book could teach you something, if only how not to write one. Of course, Eric was always going to write: not merely as an author, always a FAMOUS AUTHOR, in capitals.[6]

During those long summer holidays Eric and the Buddicom children played games together (pencil and paper games, card games and snakes and ladders were favourite pastimes), shared their hobbies and interests, experimented with chemistry, went fishing, walking and cycling. Eric also stayed with the Buddicoms on their holidays, including a number of memorable summers spent on a country estate at Ticklerton in Shropshire. Here the four of them explored the countryside together, shot rabbits and fished for perch. Continually he was storing up memories to be drawn upon years later in writing *Coming Up For Air*.

During his last two years at St Cyprian's (1915–16) Eric worked extremely hard in order to attain the necessary standard for admission to Eton. He also applied for a scholarship to Wellington College, the army school, as a fall-back position in case he failed to enter Eton. In the event, he was successful in attaining an Eton scholarship but did not achieve a sufficiently high standard to ensure him a place in the election of autumn 1916. (An 'election' is the name given to a group of ten to thirteen scholars who are admitted at any one time.) Whilst waiting for a place to become vacant, therefore, he spent nine weeks of the first term of 1917 at Wellington: an experience he described later as 'perfectly bloody'.[7] He found the regimentation and lack of privacy at Wellington abhorrent and was greatly relieved when he could enter Eton as a King's Scholar in May 1917, one month before his fourteenth birthday.

In an essay written in 1948, 'Forever Eton',[8] Orwell singled out as the outstanding merit of the school its 'tolerant and civilised atmosphere which gives each boy a fair chance of developing his individuality'. It is interesting that the adjectives he chose to describe the special atmosphere of Eton were 'tolerant' and 'civilised'; certainly the school must have made the completest contrast to St Cyprian's. At Eton he was at liberty to develop his interests, talents and friendships in a far freer atmosphere than had been possible at Eastbourne. Moreover the school had the great advantage in his eyes of providing him with a modicum of privacy and of removing from him the intense competitive pressures which had bedevilled his life at his former school.

At Eton he was a King's Scholar; that is to say, he was one of a minority, no more than seventy in number, housed in the oldest buildings of the school. Here he had a 'room' of his own, or at least a wooden stall which gave a semblance of seclusion. The other boys at the school, the 'Oppidans' (some 900 pupils) lived in dormitories in houses scattered around the town of Eton. A King's Scholar, or Colleger, was therefore a member of a privileged élite who tended to look down on the Oppidans as philistines; the Oppidans for their part looked down on the Collegers as 'swots' and prigs. Blair seems to have settled happily into this hierarchical, esoteric world and the years he spent at Eton (1917–21) were for him years of steady mental and emotional growth unencumbered by the psychological traumas he had known at St Cyprian's. Here he not only continued his friendship with Cyril Connolly – who came on from St Cyprian's in 1918 – but made several new friendships, including Denys King-Farlow and Steven Runciman. During his four-and-a-half Eton years he continued the voracious reading which was now an established pattern with him, and also continued to try his hand at the writing of poetry and short stories. To these years belong his discovery of such authors as Samuel Butler, Laurence Sterne, Bernard Shaw and Richard Garnett. He was also reading discursively in Wells and Dickens and beginning a lifelong enthusiasm for what he termed 'good bad books'[9] including *Dracula* by Bram Stoker and Guy Boothby's *Dr. Nikola*. He wrote verse and stories for two of the College periodicals with which he was closely associated, *The Election Times*, of which he was 'business manager', and *College Days*, which he and King-Farlow jointly edited. His contributions, which were usually unsigned, included poetry, short stories, parodies and humorous articles.

For most of his time at Eton Blair was a Classics scholar,

studying Latin, Greek, French, English, Mathematics, Science and Divinity. His weakest subjects were science and mathematics; those he excelled at were French and Classics (predominantly a study of Homer, Lucretius, Euripides and Horace). This statement must be qualified by emphasising that he 'excelled' in these only by comparison with his lack-lustre performance in the other subjects. Academically it cannot be claimed that he distinguished himself at Eton. He seems to have made up his mind to 'rest on his oars' during these years, if only as a reaction from the non-stop cramming he had been compelled to undergo at Eastbourne. On the whole, then, he tended to take life easily, reserving his energies for non-academic activities (including the famous Wall Game, in which he distinguished himself on a number of occasions) and his early efforts at writing. If the Eton years were not notable for intellectual attainment they made a permanent mark upon him in other directions. The Eric Blair who left the College at the end of 1921 was a much more self-assured and integrated personality than the Eric Blair who had entered it in 1917. He possessed not only an Etonian accent but a certain authority and self-possession which never left him during the remainder of his life. His wide reading – which included not only the great figures of English literature but such seminal works as Jack London's *The People of the Abyss* – had enlarged his horizons and given him an understanding and curiosity beyond his years. Above all, these had been years not only of reading and writing but of thought, discussion, questioning and argument. He had learned to sharpen his ideas in the College Debating Society and long talks with his companions; he had developed a taste for polemical discussion and statement. Though he had gained much from the experience (and it is interesting to note that though in later life he wrote bitterly of St Cyprian's he could never bring himself to write critically of Eton) he was still untried. When, in the summer of 1921, the time had come for him to make a decision concerning his future he had no definite proposal to suggest to his parents. One thing he was quite clear about was that he had no desire to proceed to a university education.

What then was he to do? There was a family conference about the problem, or, more likely, a series of family discussions extending over several weeks. Gradually the suggestion emerged that the Indian Civil Service, and in particular the Indian

Imperial Police, would be an appropriate career. The proposal had the weight of family tradition behind it: Eric's grandfather had served in India, his father had served there for many years, and his mother's family were teak merchants in Burma. Moreover, the idea commended itself to his parents since a career in the Imperial Police was eminently respectable and secure, culminating in retirement on a guaranteed pension. Eric fell in with the proposal readily enough but for very different reasons. For years he had entertained a romantic notion of going out East in the service of the empire, though this seems to have been based on his boyhood reading of Kipling rather than on an understanding of the practical realities involved. As he had been born in India he undoubtedly felt a sense of emotional kinship with that vast continent; in a sense he belonged there. And after ten years of schooling the prospect of cutting loose altogether from the academic world must have had a deep appeal for him. So he acquiesced in his parents' wishes and began the six months private cramming which was necessary before he could sit the India Office examinations in the summer of 1922. He passed the examination with 8463 marks out of a possible 12 400 – a creditable though not an outstanding performance; his highest marks were in Latin and Greek, his lowest in History – and set sail for Rangoon in October 1922. After nine months initial training at the Police Training School at Mandalay, studying law, languages, accountancy and police procedure, he was sent out to his first posting and the beginning of an ambivalent relationship with Burma which was to mark him for life.

His postings during the succeeding five years took him to widely differing regions of Burma. These included Myaungmya, a small town in the Irrawaddy Delta; Twante, further east in the Delta; Syriam, a dreary town (Orwell's word for it would have been 'beastly') surrounded by a desolate waste; Insein, a more pleasant town situated ten miles north of Rangoon; Moulmein, the third largest city in Burma; and finally Katha, a small settlement north of Mandalay. He thus had an opportunity of seeing Burma in all its moods, ranging from the featureless, swampy, mosquito-infested Delta to the comparative civilisation of Moulmein and the pleasing, temperate climate of Katha. His duties were as varied as the locations in which he served. As a police officer he was responsible for supervising stores of ammunition and equipment, training locally-recruited constables, organising night patrols, overseeing local police stations, supervising the investigation of minor crimes and deputising for his superior officers in their absence. He was frequently on tour for weeks at a time, visiting villages, inspecting stations and consulting with village headmen on judicial matters. It was an experience for which neither his Eton education nor his training at Mandalay had equipped him. Now for the first time in his life he was compelled to face demanding responsibilities, to take on-the-spot decisions and supervise the work of men older than himself. It must have been a daunting experience, particularly during the first few months when he was thrust without adequate preparation into uncongenial postings with difficult superiors who resented his Etonian background and bland manner.

There can be little question that these years in Burma made a permanent impression on the youthful Blair. The scenery made such an indelible mark on his memory that long afterwards he wrote 'The landscapes of Burma, which, when I was among them, so appalled me as to assume the qualities of nightmare, afterwards stayed so hauntingly in my mind that I was obliged to write a novel about them to get rid of them.'[10] His health was also ineradicably marred by the tropical climate: the steamy, damp atmosphere of the Delta with its impure water and constant danger of infection seems to have marked the onset of the tubercular lung ailment which dogged him for the remainder of his life. Above all, these were years of active reading and reflection which provided him with opportunities to think through his attitudes to life and literature. Despite his multifarious duties he had abundant time on his lonely sojourns to read, think and digest his experiences; away from England and English values he was free for the first time to examine himself from the outside. He carried a copy of the *Notebooks* of Samuel Butler on all his journeyings, and was also delving into the works of Tolstoy, Poe, D. H. Lawrence and Somerset Maugham. Little is known of his literary work during this time since only fragments of verse survive: two cynical love poems, 'The Lesser Evil' and 'Romance', and a tirade against imperialism beginning

> When the Franks have lost their sway
> And their soldiers are slain or fled,
> When the ravisher has his way
> And the slayer's sword is red[11]

In the absence of contemporary testimony one can only make assumptions regarding the real state of his mind during this period of his life. It seems clear that there gradually dawned upon him a profound sense of disillusionment with imperialism and with his own role within it, developing at last into a gnawing distaste for British dominion in India and elsewhere. Long afterwards he wrote: 'I gave it up partly because the climate had ruined my health, partly because I already had vague ideas of writing books, but mainly because I could not go on any longer serving an imperialism which I had come to regard as very largely a racket.'[12] Even allowing for a mature writer seeking with hindsight to impose an orderly pattern on his reasons for leaving Burma this explanation cannot be far from the truth. Though it is unlikely that Blair at the age of twenty-four had analysed his feelings or thought through the nature of imperialism in a systematic way there is no doubting his repugnance for the British presence. He had had five years in which to think out his role in life and his attitudes towards 'the white man's burden' and had come to loathe colonial rule and all that it implied: when he came to write about it in *Burmese Days* he was expressing the pent up resentment and bitterness of years of reflection. His own actions speak clearly enough for his emotions. In July 1927 he applied for leave, ostensibly on medical grounds, but in reality he seems to have determined to resign permanently from imperial service. He was granted five months leave, and it was whilst in England during this period that he submitted his formal resignation. The anger and puzzlement of his parents on hearing the news may well be imagined. From their point of view Eric was abandoning a secure career in order to pursue an uncertain, chimerical ambition of becoming a writer. Eric, however, was not to be deflected from the course on which he had embarked and, after staying with his family for some weeks (now living in retirement at Southwold on the Suffolk coast) he left for London to begin his writing career in earnest.

The Europe to which he had returned from Burma was in a state of unrest and confusion. The Trades Union Act in Britain had declared strikes and lock-outs illegal (July 1927); the German economy had collapsed in May of that year; an international conference on naval disarmament had failed to reach agreement; a young man named Adolf Hitler published the second volume of his *Mein Kampf*. Unaware that the world was about to slide into a long period of economic depression, Blair dedicated himself single-mindedly to the task of finding his niche as a writer.

During the autumn and winter of 1927–8 he lived in a cheap, austere room in a house at 10 Portobello Road, Notting Hill, next door to the poet Ruth Pitter. Here he applied himself assiduously to the composition of poems, sketches and short stories. Almost none of this material survives but it is clear from the testimony of Ruth Pitter, to whom he showed some of his work, that he was still a tiro who had yet to learn the basic techniques of his craft: his writings of this period were crude, florid and amateurish. It says much for his tenacity that although he had no success whatever with his literary efforts and must have found the experience disheartening – he had embarked on the venture with high hopes – he persevered with his writing throughout that cold winter, determined not to abandon it until his efforts met with success. In the autumn of 1927, inspired partly by the example of *The People of the Abyss* and partly by a desire 'to find some way of getting out of the respectable world altogether',[13] he went to the East End of London on the first of the expeditions among vagrants which were to occupy his time and imagination increasingly during the following five years. These expeditions culminated, after many drafts and revisions, in the book published in 1933 under the title *Down and Out in Paris and London*. In the spring of 1928 he decided to move to Paris, apparently because he had convinced himself that it was possible to live cheaper there than in London. Since he was earning no income from his writing and was living on the savings from his Burma years it was essential for him to live as frugally as possible, for he was determined to support himself and not be a burden on his parents. He lived in a cheap room in a working-class district of Paris until the end of 1929, living a simple, solitary existence and applying all his energies to writing. During this time he wrote two complete novels (one of which was possibly the first draft of the book which later became *Burmese Days*) and a number of short stories. None of this material was published. He persevered, however, deriving some encouragement from the publication of one or two articles in *Monde* and *Progrès Civique*. Although he had the satisfaction of seeing his work in print, over his own name 'E. A. Blair', his journalistic pieces were not well paid and in the late autumn of 1929 his money ran out completely. Too proud to borrow money from his parents or from his aunt Nellie Limouzin, who was living in Paris at the time, he found employment as a dishwasher at a luxury hotel, a post he held for some ten weeks. He returned to England in December 1929 and at once rejoined his mother and father at Southwold. He had little to show for his eighteen months in Paris beyond much chastening experience. There was no sign of any weakening in his resolve to become a writer. On the contrary, he was more determined than ever to pursue his chosen career.

From this point until October 1930 he was working on successive drafts of *Down and Out in Paris and London*, using his parents' home as a base but also staying for long periods with his sister and her family in Leeds. Simultaneously with the writing he was continuing his descents among the tramps of London and Kent, changing his clothes at the homes of friends and re-emerging into civilisation after expeditions of days or even weeks at a time. From March 1930 onwards he began to contribute regularly to *Adelphi*, writing book reviews, poetry and articles in an unbroken series which continued until August 1935. The editor of *Adelphi*, Richard Rees, and its literary editor, Max Plowman, befriended him and gave him much encouragement during these crucial years; Rees was later to write a fine critical study of him, *George Orwell: Fugitive from the Camp of Victory*. In April 1932, after *Down and Out* had been rejected by two leading London publishers, he realised he would have to find some means of supporting himself and took up a teaching post at The Hawthorns, a small private school at Hayes, Middlesex. It was here in the summer of 1932 that he heard from his literary agent, Leonard Moore, that Victor Gollancz was interested in publishing *Down and Out*, subject to the deletion of swear words and other minor amendments. The book was finally published in January 1933, not under his own name – which he had used for all his work hitherto and which he continued to use for his book reviews – but under the pseudonym 'George Orwell'.

It is worth pausing at this juncture to examine the significance of Blair's assumption of a pen-name, since the name itself and his adoption of it have been the subject of much critical speculation. The pseudonym was chosen with surprising casualness. In

November 1932, when *Down and Out* was already in proof, the name had still not been chosen. He wrote diffidently to his agent:

> As to a pseudonym, a name I always use when tramping etc. is P. S. Burton, but if you don't think this sounds a probable kind of name, what about
>
> Kenneth Miles,
> George Orwell,
> H. Lewis Allways.
>
> I rather favour George Orwell.[14]

He had first mooted the idea of using a pen-name a few months previously, writing with equal diffidence to Moore: 'I think if it is all the same to everybody I would prefer the book to be published pseudonymously. I have no reputation that is lost by doing this and if the book has any kind of success I can always use the same pseudonym again.'[15] Too much should not be read into the choice of the name itself. It is true that 'George' has an Englishness about it, suggesting plain speaking and common-sense, and that 'Orwell' was the name of a river he was fond of, but it has to be remembered that the name was selected by Gollancz: the publisher might equally well have chosen 'Kenneth Miles' or 'H. Lewis Allways'. What mattered to Blair was not the name as such but the second self that the name suggested and made possible; by adopting a pseudonym he symbolically turned his back on his previous existence and assumed a new persona.

It is clear that he disliked his own name 'Eric'. Writing to Rayner Heppenstall in 1940[16] he acidly observed apropos Rayner's new baby:

> ... don't afflict the poor little brat with a Celtic sort of name that nobody knows how to spell. She'll grow up psychic or something. People always grow up like their names. It took me nearly thirty years to work off the effects of being called Eric.

He disliked the name not only because he assumed it was Scottish in origin and he had a lifelong antipathy to Scottish names and authors, but also because it reminded him of the hero of *Eric, or Little by Little* by Frederic W. Farrar, a sentimental novel which he loathed. The opening paragraph of this novel might almost be taken to be a description of Eric as a schoolboy:

> Eric Williams was now 12 years old. His father was a civilian in India, and was returning on furlough to England, after a long absence. Eric had been born in India, but had been sent to England by his parents at an early age, in charge of a lady friend of his mother.

Whether he recognised an echo of himself in this eponymous hero or not, the fact remains that he detested the name and its genteel associations. The adoption of a *nom de plume* enabled him to sever himself from these associations and to assume a completely different identity, that of a writer. It also enabled him to maintain a distinction between his private and his literary life. In private he was still Eric Blair, a schoolmaster in a depressing suburban milieu. In public he was the author George Orwell, with one book already published and a second, *Burmese Days*, well on the way to completion. When, towards the end of his life, Anthony Powell asked him if he had ever considered legally adopting his pen-name, he replied: 'Well, I have, but then, of course, I'd have to *write* under another name if I did.'[17]

The distinction between the two aspects of his life, then, was important to him. (In practice it was not always possible to maintain a neat separation between the two. Friends who had known him prior to 1933 continued to call him 'Eric'; many who knew him only after his fame called him 'George'.) The point of real importance to any understanding of Orwell as a man and as a writer is this: that what had been adopted at first simply as a pen-name and with no deeper significance gradually became an actual second identity, a name synonymous with honesty, forthrightness and a militant radical attitude. The change did not happen quickly; for two or three years Blair eased himself into his new identity, writing, talking, and even dressing to conform to his new image. By 1936 the transformation was complete.

But already at the beginning of 1933 a new chapter was beginning in his life. The assumption of the name George Orwell meant that he could, symbolically and actually, sever himself from his past. St Cyprian's, Eton and Burma now belonged to a phase of his life he regarded as alien. He rejected that way of life

and all that it represented. He wanted passionately to opt out of
the life of a gentleman and assume instead the mantle of a writer.

Orwell continued teaching at The Hawthorns until September
1933. His intense dislike of Hayes is vividly expressed in a letter
he wrote to Eleanor Jaques, whose parents were neighbours of
his mother and father at Southwold:

> The most disagreeable thing here is not the job itself (it is a
> day-school, thank God, so I have nothing to do with the brats
> out of school hours) but Hayes itself, which is one of the most
> godforsaken places I have ever struck. The population seems
> to be entirely made up of clerks who frequent tin-roofed
> chapels on Sundays & for the rest bolt themselves within
> doors.[18]

During the evenings and school holidays he worked fitfully on
Burmese Days, his moods alternating between enthusiasm and the
self-doubt which was so characteristic of him. In September of
that year he transferred to Frays College, Uxbridge, a private
school for boys and girls. Although he seems to have been happier here than at The Hawthorns the work left him with little
free time to devote to his writing. By December, however, he had
completed the final version of *Burmese Days* but then fell seriously
ill with pneumonia. On recovering from this illness he decided to
abandon teaching and devote himself wholly to writing.

From January–October 1934 he lived with his parents at
Southwold, working steadily on *A Clergyman's Daughter*. During
that summer he resolved to move to London as soon as the novel
was completed. He confided to a friend:

> I am going up to town as soon as I have finished the book I am
> doing, which should be at the end of October. I haven't settled
> yet where I am going to stay, but somewhere in the slums for
> choice.[19]

In fact the address he chose was not 'in the slums' but at Hampstead, first at 3 Warwick Mansions, Pond Street, and later at 77
Parliament Hill. This was an area of London – bohemian, artis-

tic and bracing – which he loved. Here, from October 1934 to January 1936 he worked as a part-time assistant at a secondhand bookshop, Booklovers' Corner, situated on the South End Road. Since he was on duty in the shop in the afternoons only his mornings were free for writing, and he soon embarked on another novel, *Keep the Aspidistra Flying*.

In March 1935 he met Eileen O'Shaughnessy, a young woman who was later to become his wife and who played a prominent part in his life and work over the next decade. After graduating at St Hugh's College, Oxford, she had been successively a teacher, secretary and journalist. At the time she met Orwell she was studying for an MA in psychology at University College, London. Two years younger than he, she was attractive, intelligent and practical; her shrewd commonsense proved to be the perfect complement to his unusual temperament. Moreover she understood and accepted his passionate determination to become a writer and was willing to submerge her own ambitions in the interests of his own. Despite his precarious financial prospects and somewhat intimidating manner she was immediately attracted by this interesting and unconventional young man and soon accepted his offer of marriage. From this point onwards until her untimely death she became his companion and helpmate throughout the most crucial years of his life.

In January 1936 Orwell was commissioned by Victor Gollancz to make a study of poverty and unemployment in the North of England: a proposal that was to culminate in one of his most celebrated works of reportage, *The Road to Wigan Pier*. He was engaged on this project for most of that year, spending February and March travelling through the depressed areas of Lancashire and Yorkshire and then settling down to write the book, a task on which he was engaged from May until December. In April 1936 he had moved to the village of Wallington, Hertfordshire, where he combined his literary activities with husbandry and managing the tiny village shop. Wallington was to remain his home until the spring of 1940, though he retained it as a weekend cottage until 1947.

On completion of *The Road to Wigan Pier* he promptly left for Barcelona, where he was anxious to serve on the Republican side in the Spanish Civil War. He enlisted as a soldier in the militia of the POUM (Workers' Party of Marxist Unification) and served as a corporal on the Aragon front until May 1937 when he was wounded in the throat by a bullet fired by a Fascist sniper. This injury effectively ended his participation in the war and he returned to England in June to embark almost at once on his account of the conflict, *Homage to Catalonia*.

These two experiences – his journey to the coal mining areas of the North, and his participation as a militiaman in the Spanish Civil War – were of decisive importance in the making of George Orwell. It is clear from many indications in his writings that he was slow to develop, both as an artist and as a political thinker. As late as *Keep the Aspidistra Flying*, written when he was thirty-two, he was still unsure of himself politically. The combined effect of the poverty and deprivation he had witnessed at first hand in England and the overwhelming experience of Spain (the latter involving unforgettable comradeship on the one hand and the most cynical treachery on the other) shifted his convictions firmly in an ideological direction. Looking back on this period of his life a decade later he remarked that his experiences prior to 1936 'were not enough to give me an accurate political orientation. Then came Hitler, the Spanish Civil War, etc. By the end of 1935 I had still failed to reach a firm decision . . . The Spanish war and other events in 1936–7 turned the scale and thereafter I knew where I stood.'[20] The turning point, then, was Wigan and Spain rather than Burma and Paris. To express the situation in this form suggests a sudden conversion from an apolitical attitude to a radical conviction; the reality was rather less dramatic. Orwell's own words, 'The Spanish war and other events in 1936–7 turned the scale' convey accurately enough the essence of what happened: that the events of these years confirmed within him a political orientation which had been growing slowly but surely since his years in Burma and his deliberate experience of vagrancy in and around London. The impact of Spain following so soon after his journeyings among the poor and unemployed transformed his socialism from an uncertainly-held intellectual position to an emotionally-held faith, from an economic philosophy to a way of living. The difference between *The Road to Wigan Pier* and *Homage to Catalonia* is more than a difference of tone. It is the difference between a writer who is still feeling his way towards a definition of socialism as a theoretical proposition and one who is convinced that he has seen socialism in action. *Homage to Catalonia* is moreover the work of a much more assured writer, a writer with a definite point of view on social and political questions whose emotional commitment to those views is plain. From now onwards Orwell was a radical who was determined to speak out on humanitarian issues. He remained a novelist, but he was now a novelist with a mission: to combat intolerance and dishonesty in all its forms and to uphold human dignity and freedom of expression to the utmost of his powers.

Early in 1938, shortly after the completion of *Homage to Catalonia*, he fell ill with a tubercular lesion in one lung. (He discovered later that he had been tubercular since 1928 or thereabouts: the damp Burmese climate had irreparably damaged his health.) After spending some months in a sanatorium he decided on medical grounds to spend the winter in a warm climate. An anonymous donation enabled him and Eileen to stay for seven months in Morocco, where he worked on a new novel, *Coming Up For Air*, returning to England in March 1939. In the spring of that year he commenced writing a volume of essays, *Inside the Whale*, a task on which he was engaged – intermittently with gardening and rearing livestock – until December.

With the outbreak of the Second World War in September 1939 Orwell sought some means of actively supporting the war effort. The threat of invasion revived within him a strong sense of patriotism which had always been part of his make-up and it was with some bitterness that he found his applications for military service rejected on medical grounds. In an article written in the early months of the war[21] he summed up his attitude towards those intellectuals who refused to serve the government in any capacity:

> It is all very well to be 'advanced' and 'enlightened', to snigger at Colonel Blimp and proclaim your emancipation from all traditional loyalties, but a time comes when the sand of the desert is sodden red and what have I done for thee, England, my England?

Whilst seeking repeatedly for some way of making a practical contribution to the defence of his country he continued to live precariously on his income from journalism, writing book reviews for *Horizon* and *Tribune*. Since 1938 he had been projecting the idea of writing a long novel in the form of a trilogy (he completed the last part of this only, the book we know today as

Nineteen Eighty-Four) but felt strongly 'the impossibility of writing books with this nightmare going on'.[22] Unable to settle to the task of writing fiction, he moved to London with his wife in May 1940 and began to write occasional criticism for *Time and Tide*. On the formation of the Local Defence Volunteers – later renamed the Home Guard – he enrolled at once, becoming a sergeant in his local battalion. He took his duties seriously, playing his full part in weapon training, exercises and firewatching, and continued to serve as an active member until his resignation on grounds of deteriorating health in November 1943.

In August 1940 he commenced writing a novella-length essay, 'The Lion and the Unicorn', and was engaged on this task for several months. Some indication of his state of mind during this hectic period may be gauged from an entry he confided to his diary at this time:

> On Tuesday and Wednesday had two glorious days at Wallington. No newspapers and no mention of the war. They were cutting the oats and we took Marx [his dog] out both days to help course the rabbits, at which Marx showed unexpected speed. The whole thing took me straight back to my childhood, perhaps the last bit of that kind of life that I shall ever have.[23]

Early in 1941 he began contributing regularly to *Partisan Review*, an influential literary journal published in the United States, an assignment he continued until 1946. In August 1941 he commenced working full-time for the British Broadcasting Corporation, first as a Talks Assistant, and later as a Talks Producer, responsible for the compilation and production of educational programmes for transmission to India. As with the Home Guard, he approached his work conscientiously, paying particular attention to devising and editing discussions on literary topics in which he involved some of the leading intellectuals of the day including T. S. Eliot, Herbert Read and Edmund Blunden. His essay 'Poetry and the Microphone', written in 1943, contains an interesting account of his approach to educational broadcasting and his views on the implications of the radio for poetry and literature. He continued with his BBC duties for two years, simultaneously fulfilling his Home Guard commitments and contributing to *Horizon*, *Tribune*, the *New*

Statesman and other journals. By the late autumn of 1943, however, Orwell seems to have concluded that his time and energies could be better spent and he felt the urge to return to creative writing. He submitted his resignation to the BBC, adding that 'for some time past I have been conscious that I have been wasting my own time and the public money on doing work that produces no results'.[24] At the time of his resignation he had no other post in view, but before his notice expired he had been offered the literary editorship of *Tribune*, a post for which he was peculiarly fitted by his unusual combination of interests and aptitudes. Eagerly assuming his new responsibilities, he began almost at once on the writing of *Animal Farm*, a work which was to earn for him a world-wide reputation as a satirist and to invite comparison with Voltaire and Swift. He now embarked on one of the happiest periods of his life, writing regular 'As I Please' columns for *Tribune* in which he was free to comment idiosyncratically on all manner of literary, political and social issues and alternately captivating and antagonising his readers. As literary editor he had wide freedom of discretion and his column not infrequently contained opinions (on Russia, for example, then regarded as an ally) in contradiction to the official policy of the paper. But the liveliness and catholicity of the literary pages under his editorship won many new readers for *Tribune* and consolidated his reputation as a writer of unusual integrity.

After the completion of *Animal Farm* early in 1944 he wrote *The English People*, a booklet commissioned by Collins for their 'Britain in Pictures' series. He still felt unable to concentrate on the writing of a full-length novel but in the autumn of that year began planning the contents of a volume of essays. (This compilation was published in 1946 under the title *Critical Essays*.) In the meantime he and his wife had concluded that they were unable to have a family of their own and in 1944 adopted a baby son whom they named Richard Horatio Blair.

Orwell's happiness, however, was to be short lived. Early in 1945, sensing a desire to see at first hand the closing stages of the war, he terminated his appointment with *Tribune* and travelled to France and Germany as a war correspondent for the *Observer*. It was in Cologne that he received the news that his wife, who had been in poor health for some time, was dead. She had been admitted to hospital for a comparatively minor operation and had died while the anaesthetic was being administered. She was thirty-nine years of age. Orwell, grief-stricken with this news, returned at once to England. Realising that his best hope of recovery from the shock of her death was to immerse himself in activity, he completed his duties as a war correspondent, travelling widely in France, Germany and Austria. On his return he reported on the British General Election campaign for the *Observer*.

Having commenced work on the first draft of *Nineteen Eighty-Four*, he paid his first visit to the island of Jura in the Hebrides in the autumn of 1945. He had long been attracted by the idea of living in the Hebrides[25] (despite his antipathy to Scotland and all things Scottish); here, he felt, far removed from the telephone and the pressures of London he would be able to settle down to the writing of a major work of fiction. In May 1946 he settled on the island, renting a house and its surrounding farmland, intending to make Jura henceforth his permanent home. The succeeding twelve months were spent in getting the house and land in order and in gradually disentangling himself from his numerous journalistic commitments. Despite the pressures on his time he was writing some of his finest and most characteristic essays including 'Politics and the English Language', 'A Good Word for the Vicar of Bray', 'Politics versus Literature', 'How the Poor Die' and 'Lear, Tolstoy and the Fool'.

From the autumn of 1947 onwards the substance of his life was an increasingly desperate struggle against declining health. The lung infection from which he had suffered for many years began to cause him acute distress, until by October of that year he was confined to bed – having succeeded, before his health collapsed, in completing the rough draft of *Nineteen Eighty-Four*. He spent the first half of 1948 as a patient in Hairmyres Hospital, near Glasgow, receiving streptomycin treatment (then a new and expensive drug, difficult to obtain in Britain). He felt well enough to write some book reviews and was also engaged on correcting the proofs of a uniform collected edition of his works to be published by Secker & Warburg. In July he returned to Jura, working steadily on *Nineteen Eighty-Four* but aware from September onwards that he was now very ill indeed. In January 1949, having at last completed the book and typed out the final manuscript himself, he was admitted to a sanatorium at Cranham, Gloucestershire, where he remained until September. Despite being bedridden he continued to write articles and book reviews and made notes for long essays on Evelyn Waugh and Joseph Conrad and a novella to be entitled 'A Smoking Room Story'; none of the latter projects was completed. He was also reading widely, devouring the Hammonds' *The English Labourer*, Bertrand Russell's *Human Knowledge*, Hesketh Pearson's *Dickens*, Hardy's *Tess of the D'Urbervilles* and *Jude the Obscure*, Aldous Huxley's *Ape and Essence*, Dickens's *Little Dorrit*, and many others – in addition to keeping up a copious correspondence.

In September, his health having deteriorated even further, he was admitted to University College Hospital, London, where in the following month he married Sonia Brownell, then an editorial assistant on the staff of *Horizon*. 'I suppose everyone will be horrified,' he wrote to his publisher, 'but apart from other considerations I really think I should stay alive longer if I were married.'[26] By the beginning of 1950 he was making plans to travel to a Swiss sanatorium, where he felt that, given a total rest and a gentler climate, there would be at last a chance of a lasting recovery. On 21 January, however, at the age of forty-six, his lung haemorrhaged suddenly and he died of pulmonary tuberculosis. Fredric Warburg wrote of him: 'The passionate pilgrim had come to the end of the road. One of the great masters of English prose was no more.'[27]

*   *   *   *   *

In an illuminating essay on Dickens[28] Edmund Wilson has commented: 'It is necessary to see him as a man in order to appreciate him as an artist.' Much the same might be said of Orwell, for it is necessary to see his life and work as a totality in order to understand the unusual combination of circumstances – in environment, psychology and temperament – which helped to shape him as an artist and mould his distinctive attitude of mind.

He was, first of all, a quintessentially *English* writer. This was a man who loved coal fires and English cooking, Victorian furniture and high tea, a man who delighted in the novels of Dickens, Wells and Gissing, who loved the countryside and the open air and appreciated the quirkiness of such institutions as the monarchy, public schools and the Church of England. He had an acute understanding of the character of English life; he understood its tolerance, its dislike of abstract theories, its insistence on fair play and its penchant for 'muddling through'. Yet it should be noted that this Englishness was strengthened by the circumstances of his life and background: his Anglo-Indian ancestry, his years in Burma and Paris, his participation in the Spanish Civil War, all contributed to his unusual ability to see his country from the outside and to appraise its strengths and weaknesses without illusions. Much of the charm of his writings on England lies precisely in this quality of *freshness*: being simultaneously an insider and an outsider he could recognise the enduring factors in the life of the nation and discuss them with an original and penetrating insight.

Closely linked to this quality in his make-up was the fact that he chose deliberately to reject the way of life for which his background seemed to have fitted him. He was born and educated into a solid, comfortable, middle-class network with long-established traditions and a code of behaviour and attitudes to which its members were expected to conform. Orwell chose to reject this – first, by resigning from the Indian Imperial Police, then by choosing literature as his profession, then by deliberately identifying himself with the poor and deprived. The whole of his subsequent career can be seen as an elaborate attempt to renounce his background and to establish a separate identity of his own. The renunciation was so complete that it can only be described as a metamorphosis. By the time the metamorphosis was complete (and it should be remembered that the process took in all ten years, from his return from Burma in 1927 to his Spanish experience in 1937) he had acquired not only a different life-style but a set of attitudes and even a way of dressing completely in keeping with his adopted career. In the process he had acquired an unusual series of experiences which gave him a freshness of perspective quite uncharacteristic in a man of his background. In his novel *Tono-Bungay* H. G. Wells's narrator remarks:

Most people in this world seem to live 'in character' . . . They have a class, they have a place, they know what is becoming in them and what is due to them . . . But there is also another kind of life that is not so much living as a miscellaneous tasting of life. One gets hit by some unusual transverse force, one is jerked out of one's stratum and lives crosswise for the rest of the time, and, as it were, in a succession of samples.[29]

This was also Orwell's lot. The 'unusual transverse force' in his case was his passionate determination to become a writer, coupled with an equally passionate resolve to turn his back on the traditions, values and codes in which he had been so laboriously educated. The consequence of this disavowal was a receptiveness to new ideas and impressions and a concomitant willingness to abandon previously held beliefs – both refreshingly uncommon for one of his class and generation. He is the classic example of one who was brought up to accept uncritically a solid, conventional, secure mode of life who then came to question its implicit assumptions and to challenge the structure on which it is based. In essence, he was a man who tore up the roots of the conventional manner of life to which he had been born and then had to find for himself new roots appropriate to his altered way of living. His excursions among down and outs in the years 1927–32, his experiences as a dishwasher in Paris, his travels in the industrial North of England and his involvement in the Spanish Civil War were all in a sense voyages of discovery: attempts to see, hear and sample at first hand aspects of life previously unknown to him.

By birth, background and education he belonged to the bourgeoisie; by attitude and inclination he belonged to the proletariat. This unresolved tension accounts for the odd mixture of attitudes he embodied in his own person and for the sense of ambivalence which can be detected in his writings. Despising the values of the social stratum into which he was born, yet not fully accepted as a manual worker, he held feelings and reactions appropriate to both. In the diary he kept in the closing months of his life he wrote apropos 'cultivated' accents:

And what voices! A sort of over-fedness, a fatuous self-confidence ... people who, one instinctively feels, without even being able to see them, are the enemies of anything intelligent or sensitive or beautiful. No wonder everyone hates us so.[30]

The use of the word 'us' in the last sentence is revealing: clearly Orwell felt that his accent identified him as a member of a privileged class. Contrast this with his comment on arriving in revolutionary Barcelona in December 1936:

All this was queer and moving. There was much in it that I did not understand, in some ways I did not even like it, but I recognised it immediately as a state of affairs worth fighting for.[31]

It is this combination in Orwell of an acute understanding of middle class society – an understanding which could only stem from having seen it intimately from the *inside* – and a complete emotional identification with the underdog, which provides his books with their energising force and makes him so rewarding a writer to study in depth.[32]

Rayner Heppenstall, who knew him well in the 1930s, has remarked in a memoir:

To us it was a curious mind, satirically attached to everything traditionally English, always full of interesting and out-of-the-way information like *Tit-Bits*, but arid, colourless, devoid of poetry, derisive, yet darkly obsessed. There underlay it all some unsolved equation of love and hate, some memory of childhood nursed through Eton, through Burma, taken out and viewed secretly in Paris kitchens or upon the thresholds of doss-houses.[33]

The precise origin of this 'unsolved equation of love and hate' has not been established but there seems little doubt of its reality. Embedded deep within his make-up was a profound pessimism, a revulsion against human bestiality which inhibited him from close friendships and darkened the closing years of his life. The only individual who succeeded in breaking through this defensive crust was his first wife, Eileen, who understood him fully and appreciated the complex of forces which had made him what he was. She and she alone had the ability to see through his moods and penetrate to the 'crystal spirit' which lay beneath.

An essentially private man – he could be aloof and taciturn in certain moods and had few really close friendships – he requested in his will that no biography of him should be written. This request may have been prompted by a natural reticence, or possibly by a feeling that he had himself told all that was necessary of his life story in the autobiographical section of *The Road to Wigan Pier*. But such an odd request is entirely in keeping with his quixotic temperament. He was a man who 'kept himself to himself ', who attached little importance to material possessions and felt that his life was of value only in the sense that he was a writer. To him his literary work came before all else: before personal friendships, before his marriage, before his own health and happiness. 'Writing a book,' he observed, 'is a horrible, exhausting struggle, like a long bout of some painful illness. One would never undertake such a thing if one were not driven on by some demon whom one can neither resist nor understand.'[34] He was indeed driven by a demon: a consuming passion to write which indirectly contributed to his death but which has earned for him a place alongside the great radical writers of the past.

Viewing his life and achievement in perspective one cannot but derive encouragement from the story of this unusual, complex, engaging man. One has a deep sense of unfulfilled potentialities, an awareness that, had he lived, he could have accomplished much more in the fields of satire, allegory and radical journalism – fields which he had made so much his own. Unquestionably he would have gone on to write novels and essays in that spare, direct, astringent prose for which he is best remembered. Yet there is so much in his life and work for which posterity has reason to be grateful. Through his insistence on moral values in an age of materialism, his emphasis on human decency, his detestation of tyranny and intolerance and his abiding faith in the common man he merits an honoured place in twentieth-century ideas as a man who fought throughout his career for the integrity of the human spirit. The entire weight of his energies over a span of twenty years was devoted to an insistence on fraternity, honesty and tolerance in all aspects of living and to the exposure of any erosion of these values – whether in language, political action, ideology or daily life. He should be remembered not simply as the author of *Animal Farm* and *Nineteen Eighty-Four* but as a man who strived honourably to guide his actions, public and private, by the truth. In doing so he gave us some fine and memorable novels, documentaries and essays and the memory of a fiercely independent and uncompromising spirit.

Orwell's Literary Achievement

Orwell is now acknowledged as one of the most significant writers of the twentieth century. Few observers would have forecast on the evidence of his early work that thirty years after his death his works would be available in numerous editions and in many languages and that he would be regarded as 'a world figure, a name to set argument going wherever books are read'.[35] Until 1945 his reputation rested on his early novels together with *The Road to Wigan Pier* which, due in large measure to the Left Book Club, had enjoyed a very wide circulation. Sales of *Homage to Catalonia* by comparison had been very small indeed. At the end of the Second World War, then, he was regarded as a comparatively minor novelist with a gift for documentary reportage and an essayist of some promise. The publication of *Animal Farm* brought his name before a considerably wider readership both in the English-speaking world and beyond. Comparisons began to be made with *Gulliver's Travels* and the satires of Voltaire; critics were slowly beginning to recognise an unusual and original talent. *Animal Farm* was followed by many major essays which consolidated his growing reputation as a force to be reckoned with in English literature. Such essays as 'How the Poor Die', 'Politics and the English Language', 'Lear, Tolstoy and the Fool' and 'Writers and Leviathan', together with his prolific journalism for *Tribune*, the *Observer* and other papers earned him respect and admiration as an essayist in the vein of Hazlitt and Stevenson. With the publication of *Nineteen Eighty-Four* in 1949 his stature as a major literary figure was secure. The adjective 'Orwellian' was added to the language and his early works began to be rescued from the temporary oblivion into which they had fallen. Today his reputation has never been higher and shows no sign of diminishing. Film and television adaptations of his novels have brought his work before a vast audience and it is estimated that *Animal Farm* and *Nineteen Eighty-Four* have each sold in excess of ten million copies. At the time of writing everything of significance by Orwell is available in both hardback and paperback editions and his work continues to sell at a vigorous rate. Today he is acknowledged as one of the most distinctive voices of our age and as a worthy successor to the great radical writers of the past. Anthony Burgess wrote of him: 'His radicalism was of a nineteenth-century kind, with a strong tinge of something older – the dissenting spirit of Defoe and the humane anger of Swift.'[36]

His literary achievement may usefully be examined under four heads: as novelist, as essayist and political writer, as journalist, and as satirist. Whilst this division permits an orderly discussion it should be borne in mind that it is arbitrary and imposes a pattern on a corpus of writing which does not always fall into such neat categories. There is no rigid dividing line in Orwell's life and work between aesthetic and polemic. His whole life was a complex interplay between the two and it is precisely this aspect – the continuous fusion of an artistic with a political intelligence – which makes him a writer of such unusual and compelling interest.

*   *   *   *   *

In an essay written in 1948 he defined a novel as

> a story which attempts to describe human beings, and – without necessarily using the techniques of naturalism – to show them acting on everyday motives and not merely undergoing strings of improbable adventures. A true novel, sticking to this definition, will also contain at least two characters, probably more, who are described from the inside and on the same level of probability – which, in effect, rules out the novels written in the first person.[37]

If one accepts this definition it becomes readily apparent that few of his novels can be said to conform to it: indeed *Burmese Days* is possibly the only one which fulfils each of Orwell's requirements. Yet in acknowledging this one is simultaneously aware that there are present in each of his works of fiction qualities of vitality and readability which outweigh their defects on strictly literary criteria; each possesses an inner strength which redeems its shortcomings. There is no doubt that most of his novels can be faulted on grounds of structure or characterisation or both; despite this the fact remains that he is one of the few writers of his generation whose work is seen to be of continuing relevance and whose fiction continues to be studied and enjoyed by readers living in a fundamentally different social climate. Clearly, then, his fiction must possess qualities, both literary and extra-literary, which outweigh their limitations. Why is it, for example, that a novel such as *A Clergyman's Daughter*, which most critics find embarrassingly clumsy in its execution and is flawed by structural weaknesses which impair it as a coherent work, has been in constant demand since its reprinting in 1960 (its first publication since Orwell's death) and that its sales show no signs of diminishing? Why is it that though his novels sin against the canons of the art as defined by Henry James and even by himself they continue to be read whilst those of some of his more fashionable contemporaries have lapsed into disregard?

It is apposite at this juncture to raise the question: to what extent was he an original writer? To what extent was he working within the accepted forms of the English novel? It seems clear from internal evidence and from his own statements that at the outset of his career as a novelist he intended to conform to conventional standards of the genre:

> I wanted to write enormous naturalistic novels with unhappy endings, full of detailed descriptions and arresting similes, and also full of purple passages in which words were used partly for the sake of their sound. And in fact my first complete novel, *Burmese Days*, which I wrote when I was thirty but projected much earlier, is rather that kind of book.[38]

As a novelist in the accepted sense Orwell's achievement has been overshadowed by the enormous popular success of *Animal Farm* and *Nineteen Eighty-Four*. The deserved fame of these two works has tended to obscure his performance as a novelist *per se*, where his contribution is felt to be accomplished but uninspired. At first sight he does seem to be a curious example of a writer continuing well into the twentieth century the conventions of the

Victorian novel (he agreed only with reluctance to delete the phrase 'it now remains to tell' from the manuscript of the final chapter of *Burmese Days*, telling his agent 'I hate a novel in which the principal characters are not disposed of at the end').[39] The novels of his middle period – *Burmese Days*, *A Clergyman's Daughter* and *Keep the Aspidistra Flying* – are conventional in the sense that they do not depart from the established usages of the genre and show little awareness of contemporary trends in literature. Franz Kafka's *The Trial* had been published in 1924; H. G. Wells's *The World of William Clissold* in 1926; Virginia Woolf's *To the Lighthouse* in 1927; Hesse's *Narziss and Goldmund* in 1930. Throughout the 1920s writers in England and Europe were seeking to escape from the confines of the novel as exemplified by the great nineteenth-century practitioners, to widen its scope and approach it from fresh angles. Orwell seems to have been unaware of this process until his own literary apprenticeship came to an end with the publication of his first book. By that time (1933) he had established a style of his own and had worked out his own conception of what a novel should or should not be. By the time he encountered the novels of Joyce he had completed his own first novel and was in the throes of his second. On this interpretation his novels are seen as belonging firmly in the English tradition of Dickens, Gissing and Wells and as being virtually uninfluenced by the more experimental writing of Lawrence, Proust and Virginia Woolf. To the extent that this judgement is accurate it is a reflection of the literary influences upon him and of his background as a writer whose apprenticeship took place largely outside England. The novelists who influenced him most deeply – apart from Dickens, Gissing and Wells, for each of whom his admiration was profound[40] – were Fielding, Charles Reade, Samuel Butler, Zola and Flaubert. The principal literary influences upon him throughout his adolescence and early manhood were in the naturalistic tradition and it was not until 1933, at the age of thirty, that he read for the first time James Joyce's *Ulysses*: a work which exercised a deep influence on his attitude of mind and approach to literature.

Whilst superficially the novels which followed *Burmese Days* are equally unexperimental in form, closer examination reveals indications of an original mind seeking to achieve a literary form appropriate to the needs of the twentieth century and which would permit the discussion of contemporary issues within its overall framework. Seen in this light *A Clergyman's Daughter*, *Keep the Aspidistra Flying* and *Coming Up For Air* are less derivative than appears on first reading and merit far more serious attention than they have yet received.

A Clergyman's Daughter, which in later years he came to disparage and claimed to have written 'simply as an exercise',[41] is marred by faults of which Orwell himself was well aware and yet remains a most interesting attempt to explore the mind and behaviour of a woman in impoverished circumstances. The most valuable part of the book from his own standpoint was the third chapter – the Trafalgar Square sequence, written entirely in dialogue (and whilst he was still heavily influenced by *Ulysses*) – and this is undoubtedly a powerful piece of writing, closely observed and haunting in its imagery – though it does not blend easily with the remainder of the novel. But from the point of view of his development as a writer, learning the craft of the novelist through a painful process of trial and error, the most enduring aspect of the book is the creation of the central character, Dorothy Hare. In creating a heroine deliberately removed from his own background, in exploring her religious and emotional doubtings and examining her attitudes towards her contemporaries he was widening the horizons of the English novel and at the same time gaining self-confidence and maturity in the art of the storyteller. In a letter to Henry Miller apropos the book he confided 'I made some experiments in it that were useful to me'.[42] It is clear, then, that whilst he freely acknowledged its imperfections he was conscious that the act of writing it had been a salutary experience through which he had gained insights he could have gained in no other way. (It is significant in this connection that he resisted the temptation to cast the story in the form of a first-person narrative: the third-person form permitted him to see Dorothy Hare from the outside and thus to achieve a larger measure of detachment.) Whilst structurally and thematically *A Clergyman's Daughter* is perhaps the least satisfactory of the novels it is of far more significance than his own dismissal of it as a 'silly pot-boiler'[43] would suggest. There is no question that he found the writing of it an extraordinarily difficult undertaking but in the process he achieved one of the few convincing portraits of life in a small provincial town (the whole of Chapter 1, a novella-length description of Knype Hill, is an excellent example of his technique of realistic observation and of his gift for penetrating beneath the surface of English life) and a sustained attempt to reach inside the mind of a thoughtful young woman in her search for fulfilment.

Keep the Aspidistra Flying, which again was disowned by Orwell in later life, was conceived at the time as a 'work of art'[44] and written and revised with great care. Its manifest weaknesses – a constant harping on money, an obsessive self-pity and a rather contrived plot – have tended to distract attention from its real strengths as a work of fiction which sought to draw attention to the sense of disintegration experienced by many in the England of the 1930s. Skilfully interwoven into the surface narrative are a series of leitmotifs which dominated his life, to greater or lesser degree, for many years to come. There is, firstly, an overwhelming awareness of the inherent unhealthiness and artificiality of urban civilisation: a civilisation heavily dependent upon drugs, advertising and prefabricated entertainment:

He gazed out at the graceless street. At this moment it seemed to him that in a street like this, in a town like this, every life that is lived must be meaningless and intolerable. The sense of disintegration, of decay, that is endemic in our time, was strong upon him. Somehow it was mixed up with the ad-posters opposite . . . But what is behind the grin? Desolation, emptiness, prophecies of doom.

Closely linked with this awareness of decay, of a fundamental malaise at the heart of society, is a sombre acknowledgement of the imminence of war. At numerous points in the novel Orwell reveals a sense of foreboding at the impending threat of aerial warfare; there is an atmosphere of brooding menace, a vision of 'Enemy aeroplanes flying over London; the deep threatening hum of the propellors, the shattering thunder of the bombs'. Written long before his experiences in Spain, the novel is rich in the imagery of warfare and displays a vivid recognition of the power of the bombing aeroplane as a symbol of destructiveness. A third leitmotif is the concern with the corruption of language, a theme which came increasingly to the forefront of his literary and political concerns in the years following the Spanish Civil War. Gordon Comstock's experience as a copywriter in an advertising agency is an immense disillusionment, convincing him of the cynicism of much modern advertising and the ease with which language can be corrupted through the use of slogans and metaphors. Newspeak and the Ministry of Truth are clearly foreshadowed in the New Albion Publicity Company. Finally there is the predominant theme of poverty which provides the novel with its moving and energising force. Not since Gissing's *New Grub Street* (1891) has there been a more profound study of the loneliness, unhappiness and alienation engendered by poverty. It is this deeply human concern with the lack of money and its moral and physical consequences which infuses the novel with its poignancy and will ensure a readership for it for generations to come.

Coming Up For Air, possibly the most imaginative and satisfying of Orwell's novels, has an unusual structure which has effectively obscured its stature as a Bildungsroman. It belongs in fact to a distinguished literary tradition: the novel of development, of which the most representative examples are *David Copperfield*, *Great Expectations*, *Tono-Bungay* and *Sons and Lovers*.[45] That is, it belongs to a genre in which the life of the hero is traced from childhood through adolescence to maturity and which illustrates the manner in which the hero responds to his experiences and is changed by them. Throughout *Coming Up For Air* George Bowling is at pains to describe the experiences and influences which helped to shape his character and outlook. He relates at length his home background, his childhood adventures, his reading, his emotional development, his attitude to life and reflections on all that life has taught him.

Writing to Jack Common whilst the book was in progress Orwell confided: 'it's suddenly revealed to me a big subject which I'd never really touched before and haven't time to work out properly now . . . I have very dimly in my mind the idea for an enormous novel in several volumes and I want several years to plan it out in peace.[46] From what is known of this project, the provisional title of which was *The Quick and the Dead*, the 'big subject' which he intended to explore in greater depth and which had been revealed to him during the writing of *Coming Up For Air* was the manner in which the life and personality of an individual can be shaped by his emotional development. The theme is treated at some length in *Coming Up For Air* which – partly due to the ebullient character of the narrator, and partly because of the first-person narration – is the most frank of the pre-war novels on matters of sex and morality.

In relating the life story of George Bowling he was making a significant contribution to the Bildungsroman as a literary form and was doing so in a manner which represented a radical departure from his previous fiction. The fact that it is written throughout in a simple, colloquial, direct style should not blind the reader to its literary merits. Its apparent simplicity is deceptive; the style was not arrived at without much travail and was the result of a long process of artistic searching.

Not only has Orwell been underestimated as a storyteller but also as a creator of character. It is widely assumed that John Flory, Gordon Comstock and George Bowling are simply projections of himself and that in each of these characters he was portraying his own *alter ego*, a mouthpiece for his opinions on current social and political issues. It will be demonstrated in this *Companion* that in fact his achievements in the field of characterisation are more substantial and subtle than is usually acknowledged and that each of his central figures is a composite portrait rather than a direct self-projection. Flory, Comstock and Bowling certainly embody some of Orwell's own attitudes but each is in the last analysis a *fictional* creation, an imaginary personality deliberately distanced from the author. Both Flory and Comstock can be regarded as self-portraits *only* to the extent that they depict representations of Blair/Orwell as he might have been had his life taken a different course. Had he remained in Burma, for example, it is conceivable that he could have degenerated in time into a figure approximating to the embittered figure of John Flory. Had his apprenticeship as a writer continued to be the failure it undoubtedly was during the years 1928–32 it is conceivable that he could have become in time a figure not unlike Gordon Comstock. The essential point is that both characters embody elements of self-pity and shallowness which we know to be uncharacteristic of their creator. Orwell did not remain in Burma but deliberately severed himself from a life which he had come to loathe; he did not, as Comstock did, abandon writing in the face of repeated rejection slips but persevered in spite of every discouragement. George Bowling is a more complex figure than the heroes of the earlier novels for whilst he embodies many of Orwell's opinions he is totally different in personality and background. In his anxiety to create a credible narrator who would not be identified with himself Orwell deliberately distances himself from Bowling by placing him in a quite different environment from his own and investing him with traits and attitudes representative of his milieu. The result is a genuine creation, as memorable in its own way as the Grossmiths' Charles Pooter or Bennett's Denry Machin.

His critics are on firmer ground in drawing attention to a certain lack of perceptiveness in his treatment of women. There are few convincing female characters in the novels; most are competently drawn but lack those touches of realism which truly memorable characters possess. If one thinks, for example, of Elizabeth Lackersteen in *Burmese Days*, Elsie Waters and Hilda Vincent in *Coming Up For Air* and Julia in *Nineteen Eighty-Four* one is aware of a lack of solidity in the execution: the reader senses that the author is gifted with vivid descriptive powers and can evoke an atmosphere with unforgettable vigour but is less successful in imagining character or in presenting a realistic picture of an emotional relationship. The outstanding exception to the rule is Rosemary in *Keep the Aspidistra Flying*, a portrait which is all the more convincing for being drawn from life (although again it should be noted that Rosemary is not based on any one individual but on a number of women who entered Orwell's life in the years 1934–5). This exception apart, it seems fair to say that on the whole his greatest strength as a novelist lay in the depiction of atmosphere and that he was least successful in the presentation of adult relationships.

As a naturalistic writer in the vein of Zola his undoubted talent lay in the power to evoke a setting with such clarity that the picture remains in the mind long after the book has been laid aside. One thinks of the white man's club in *Burmese Days*, Gordon Comstock's lodgings in *Keep the Aspidistra Flying*, the hop-picking sequence in *A Clergyman's Daughter*, the childhood fishing idyll in *Coming Up For Air*: these are described in prose of such vigour that the episodes as a whole come to life in an extraordinary way and animate the novels with unusual force. When he remarked at the end of his life that 'I am not a real novelist anyway'[47] he was referring to the craft of the novel in the sense of the creation of character and the depiction of nuances of behaviour. He was perceptive enough to recognise that in this regard he was not a 'real novelist' in the sense that Dickens and Trollope were. Yet in making this observation he was obscuring his very real achievement as a descriptive writer, perhaps the finest writer of lucid prose of this century. One does not turn to

Orwell for profound studies of human nature or conduct; his strength does not lie in these fields. His strength lies rather in the vivid presentation of location and background, in the description of 'the physical memories, the sounds, the smells and the sur- faces of things',[48] in the illumination of moods and environments ignored by writers who had not undergone his own experiences of poverty and humiliation.

Each of the novels is in a sense a study in failure. John Flory in *Burmese Days*, Dorothy Hare in *A Clergyman's Daughter*, Gordon Comstock in *Keep the Aspidistra Flying*, George Bowling in *Coming Up For Air* and Winston Smith in *Nineteen Eighty-Four* are all examples of a central character who seeks to change the circums- tances of his or her own life but ultimately fails. Flory is rejected by the woman he loves and commits suicide in a mood of humili- ation and disappointment; Dorothy fails in her attempt to escape from a life of penury and relapses into a world of humdrum domesticity; Comstock makes a determined attempt to free him- self from a society tainted by money but fails utterly, finally abandoning all his principles in the interests of respectability; Bowling's attempt to recreate the idyll of his childhood spells complete disillusionment and he returns to a lifeless marriage in which he feels himself entrapped; Winston Smith abandons his lonely struggle against the system and ends his days a broken and dispirited man. These studies in failure owe much to Gissing but are in the sharpest contrast to the novels of Dickens and Wells, most of whose heroes succeed in resolving their struggles with life. Does the comparative greyness revealed in the novels indicate a fundamentally pessimistic cast of mind? It is at least arguable that the dourness of the novels is indicative of neither optimism nor pessimism – for all his life was an interplay of the two – but rather of an intrinsic concern for the grimmer aspects of life and an emotional identification with the underdog. In an essay on Gissing written towards the end of his life Orwell wrote: 'we must be thankful for the piece of youthful folly which turned him aside from a comfortable middle-class career and forced him to become the chronicler of vulgarity, squalor and failure'.[49] In his own way Orwell was a supremely successful chronicler 'of vulgarity, squalor and failure'. He illuminated in his novels aspects of life rarely touched upon by writers of his generation and did so with a realism and honesty that are wholly com- mendable. His unusual combination of experiences inevitably gave his writing a freshness and peculiarity of approach not shared by the novelists of his generation (Connolly, Greene, Isherwood and Waugh). His years in humdrum occupations – as a private tutor, as a teacher in wretched private schools, as a shop assistant – coupled with his experience of poverty in Paris and London meant that he could not simply *describe* failure but could *understand* it, having seen it intimately and sympathetically from the inside. His deliberate disavowal of the life of a gentleman – as witnessed, for example, in his conscious decision not to pursue a university education, his rejection of Eton and public-school values, the abandonment of his imperial career in Burma and his symbolic adoption of a pseudonym – meant that he could write freely and sympathetically on the themes which lay closest to his imagination and interests: the debilitating effects of poverty, the regimentation and artificiality of modern life, the quest for a satisfying rationale based upon human decency and, above all, the need for freedom and justice in an age of totalitarianism. These were the concerns which motivated him as a man and as a writer and which animate his novels with a distinctive voice.

Orwell has been described as 'probably the best writer of reportage in a whole generation'. His three full-length works of reportage are now accepted as classics of their kind, in spite of the fact that each is flawed by structural imperfections similar to those found in the novels.

At first sight it may seem odd that Orwell's documentaries remain readable and relevant today when the issues which inspired them have long since changed beyond recognition. Vagrancy and poverty are no longer pressing social problems in England; unemployment, though widespread, is no longer associated with wretched housing and deprivation; the Spanish Civil War ended in 1939 with defeat for the Republicans and is now no more than a fading memory. Many of the issues he wrote about so cogently and eloquently – Fascism, imperialism, colonialism, the Second World War – are now matters of history and no longer have the burning topicality they had in his lifetime. Despite this his books and essays continue to be read: why is this? There are, I suggest, two reasons. First, his writings continue to be in demand because he was preoccupied with fundamental human problems. His close friend Richard Rees observed: 'The reason why his books are still alive and seminal, when so many portentous works of Socialist and Marxist propaganda have been forgotten, is that he dealt with permanent as well as with temporary problems'.[50] The central issues which so exercised him as man and writer – freedom of thought, justice, individual liberty, the insidious growth of totalitarianism – remain equally relevant today. They may appear in different forms from those Orwell knew but they remain essentially and recognisably the same. It is these basic human concerns which underlay all his work and will continue to ensure an audience for it despite the far-reaching social and political changes since his death. Reflecting on his life and achievement one is repeatedly struck with his deeply felt sense of justice. Flowing behind and through his political writings is a passionately strong sense of right and wrong, a concern for fairness and honesty which is so strong and consistent that it could be described as his hallmark.

Second, almost all his published writings from the major books and essays to the smaller articles and book reviews possess literary qualities which raise them above the level of journalism. He himself remarked apropos his work: 'I could not do the work of writing a book, or even a long magazine article, if it were not also an aesthetic experience'.[51] Numerous examples could be cited of this aesthetic quality in his work. One example must here suffice, selected almost at random; it is a paragraph from Chapter 4 of *Homage to Catalonia*:

> But there were mornings when the sight of the dawn among the mountain-tops made it almost worth while to be out of bed at godless hours. I hate mountains, even from a spectacular point of view. But sometimes the dawn breaking behind the hill-tops in our rear, the first narrow streaks of gold, like swords slitting the darkness, and then the growing light and the seas of carmine cloud stretching away into inconceivable distances, were worth watching even when you had been up all night, when your legs were numb from the knees down, and you were sullenly reflecting that there was no hope of food for another three hours.

Such a paragraph is completely irrelevant to any discussion of the Spanish Civil War, nevertheless he feels that his account of his experiences at the front would be incomplete without it. In the context of the chapter as a whole it is merely an aside, a respite from the grim reality of trench warfare, but it adds immeasurably to the stature of the book from a literary stand-point. (It is entirely characteristic of Orwell that the lyrical description of the dawn with its 'first narrow streaks of gold, like swords slitting the darkness' is prefaced with the deprecatory 'I hate mountains, even from a spectacular point of view'.) Similar descriptive passages can be found at many points in the documentary books and essays. They are indicative of an intelligence for whom simple reportage and observation are not sufficient in themselves, a writer determined to make each of his works a medium for artistic expression. It is for this reason that the reportage and essays continue to be read and enjoyed.

An interesting aspect of his documentary essays and works of social reportage is that in each case the process being recorded is a transition from ignorance to enlightenment. In works such as *Down and Out*, *The Road to Wigan Pier*, *Homage to Catalonia* and 'A Hanging' both reader and author commence in a state of ignor-ance: the experience being unfolded is that of Orwell's own edu-cation which is described as if the reader is himself sharing in the process. At the commencement of *Down and Out* the narrator has no experience of poverty in either Paris or London, but he shares his knowledge with the reader as his adventures unfold; simi-larly, in *Homage to Catalonia* the 'I' has no experience of warfare at the outset of the book but describes all that happens to him as it were contemporaneously. The effect of immediacy is all the more remarkable when one recalls that each of these works was written months (and, in some cases, years) after the events described. As an important consequence of this technique his attitude from the outset of the documentaries is one of innocence: he does not adopt a stance until he has established the facts for himself; only then is he in a position to take sides. A further consequence is that none of the documentaries begins with the educational process. On the contrary, each commences with straightforward description rather than analysis. Thus the open-ing section of *Down and Out* is a description of his Paris hotel and his fellow lodgers; the first chapter of *The Road to Wigan Pier* is a detailed account of his lodgings in rooms above a tripe shop in Wigan; *Homage to Catalonia* commences with his meeting with an Italian militiaman in the Lenin Barracks in Barcelona; 'A Hang-ing' opens with a description of a Burmese morning outside the condemned cells. This technique is of course deliberate and is an illustration of the manner in which Orwell sets out to achieve a direct relationship between author and reader. By commencing with observation rather than argument he establishes confidence with the reader; one senses that here is a writer to be trusted. Had he analysed the situation in the opening chapter (as he must have been tempted to do, particularly where, as in *Homage to Catalonia*, he held strong views on the issues involved) the reader's confidence would be markedly diminished.

George Woodcock remarked of Orwell that 'he and Swift belonged to the same literary tradition, that of English Tory dissent'.[52] His finest essays are now acknowledged to be classics of English prose and he is numbered among that select band of dissenting writers which includes not only Swift but also Cobbett and Defoe. The influence of all three upon his work can be discerned in that lucid, transparent style – at once simple and eloquent – by which he is best remembered and which is associated indelibly with his name. Embedded in each of the essays, even the minor ones, are flashes of vivid Orwellian writing:

> And the whole atmosphere of the poor quarters of Paris as a foreigner sees them – the cobbled alleys, the sour reek of refuse, the bistros with their greasy zinc counters and worn brick floors, the green waters of the Seine, the blue cloaks of the Republican Guard, the crumbling iron urinals, the peculiar sweetish smell of the Metro stations, the cigarettes that come to pieces, the pigeons in the Luxembourg Gardens – it is all there, or at any rate the feeling of it is there.

This passage, taken from the opening pages of 'Inside the Whale', is a characteristic example of his technique as a documentary writer. There is the emphasis on smells: the 'sour reek' of refuse, the 'peculiar sweetish smell' of the tube stations; there is the insistence on details which remain in the memory: 'the bistros with their greasy zinc counters and worn brick floors', 'the crumbling iron urinals', 'the cigarettes that come to pieces'. The paragraph has a deceptive simplicity which makes it appear simply as a random catalogue of impressions. In fact it is a carefully composed summary of those aspects of Paris which Orwell found unforgettable and which he wished to share with his readers. The vivid contrast of colours – 'the green waters of the Seine', 'the blue cloaks of the Republican Guard', 'the pigeons in the Luxembourg Gardens' – heighten the effectiveness of the sentence as a whole and add to its impact as a descriptive accumulation. This example could be repeated many hundreds of times and is indicative of the care with which he assembled his essays and documentaries.

One of the reasons why his essays have made such a deep and lasting impression is that the reader is involved, both intellectually and emotionally, from the outset: he seeks to engage the interest and sympathies of his audience, to arouse their concern for his subject and enlist their support for his cause. Consider his technique, for example, in the following opening sentences:

> In Moulmein, in Lower Burma, I was hated by large numbers of people – the only time in my life that I have been important enough for this to happen to me.
>
> ['Shooting an Elephant']

> Most people who bother with the matter at all would admit that the English language is in a bad way, but it is generally assumed that we cannot by conscious action do anything about it.
>
> ['Politics and the English Language']

> As I write, highly civilised human beings are flying overhead, trying to kill me.
>
> ['The Lion and the Unicorn']

> The Spanish war has probably produced a richer crop of lies than any event since the Great War of 1914–18, but I honestly doubt . . . whether it is the pro-Fascist newspapers that have done the most harm.
>
> ['Spilling the Spanish Beans']

In each instance the effect is to engage the reader's interest and curiosity through an arresting statement which demonstrates his own concern or implicitly challenges accepted attitudes. In the first example, the statement 'I was hated by large numbers of people' is deliberately followed by the satirical aside 'the only time in my life that I have been important enough for this to happen to me'. Immediately the reader's attention is aroused:

what was the cause of this hatred? What exactly happened in Moulmein? Who is the 'I' who relates this narrative in such a graphically matter-of-fact way? The technique in the second example is quite different though no less effective. Implicit in the introductory sentence is the assumption that though 'the English language is in a bad way' some positive action can be taken to reverse the process of decline: again, the effect is to arouse curiosity and encourage the reader to pass on to the succeeding paragraphs. (It should be noted in passing that his use of 'Most people' rather than 'Many people' is entirely characteristic; 'many' is probably more accurate, but 'most' is undoubtedly more effective in the context.) In the next example he deliberately commences his essay with a statement designed to shock: 'As I write, highly civilised human beings are flying overhead, trying to kill me'. Note that Orwell considers it necessary to remind his audience that Nazi airmen are 'highly civilised' (and not, by definition, barbarians); the use of the phrase 'human beings' must surely be quite deliberate: he is consciously reminding us of the Nazis common humanity with ourselves. What is even more remarkable about this sentence is that it forms the opening statement in a pamphlet concerned primarily not with the conduct of the war with Germany but with a definition of the English character and a discussion of the probable shape of post-war reconstruction. In place of a dispassionate appraisal of national characteristics he chose to commence the essay with this arresting statement as a reminder of the exceptional times in which he and his readers were living. The fourth example makes use of another Orwellian device: having informed his readers that the Spanish Civil War has 'produced a richer crop of lies than any event since the Great War' he then concludes that the *anti*-Fascist newspapers have done the most harm; a conclusion diametrically opposed to that presented in the English press and one calculated to cause annoyance, if not disbelief. Again, the effect is to engage interest. One senses the presence of an unusual individual voice, a man who has something pertinent to say and expresses himself in language of refreshing clarity and directness.

The outstanding attribute of Orwell as an essayist is his *compassion*: it would be difficult to name any other political writer of this century who has demonstrated so powerfully his concern for the underdog, his anger at injustice and unfairness or his anxiety to establish the truth behind infringements of individual liberty. Whether he is discussing fundamental issues of politics or litera- ture, or the host of mundane topics in which he displayed such an intense interest – the coming of spring, the quality of Wool- worth's roses, the cost of books, English cooking – one is aware of a compassionate intelligence, deeply concerned or angry and eager to communicate his feelings to the reader. This concern (one might almost describe it as righteousness) sprang directly from the moral stance he adopted throughout his writing life and particularly from 1936 onwards: he was essentially a moralist. This ethical stance derived not from any religious conviction (though he respected the language and traditions of the Church of England) but rather from the radical tradition of Winstanley and John Ball to which he felt he belonged. The distinguishing feature of his essays is a strong sense of tolerance, an insistence on liberty and a passionate adherence to principle.

The use of the phrase 'English Tory dissent' in Woodcock's description of Orwell is extremely interesting. There is no doubt that there was an 'old-fashioned' side of Orwell – as witnessed, for example, in his dislike of twentieth-century technology, his deep love of the English countryside, his enthusiasm for garden- ing and rural pursuits, his strong sense of patriotism (as distinct from nationalism) and his nostalgia for the unchanging world he had known in his Edwardian childhood. In his personal life this evidenced itself in his decision to become a village shopkeeper after his marriage, his dislike of the radio and urban civilisation, his enthusiasm for Victoriana and old-fashioned furniture. In his writing life it came to the fore in such essays as 'Some Thoughts on the Common Toad', 'A Good Word for the Vicar of Bray' and 'Pleasure Spots', in his espousal of Kipling, Dickens and Gissing, and in his willingness to take up the cudgels on behalf of all manner of unorthodox and unpopular causes. Cyril Connolly described him as 'a revolutionary who was in love with the 1900s'; Conor Cruise O'Brien described his character as that of 'an English conservative eccentric'. To draw attention to this aspect of Orwell is not to diminish his achievement nor to cast doubts on his sincerity as a socialist; it is simply to underline the complexity of his personality: to emphasise again that he was by no means an uncomplicated, straightforward man. George Gis- sing's *The Private Papers of Henry Ryecroft* has been described as 'the testament of a man who loved everything venerable in England, from open fires to church bells'.[53] Much the same remark could be applied to *Coming Up For Air*, to such essays as 'The Moon Under Water' and many of the 'As I Please' articles. When one takes into account his nostalgia for the past, his refusal to ally himself with those who advocated the abolition of the monarchy or the public schools, his respect for the formalities and conventions of English life, one questions whether 'Whig' might be more accurate than 'Tory' as an epithet for him. Was Orwell a Whig in the manner of Burke rather than a truly radical thinker? Orwell's detestation of tyranny, intolerance, dishonesty and injustice was unquestionably sincere and deeply felt; but one questions how far he would have welcomed radical changes in the basic fabric of life.

Parallel with his conservatism in many aspects of life is his amateurism – using the word not in a derogatory sense but as 'one who cultivates a particular study or art for the love of it'. He was not a systematic or philosophical thinker in the same sense as H. G. Wells, Bertrand Russell or H. J. Laski. One would look in vain in his work for any profound philosophical or psychological analysis. Yet, paradoxically, in this very amateurism lay his greatest strength. Precisely because he wrote as a lay observer rather than a specialist he approached his themes with a freshness and originality unusual in political writing; whilst his essays frequently provoke disagreement they command respect as the work of an honest writer determined at all costs to tell the plain truth as he saw it. This quality of freshness may be illustrated by his essays, 'The Lion and the Unicorn' and 'The English People', in which he examined English national characteristics with an invigorating honesty and from the vantage point of a sympathetic yet shrewd observer. To write dispassionately of the traits and foibles of one's own country demands an unusual degree of truthfulness and objectivity; Orwell possessed these qualities in abundance. He owed them partly to his experiences, which had broadened his imagination and outlook in a manner quite untypical for one of his background; partly to his perfervid reading, and his desire to fashion a style of his own by which he would be remembered; partly to his lack of any formal philosophical education; but above all to his own highly idiosyncratic personality, with its insistence on fairness and plain speaking at all costs. His astringent manner of argument gives a cutting edge to his polemical writing which is at once refreshing and provocative.

It is for these qualities, then, that his essays and documentaries will continue to be read. In an age of conformity and ideology the freshness of his approach will earn for his non-fiction writings a new and wider audience. Readers who were too young to remember the immense social and political issues which so exercised his life will turn to him with respect and understanding, sensing that for all his faults – his tendency to generalise, to make sweeping judgements based on his own predilections, to exaggerate occasionally for the sake of effect – he remains a voice to be trusted, a man who wrote with anger and compassion on the problems of his time and elevated political writing into an enduring form of art.

It is easy to overlook the fact that Orwell's literary achievement is far more substantial than the six novels and three full-length documentaries associated with his name. Throughout his literary career he was a prolific journalist, producing a very considerable quantity of book reviews, articles and memoranda of which much (but by no means all) is preserved in the *Collected Essays, Journalism and Letters*. The sheer volume of this work is difficult to comprehend. During the period July 1943 to December 1945 he wrote book reviews and short articles totalling some 110 000 words, often sitting at his typewriter until the early hours of the morning. Much of this material was for prestigious journals such as the *Observer* and the *Manchester Evening News* but a considerable amount was written for small magazines with limited circulations; for these he received a token payment only. His themes ranged from fundamental questions of world politics to all those aspects of daily life which fascinated him so much: curious items of information culled from obscure books and from conversations with friends, superstitions, the climate, wild life, words and their meanings, and the extraordinary diversity of incident and behaviour in wartime London.

His interest in journalism had commenced as a struggling writer in Paris in the late 1920s (one of his very earliest pieces, 'A Farthing Newspaper',[54] published in *G. K.'s Weekly* on 29 December 1928, has been preserved for posterity). His book reviews for the *Adelphi* are much more assured pieces of writing.

In these Orwell made full use of his wide reading and produced with apparent effortlessness a series of carefully composed reviews in the best traditions of pithy literary criticism. What is notable in these reviews is that he did not hesitate to introduce elements of controversy, nor to criticise established literary figures. Appraising J. B. Priestley's *Angel Pavement*, for example, he wrote:

> But unfortunately, a novelist is not required to have good intentions but to convey beauty. And when one has finished applauding Mr. Priestley's effort to make clerks and typists interesting, one must add that the effort does not, even for a single page, come off. It is not that he writes ineptly, or is lumpishly dull, or consciously plays for cheap effects; it is simply that his writing does not touch the level at which memorable fiction begins.[55]

Continually when reading his reviews one is struck by his felicity in drawing attention to unusual or interesting aspects of the book under discussion, his ability to make apposite comparisons with other novels, the ease with which he places works in their literary and intellectual context. Throughout his apprentice years as a novelist he was writing book reviews for the *Adelphi* and other journals in which he thought aloud on the problems of construction and form he was wrestling with in his own work. Even when discussing works which have since faded into obscurity his observations are still worth reading for their insight and vigour. This skill in reviewing (which he satirised in a brilliant essay, 'Confessions of a Book Reviewer') continued throughout his life; even when gravely ill in 1948 he found the energy to write assessments of books by Oscar Wilde, Graham Greene, Osbert Sitwell, Jean-Paul Sartre and T. S. Eliot. He was a bibliophile in the sense that he was totally at home in the world of books, yet he never lost sight of the value of literature as a means towards the enrichment of life and the fuller understanding of human character.

His articles – as distinct from his major essays, which are frequently anthologised and widely known – are perhaps little read today although they reveal the breadth of his interests and the unusual catholicity of his reading. In them he revealed his interest in writers as diverse as Charles Reade, Rudyard Kipling, Arthur Koestler, Tobias Smollett, Mark Twain and Joseph Conrad. In this shorter work he also displays his ability to write lucidly and provocatively on a bewildering range of major and minor topics: the pamphlet as a literary genre, the techniques of discussing poetry on the radio, a reassessment of Thackeray as a novelist, propaganda and its influence upon language, freedom of the press, holiday resorts, the English murder, the cost of smoking, and so on and so on. The overwhelming impression one receives from reading through this material is of a vigorous intellectual *curiosity*, of a mind acutely interested in the world around him and determined to pursue its peculiarities into the remotest corners of life. At the moment when he was shot on the Aragon front almost his first thought was 'a violent resentment at having to leave this world which, when all is said and done, suits me so well'.[56] It is clear that though Orwell was impractical and rather innocent in some respects he retained a lively interest in the panorama of life and felt a deep concern for the injustices and unfairness he saw all around him. This sense of commitment is revealed at many points in his journalism and indicates a refusal to detach himself from the mainstream of life. In this he was the antithesis of Henry Miller, despite his strong admiration for Miller's work. The journalism is the work of a man whose love of literature is only too manifest, but is at the same time actively involved in the social, political and cultural life of his time. Arthur Koestler described him as 'the only writer of genius among the *litterateurs* of social revolt between the two wars'.[57]

Orwell's lifelong admiration for the satires of Jonathan Swift found expression in the two masterly works for which he is most renowned, *Animal Farm* and *Nineteen Eighty-Four*. The impact of these works on the twentieth-century consciousness has been profound. It is not merely that words and phrases from them – such expressions as 'Newspeak', 'doublethink', 'all animals are equal' – are now accepted additions to our vocabulary, but that his rationale of totalitarianism has made such a far-reaching impression on modern political thought. Whilst *Animal Farm* is now accepted as a classic study of 'the revolution betrayed' (and an allegory as timeless as Voltaire's *Candide*), *Nineteen Eighty-Four* is increasingly recognised as a thoroughgoing critique of the totalitarian philosophy, a profound indictment of the doctrine that might is right. The regime which ultimately defeats Winston Smith is akin to the 'vast pitiless mechanism'[58] of Wells's *The Island of Doctor Moreau* or the anonymous powers which frustrate Kafka's lonely heroes. As a study and critique of totalitarianism Orwell's satire ranks beside the work of Arthur Koestler, Ignazio Silone and Franz Borkenau; yet its influence has been far greater than that of his contemporaries since both *Nineteen Eighty-Four* and *Animal Farm* are myths which have become part of the intellectual and imaginative stock of modern man. Not only are both works seminal studies of tyranny but each is a moving essay on the theme of the outcast, the uprooted individual in conflict with forces he does not understand. When Boxer's eyes fill with tears in his disillusionment with the revolution and Winston Smith wanders through desolate London searching for companionship the reader identifies with them, recognising the loneliness and alienation which are persistent themes in the literature of our times.

Orwell concluded a memorable essay on Swift[59] with these words:

Swift did not possess ordinary wisdom, but he did possess a terrible intensity of vision, capable of picking out a single hidden truth and then magnifying it and distorting it. The durability of *Gulliver's Travels* goes to show that if the force of belief is behind it, a world-view which only just passes the test of sanity is sufficient to produce a great work of art.

These observations have a striking relevance to *Animal Farm* and *Nineteen Eighty-Four*. Orwell, in common with Swift, possessed 'a terrible intensity of vision'. This was a vision which had haunted him since his experiences in Spain in 1936–7. It was a vision of all-powerful regimes, sustained in power by a conviction of the absolute rightness of dogma, possessed with the ability to manipulate truth through the control of all means of communication. Such regimes, he believed, would control both the past and the present through their ability to alter the historical record in their own interests; would ruthlessly suppress any challenge to their authority from within; would not hesitate to distort the truth to comply with official doctrines; and could only be overcome by vigilance and, in the last analysis, by the use of force. This vision was indeed 'sufficient to produce a great work of art'. In common with other satires which have stood the test of time – *Gulliver's Travels*, *Candide*, *Erewhon* – Orwell's are not allegories concerning the future but the present: in each his method is to select a number of tendencies prevalent or incipient in the contemporary world, to isolate these, and exaggerate them for didactic purposes. Thus, television becomes the telescreen, the Gestapo and the OGPU become the Thought Police, and so on. The result is the creation of a wholly consistent world which has the capacity both to stimulate thought and entertain.

X   In assessing Orwell's stature as a satirist it is easy to underestimate the imaginative significance of *Nineteen Eighty-Four*. His very success in extrapolating from present trends has led some critics to overlook his creative achievement in describing a totally believable world animated with a terrifying logic of its own. The intellect refuses to accept that such a world could be possible; yet the rationale of his creation is such as *to suspend disbelief*. No book could exercise such an impact which did not possess unusual literary and imaginative qualities. Though it can be faulted on the grounds of its pessimism its capacity to haunt the imagination, to compel the reader to examine afresh questions of language and to foster a critical approach to ideology will ensure for it a niche in the cultural history of our age. It has a permanent place in literary history – alongside Wells's *The Time Machine*, Kafka's *The Castle* and John Fowles's *The Magus* – as one of those enduring myths which illuminate the problems of twentieth-century man.

$$* \quad * \quad * \quad * \quad *$$

It is in such terms, then, that one might attempt to assess the literary achievement of George Orwell. What is so extraordinarily significant about his life and work is that, despite its shortcomings, his stature as a novelist and essayist is now greater than ever and he has joined that select company of writers – Lawrence, Joyce and Kafka among them – whose work has exercised, and continues to exercise, a profound influence on English literature. The weaknesses inherent in his writings: an indifference to music and art, a tendency to sweeping generalisations, an occasional propensity to sadism, are far outweighed by their strengths. Indeed it seems safe to say that the qualities of honesty and lucidity which he felt to be so important will earn for his work a continuing reputation in the years ahead and that readers will turn afresh to his books and essays in search of that compelling prose, that crystalline sharpness, for which he is best remembered.

There are many unanswered questions which scholars will continue to debate. Was he on the whole an optimistic or a pessimistic writer? Was he a genuinely radical thinker or simply anxious to conserve the best of the past? Would he have continued writing satires after *Nineteen Eighty-Four*? To these and other questions there can be no final answers. All that can be said with confidence is that his work belongs in one of the central traditions of English letters, that his preoccupation with human decency was wholly honourable, and that future generations will honour him for his straightforwardness and lack of pretension in an age of cynicism.

Reflecting on his life and achievement one cannot but regret that his life was cut short at the age of forty-six, when he was clearly at the height of his powers and had so much still to give. Had he lived, he would assuredly have produced more novels, essays and documentaries in that inimitable style and continued to write articles commenting trenchantly on the issues of the day. Yet despite the brevity of his writing career the volume and diversity of his achievement is remarkable. When one reflects on the power of his writings to challenge and inspire, their incisive intelligence, their outspokenness and abundant humanity, one realises anew that comparisons with Swift, Defoe and Voltaire are not unjustified. Orwell has been described as 'the wintry conscience of a generation'.[60] He was that and much more. He was one of the few writers of this century to awaken his readers to a sense of the beauty of language and the corrupting effects of its misuse; to create a vision of human fraternity and of the misery caused by poverty and deprivation; to insist on tolerance, justice and decency in human relationships; to warn against the increasing artificiality of urban civilisation. Above all he presented a devastating critique of totalitarianism, warning with eloquence and anger of erosions of liberty and helping his readers to recognise tyranny in all its forms. For this and for the shining honesty of his prose posterity has reason to be grateful.

A George Orwell Dictionary

This dictionary is an alphabetically arranged guide to Orwell's books, essays and poems. Reviews of books will be found collected together under the heading 'Book Reviews'. Details of first publication are given where these are known.

The following examples are used throughout the dictionary:

CEJL	*Collected Essays, Journalism and Letters*
Crick	Crick, Bernard, *George Orwell: A Life*
NEW	*New English Weekly*
NS	*New Statesman and Nation*
Standard	*Evening Standard*

ANIMAL FARM A satire written in the form of an allegory, composed during the winter of 1943–4 and published in 1945. The story, which is a critique of dictatorship in general and of the USSR in particular, follows in the literary tradition of Voltaire's *Candide* and Swift's *Gulliver's Travels*.

ANTISEMITISM IN BRITAIN [*Contemporary Jewish Record*, April 1945] An examination of anti-Jewish prejudice and its psychological roots.

ARTHUR KOESTLER [Written September 1944] A discussion of the novels of Arthur Koestler, with particular reference to *Darkness at Noon*. He is seen as extremely significant because 'there is almost no English writer to whom it has happened to see totalitarianism from the inside'.

THE ART OF DONALD McGILL [*Horizon*, February 1942] An examination of comic postcards from a sociological standpoint. The essay includes the memorable sentence: 'If you look into your own mind, which are you, Don Quixote or

Sancho Panza?' (Orwell had been interested in comic post-cards for many years and collecting them was one of his hob-bies.)

AS I PLEASE From December 1943 until February 1945, and again from November 1946 until April 1947, Orwell contri-buted a regular column to *Tribune* under the title 'As I Please'. The column reflected the diversity of his interests and enthusiasms, ranging widely over politics, literature and cur-rent affairs. The articles are reproduced almost complete in *CEJL*.

AS ONE NON-COMBATANT TO ANOTHER [*Tribune*, 18 June 1943] A satirical poem replying to verses by Alex Comfort which had criticised a number of literary figures of the day. In a letter to Comfort following the exchange Orwell commented: 'I was only making a political and perhaps moral reply, and as a piece of verse your contribution was immensely better'.

AWAKE! YOUNG MEN OF ENGLAND [*Henley and South Oxfordshire Standard*, 2 October 1914] A patriotic poem composed whilst a schoolboy at St Cyprian's. The text is reproduced in Stansky and Abrahams, *The Unknown Orwell*, and also in Crick.

BENEFIT OF CLERGY [Written June 1944] A review of Salvador Dali's autobiography in which Orwell raises the question of whether 'the artist is to be exempt from the moral laws that are binding on ordinary people'.

BOOK REVIEWS Orwell wrote a considerable number of book reviews, of which the following are included in *CEJL*:

Adam, Karl	*The Spirit of Catholicism*
Aldington, Richard	*Death of a Hero*
Anand, Mulk Raj	*The Sword and the Sickle*
Asch, Scholem	*The Calf of Paper*
Ashton, Helen	*Dr. Serocold*
Asquith, Margot	*Autobiography*
Atholl, Duchess of	*Searchlight on Spain*
Bartimeus	*Naval Occasions*
Basily, N. de	*Russia under Soviet Rule*
Blunden, Edmund	*Cricket Country*
Borkenau, Franz	*The Spanish Cockpit*
	The Communist International
	The Totalitarian Enemy
Brockway, Fenner	*Workers' Front*

Brogan, Colm	*The Democrat at the Supper Table*
Burdett, Osbert	*The Two Carlyles*
Byrne, Donn	*Hangman's House*
Cain, Paul	*Fast One*
Casado, S.	*The Last Days of Madrid*
Churchill, Winston S.	*Their Finest Hour*
Cohen, Albert	*Nailcruncher*
Collis, Maurice	*Trials in Burma*
Common, Jack	*The Freedom of the Streets*
Connolly, Cyril	*The Rock Pool*
Conrad, Joseph	*Almayer's Folly*
	The Nigger of the Narcissus
	Typhoon
Crozier, F. P.	*The Men I Killed*
Curle, Richard	*Who Goes Home?*
Davies, W. H.	*Collected Poems*
du Bos, Charles	*Byron and the Need of Fatality*
Eliot, T. S.	*Burnt Norton*
	East Coker
	The Dry Salvages
	Notes towards the Definition of Culture
Fielden, Lionel	*Beggar My Neighbour*
Forster, E. M.	*A Passage to India*
Fraenkel, Michael	*Bastard Death*
Galsworthy, John	*Glimpses and Reflections*
Garstin, Crosbie	*The Owls House*
Goldsmith, Oliver	*The Vicar of Wakefield*
Green, F. C.	*Stendhal*
Green, Julian	*Midnight*
	Personal Record
Greene, Graham	*The Heart of the Matter*
Hart, B. H. Liddell	*The British Way in Warfare*
Hay, Ian	*A Safety Match*
Hayek, F. A.	*The Road to Serfdom*
Henderson, Philip	*The Novel Today*
Hilton, Jack	*Caliban Shrieks*
Hitler, Adolf	*Mein Kampf*
Jacobs, W. W.	*Odd Craft*
Jellinck, Frank	*The Civil War in Spain*
Jesse, F. Tennyson	*The Story of Burma*
Koestler, Arthur	*Spanish Testament*

Lawrence, D. H.	*The Prussian Officer*
Lewis, Sinclair	*Our Mr. Wrenn*
Low, Mary	*Red Spanish Notebook*
Lunn, Arnold	*Spanish Rehearsal*
Lyons, Eugene	*Assignment in Utopia*
Mass Observation	*The Pub and the People*
Miller, Henry	*Tropic of Cancer*
	Black Spring
	The Cosmological Eye
Mitchell, Mairin	*Storm over Spain*
Montague, C. E.	*A Hind Let Loose*
Moore, George	*Esther Waters*
Morley, F. V.	*War Paint*
Mumford, Lewis	*Herman Melville*
Noyes, Alfred	*The Edge of the Abyss*
O'Casey, Sean	*Drums under the Windows*
Palinurus	*The Unquiet Grave*
Peers, E. Allison	*Catalonia Infelix*
Priestley, J. B.	*Angel Pavement*
Read, Herbert	*A Coat of Many Colours*
Reade, Winwood	*The Martyrdom of Man*
Roberts, Kenneth	*The Lively Lady*
Russell, Bertrand	*Power: A New Social Analysis*
Sanderson, Lady	*Long Shadows*
Sartre, Jean-Paul	*Portrait of the Antisemite*
Sayers, Dorothy L.	*Gaudy Night*
Sheed, F. J.	*Communism and Man*
Shute, Nevil	*Landfall*
Sinclair, Upton	*The Jungle*
Sitwell, Edith	*Alexander Pope*
Sitwell, Osbert	*Great Morning*
Sommerfield, John	*Volunteer in Spain*
Teichman, Sir Eric	*Journey to Turkistan*
Timmermans, R.	*Heroes of the Alcazar*
Wilde, Oscar	*The Soul of Man under Socialism*
Wodehouse, P. G.	*My Man Jeeves*
Wolfe, Lawrence	*The Reilly Plan*
Woller, Johann	*Zest for Life*
Zamyatin, E. I.	*We*
Zilliacus, K.	*The Mirror of the Past*

BOOKSHOP MEMORIES [*Fortnightly*, November 1936] In this essay Orwell looks back with whimsical detachment to his days as a bookshop assistant in Hampstead and describes his feelings on thinking over this period in his life (October 1934–January 1936). (Cf. Chapter 1 of *Keep the Aspidistra Flying*.)

BOOKS VS. CIGARETTES [*Tribune*, 8 February 1946] An examination of the cost of books compared with that of cigarettes and other forms of entertainment. (It is entirely characteristic of Orwell's thoroughness that in order to arrive at a figure for the annual cost of reading he made a detailed inventory of his own library.)

BOYS' WEEKLIES [*Horizon*, March 1940] Written in 1939, 'Boys' Weeklies' is a discussion of boys' comics, particularly those featuring Billy Bunter and Greyfriars school. Orwell analyses the stories from both literary and sociological standpoints and discusses their influence upon readers. The essay provoked a lengthy reply from the author of the Billy Bunter stories, Frank Richards.

BURMESE DAYS Orwell's first novel, published in 1934. The book is based on his experience as a policeman in Burma during the years 1922–7 and expresses his revulsion against imperialism. In 1936 he described it in a letter to Henry Miller as 'the only one of my books that I am pleased with'.

BURNHAM'S VIEW OF THE CONTEMPORARY WORLD STRUGGLE [*New Leader*, 29 March 1947] A discussion of *The Struggle for the World* by James Burnham and of the likelihood of a Third World War.

CATASTROPHIC GRADUALISM [*Common Wealth Review*, November 1945] An examination and refutation of the Theory of Catastrophic Gradualism, i.e., the idea that social change cannot be achieved without violence and injustice.

CHARLES DICKENS Written in 1939 this, the longest of Orwell's essays, is an extended discussion of Dickens's strengths and weaknesses as a novelist and an analysis of his literary techniques. The essay is of seminal importance as an indication of Orwell's approach to literature and of his indebtedness to Dickens.

CHARLES READE [*NS*, 17 August 1940] A discussion of Reade's merits as a writer. Orwell describes his own favourite Reade novel *Foul Play* and concludes that its attraction is 'the charm of useless knowledge'.

A CLERGYMAN'S DAUGHTER Published in 1935, this was Orwell's second novel. It relates the story of Dorothy Hare, the daughter of an impoverished rector, and of her quest for emotional fulfilment. The novel incorporates Orwell's experiences of hop-picking in Kent and of teaching in private schools. In later years he repudiated the book and would not permit it to be reprinted during his lifetime.

CLINK Written in August 1932 and not published in Orwell's lifetime, 'Clink' describes his unsuccessful attempts to be imprisoned for drunkenness. The style is similar to that of *Down and Out* and should be compared with 'The Spike' as an interesting early example of his documentary technique.

COLLECTED ESSAYS An omnibus volume published in 1961 containing the essays included in *Critical Essays*, *Shooting an Elephant and other essays* and *England Your England*.

COMING UP FOR AIR In this novel, published in 1939, Orwell expressed his forebodings concerning the rise of totalitarian regimes. The story is memorable for the evident nostalgia of the narrator as he looks back on his idyllic childhood in Lower Binfield [Henley-on-Thames] during the years prior to 1914.

COMMON LODGING HOUSES [*NS*, 3 September 1932] A factual description of municipal night-shelters in London. The essay is a summary of his researches into lodging houses and should be compared with Chapters 24 and 25 of *Down and Out*.

CONFESSIONS OF A BOOK REVIEWER [*Tribune*, 3 May 1946] A quasi-humorous account of the practicalities of book reviewing.

CONRAD'S PLACE AND RANK IN ENGLISH LETTERS [*Wiadomosci*, 10 April 1949] A short appraisal of Conrad's stature as a novelist. During the last year of his life Orwell began making notes for a long essay on Conrad which he intended to include in the collection *Shooting an Elephant and other essays* but this was not completed.

THE COST OF LETTERS [*Horizon*, September 1946] Orwell's answers to a questionnaire on writing as a livelihood. 'If one wants to be primarily a *writer*, then, in our society, one is an animal that is tolerated but not encouraged – something rather like a house sparrow – and one gets on better if one realises one's position from the start.'

CRITICAL ESSAYS An anthology published in 1946 and containing the following essays:

Charles Dickens
Boys' Weeklies
Wells, Hitler and the World State
The Art of Donald McGill
Rudyard Kipling
W. B. Yeats
Benefit of Clergy
Arthur Koestler
Raffles and Miss Blandish
In Defence of P. G. Wodehouse

DECLINE OF THE ENGLISH MURDER [*Tribune*, 15 February 1946] Orwell argues that 'our great period in murder, our Elizabethan period, so to speak, seems to have been between roughly 1850 and 1925', and notes that the prevalent type of crime is less emotional than the sensational murders of the past.

DEMOCRACY IN THE BRITISH ARMY [*Left Forum*, September 1939] A plea for the democratisation of the British armed forces and a discussion of the factors militating against fundamental changes in military organisation.

DICKENS, DALI AND OTHERS The American title of the collection published in England under the title *Critical Essays*.

DOWN AND OUT IN PARIS AND LONDON Orwell's first book, published in January 1933. It is an account of his experiences of poverty in Paris and London between 1929 and 1931. Although the book was extensively reviewed it soon went out of print and it did not become widely known until its publication as a paperback (by Penguin Books) in 1940.

A DRESSED MAN AND A NAKED MAN [*Adelphi*, October 1933] A poem of ten verses describing a bargain over a lodging-house fire: a man agrees to exchange his clothes in return for the price of a meal.

ENGLAND YOUR ENGLAND The English edition of the collection published in the United States under the title *Such, Such Were the Joys*. In this edition 'Such, Such Were the Joys' was omitted, and Chapter 2 of *The Road to Wigan Pier* (under the title 'Down the Mine') was included.

THE ENGLISH PEOPLE A booklet published in 1947 (but written in 1944), commissioned by Collins for their series 'Britain in Pictures'. The booklet is divided into six sections: 'England at First Glance', 'The Moral Outlook of the English People', 'The Political Outlook of the English People', 'The English Class System', 'The English Language' and 'The Future of the English People'. Whilst covering broadly similar ground to *The Lion and the Unicorn* Orwell frequently employs different arguments: the two publications therefore represent an interesting case-study in the development of his thought.

A FARTHING NEWSPAPER [*G.K.'s Weekly*, 29 December 1928] Reviews a Paris newspaper, the *Ami du Peuple*, which is published at a price of a farthing, and exposes the fact that it is financed by industrial capitalists.

FREEDOM OF THE PARK [*Tribune*, 7 December 1945] A defence of freedom of speech and of the right to sell minority newspapers in Hyde Park.

THE FRONTIERS OF ART AND PROPAGANDA [*Listener*, 29 May 1941] A discussion of the relationship between literature and propaganda and an assertion that 'propaganda in some form or other lurks in every book, that every work of art has a meaning and a purpose'.

FUNNY, BUT NOT VULGAR [*Leader*, 28 July 1945] Orwell argues that the great age of English humorous writing was the first three quarters of the nineteenth century and discusses the reasons why 'there is not and has not been for decades past, any such thing as a first-rate humorous periodical'.

GEORGE GISSING [Written May–June 1948] An appraisal of Gissing's novels, dealing in particular with *New Grub Street* and *The Odd Women*. Orwell concludes that he was 'exceptional among English writers . . . I am ready to maintain that England has produced very few better novelists'.

GOOD BAD BOOKS [*Tribune*, 2 November 1945] A discussion of the good bad book: 'that is, the kind of book that has no literary pretensions but which remains readable when more serious productions have perished'. He argues that the supreme example of the good bad book is *Uncle Tom's Cabin*.

A GOOD WORD FOR THE VICAR OF BRAY [*Tribune*, 26 April 1946] A plea to his readers to have sufficient foresight to plant trees for future generations to enjoy.

A HANGING [*Adelphi*, August 1931] A description of the execution of a Hindu for an unspecified crime and the realisation on the part of the narrator of the inherent wrongness of capital punishment. 'A Hanging' is the only essay signed with his real name (i.e., written prior to 1933, when he adopted his pseudonym) which Orwell permitted to be reprinted.

HOMAGE TO CATALONIA A documentary account of his experiences as a militiaman during the Spanish Civil War (Orwell served on the Aragon front from January–June 1937). Cf. 'Looking Back on the Spanish War' and 'Notes on the Spanish Militias'.

HOP-PICKING Written in October 1931 and not published in Orwell's lifetime, this is cast in the form of a diary covering the period 25 August to 8 October 1931. It describes a sojourn of several weeks in the hop-fields of Kent and the picaresque adventures of Orwell and his companions *en route*. Some of the material was adapted to form part of Chapter 2 of *A Clergyman's Daughter*.

HOW THE POOR DIE [*Now*, November 1946] A graphic account of his stay in a Paris hospital in 1929 when he was seriously ill with pneumonia.

A HUNDRED UP [*Observer*, 13 February 1944] Reflections on the hundredth anniversary of the publication of Dickens's *Martin Chuzzlewit*.

IN DEFENCE OF COMRADE ZILLIACUS [Written autumn 1947] A criticism of *Tribune* for 'having no definite and viable foreign policy' and for the ambiguity of its editorial policy towards the USSR.

IN DEFENCE OF ENGLISH COOKING [*Standard*, 15 December 1945] Orwell lists the English dishes which cannot be obtained outside Britain and vigorously defends English cooking against the charge of imitativeness.

IN DEFENCE OF P. G. WODEHOUSE [*Windmill*, July 1945] A discussion of Wodehouse, his achievement as a novelist, and the mental atmosphere of the Bertie Wooster novels. Orwell defends Wodehouse against the charge of aiding the Nazis.

IN DEFENCE OF THE NOVEL [*NEW*, 12 and 19 November 1936] A discussion of the reasons for the decline in the prestige of the novel and a plea for more intelligent reviewing of new novels.

IN FRONT OF YOUR NOSE [*Tribune*, 22 March 1946] A discussion of the widespread tendency to ignore facts which are obvious and unalterable, and to hold irreconcilable attitudes: these contradictions are 'all finally traceable to a secret belief that one's political opinions . . . will not have to be tested against solid reality'.

INSIDE THE WHALE Written in 1939, 'Inside the Whale' is an extended discussion of Henry Miller's novel *Tropic of Cancer* and an analysis of two schools of thought which Orwell detects in the literary world: those who are 'inside the whale', i.e., who realise that they are powerless to influence world affairs and are content simply to record them; and those 'outside the whale' who feel it is a writer's duty to play an active role in politics.

INSIDE THE WHALE AND OTHER ESSAYS A collection of three essays published in 1940: 'Inside the Whale', 'Charles Dickens' and 'Boys' Weeklies'.

INTRODUCTIONS Orwell contributed the following introductions, all of which are reprinted in *CEJL*:

London, Jack	*Love of Life and Other Stories*
Merrick, Leonard	*The Position of Peggy Harper*
Orwell, George	*Down and Out in Paris and London* (French edition)
	Animal Farm (Ukrainian edition)

KEEP THE ASPIDISTRA FLYING Published in 1936, this was Orwell's third novel. The book incorporates his experiences as a bookshop assistant in London and the tribulations of his literary apprenticeship.

KITCHENER [*Henley and South Oxfordshire Standard*, 21 July 1916] A patriotic poem composed whilst a schoolboy at St Cyprian's. The text is reproduced in Stansky and Abrahams, *The Unknown Orwell*, and also in Crick.

LEAR, TOLSTOY AND THE FOOL [*Polemic*, March 1947] A discussion of Tolstoy's critical pamphlet *Shakespeare and the Drama* in which Orwell vigorously defends Shakespeare against Tolstoy's polemic.

THE LIMIT TO PESSIMISM [*NEW*, 25 April 1940] A review of Malcolm Muggeridge's *The Thirties* and a critique of the pessimism inherent in the argument that 'every attempt to establish liberty leads directly to tyranny'.

THE LION AND THE UNICORN A booklet published in London in

1941, the first volume in a series – the Searchlight Books – edited by Orwell and T. R. Fyvel. The booklet, which is divided into three parts – 'England Your England', 'Shopkeepers at War' and 'The English Revolution' – discusses English national characteristics and the need for radical social changes in Britain within the context of the war effort. 'England Your England' was later reprinted as a separate essay.

LITERATURE AND THE LEFT [*Tribune*, 4 June 1943] Orwell asserts that the Socialist movement has alienated the literary intelligentsia, 'partly by confusing tracts with literature, and partly by having no room in it for a humanistic culture', and criticises the tendency to judge a writer by his political beliefs.

LITERATURE AND TOTALITARIANISM [*Listener*, 19 June 1941] A discussion of the implications of totalitarianism upon literature and freedom of thought: 'if totalitarianism triumphs throughout the world, literature, as we have known it, is at an end'.

LONDON LETTERS A series of articles which Orwell contributed to the *Partisan Review* (New York) at regular intervals from January 1941 to the summer of 1946. The letters comment on the changing political and military situation and discuss their implications for Britain and America.

LONDON PLEASURES The title of a long poem by Gordon Comstock, the central character in *Keep the Aspidistra Flying*. The poem was published in *Adelphi* in November 1935 under the title 'St. Andrews Day, 1935' although it is not included in *CEJL*.

LOOKING BACK ON THE SPANISH WAR [*New Road*, 1943] Orwell reflects on his experiences as a soldier during the Spanish Civil War and discusses the wider implications of the conflict. The essay includes his poem in memory of the Italian militiaman he had befriended, concluding with the words:

> But the thing that I saw in your face
> No power can disinherit:
> No bomb that ever burst
> Shatters the crystal spirit.

MARK TWAIN – THE LICENSED JESTER [*Tribune*, 26 November 1943] A discussion of the life and work of Mark Twain, in which he regrets that Twain's 'best and most characteristic' books, *Roughing It*, *The Innocents at Home*, and *Life on the Mississippi* are little remembered today. (Orwell retained a lifelong interest in Twain and his essays and letters contain frequent references to him. In 1935 he considered the idea of writing a short biography of Twain but failed to find a publisher for such a project.)

MARREKECH [*New Writing*, Christmas 1939] Written in the spring of 1939 when Orwell and his wife were staying at Marrakech, Morocco, this is a vivid pen-picture of poverty, dirt and starvation in North Africa. 'When you walk through a town like this . . . when you see how the people live, and still more how easily they die, it is always difficult to believe that you are walking among human beings.'

THE MEANING OF A POEM [*Listener*, 12 June 1941] A discussion of the poem 'Felix Randal' by Gerard Manley Hopkins and of the techniques involved in analysing its meaning.

THE MOON UNDER WATER [*Standard*, 9 February 1946] A description of Orwell's ideal public house: 'its whole architecture and fittings are uncompromisingly Victorian . . . everything has the solid comfortable ugliness of the nineteenth century'. After describing the attractive features of the inn he reveals that it is imaginary.

MY COUNTRY RIGHT OR LEFT [*Folios of New Writing*, Autumn 1940] Orwell discusses his emotional attitudes to the First and Second World Wars and his reasons for supporting the resistance to Hitler: 'There is no real alternative between resisting Hitler and surrendering to him, and from a Socialist point of view I should say that it is better to resist'.

MY EPITAPH BY JOHN FLORY An excerpt from an early unpublished draft of *Burmese Days*. The excerpt, unlike the novel itself, is written in the first person and contains Flory's request that his epitaph shall be carved 'on the bark of some great peepul tree above my head'. Stansky and Abrahams date the fragment as having been written early in 1930. (Cf. *The Unknown Orwell*, 189.)

NEW WORDS [Circa 1940] The thesis of this article is that 'from the point of view of exactitude and expressiveness our language has remained in the Stone Age'. He advocates the deliberate invention of new words to facilitate more unambiguous communication.

A NEW YEAR MESSAGE [*Tribune*, 5 January 1945] Orwell defines

Tribune's literary policy and defends the decision to print fewer short stories and to devote more space to essays on literary and general subjects (he was literary editor of the paper from November 1943 to February 1945).

A NICE CUP OF TEA [*Standard*, 12 January 1946] Contains precise directions for making 'the perfect cup of tea'. The directions consist of eleven points, 'every one of which I regard as golden'.

NINETEEN EIGHTY-FOUR Orwell's last completed novel, published in 1949, and the book by which he is most likely to be remembered. He commenced work on it in August 1946 but its composition was continually delayed due to his serious illness; it was not completed until November 1948. The book describes England ruled by a totalitarian dictatorship: a society in which thought is controlled and language is manipulated in the interests of the state. Cf. his essay 'Prophecies of Fascism'.

NO, NOT ONE [*Adelphi*, October 1941] A review of the novel *No Such Liberty* by Alex Comfort and a critique of arguments for pacifism.

NONSENSE POETRY [*Tribune*, 21 December 1945] A discussion of the nonsense rhymes of Edward Lear and of their influence on literature. Cf. 'Lear, Tolstoy and the Fool'.

NOT COUNTING NIGGERS [*Adelphi*, July 1939] A review of Clarence Streit's *Union Now* (which advocated a federal union of the democratic states opposed to Nazism) and a criticism of the implied exclusion of the subject peoples of Asia and Africa.

NOTES ON NATIONALISM [*Polemic*, October 1945] A detailed discussion of nationalism and of the principal characteristics of nationalist thought. Orwell concludes that it is possible to struggle against prejudice and xenophobia but 'that this is essentially a *moral* effort'.

NOTES ON THE SPANISH MILITIAS These notes, found among Orwell's papers after his death, describe the ideological differences between the various Spanish militias. For a full understanding of the complexities of the Spanish Civil War the notes should be read in conjunction with Chapters 5 and 11 of *Homage to Catalonia*.

NOTES ON THE WAY [*Time and Tide*, 6 April 1940] Comments upon Malcolm Muggeridge's *The Thirties*, Hilaire Belloc's *The Servile State* and Aldous Huxley's *Brave New World* and concludes with the reflection that the outlook for mankind is one of totalitarianism unless a belief in human brotherhood can be reinstated.

ON A RUINED FARM NEAR THE HIS MASTER'S VOICE GRAMOPHONE FACTORY [*Adelphi*, April 1934] A poem of nine verses describing the mixed feelings of the narrator on observing the despoliation of the countryside by industrialisation. The poem was included in *The Best Poems of 1934*.

ON KIPLING'S FARM [*NEW*, 23 January 1936] A short summary of Kipling's achievement in which Orwell pays warm tribute to the influence of his books upon his own development. 'But now that he is dead, I for one cannot help wishing that I could offer some kind of tribute – a salute of guns, if such a thing were available – to the story-teller who was so important to my childhood.' Cf. 'Rudyard Kipling'.

OYSTERS AND BROWN STOUT [*Tribune*, 22 December 1944] A discussion of Thackeray as a novelist, journalist and writer of burlesques.

PAMPHLET LITERATURE [*NS*, 9 January 1943] A review of fifteen tropical pamphlets and a discussion of the revival of the pamphlet as a literary form. (Over a period of many years Orwell accumulated a substantial collection of pamphlets; this is now housed in the British Library.)

PLEASURE SPOTS [*Tribune*, 11 January 1946] A criticism of the artificiality and regimentation of modern pleasure resorts: 'man only stays human by preserving large patches of simplicity in his life'.

POETRY AND THE MICROPHONE [*New Saxon Pamphlet*, March 1945] Orwell discusses the techniques involved in the broadcasting of poetry and argues that, imaginatively handled, radio could play an important role in the popularising of literature. The article stemmed directly from his work in broadcasting literary programmes to India.

POLITICS AND THE ENGLISH LANGUAGE [*Horizon*, April 1946] One of Orwell's most significant and characteristic essays, this is an analysis of the erosion of the English language through the use of meaningless words, dying metaphors and pretentious diction. He argues that political discussion in particular has become debased through careless and imprecise language.

THE POLITICS OF STARVATION [*Tribune*, 18 January 1946] Deplores the famine in Europe and argues in favour of increas-

ing the food supply to Germany. 'Whatever the ultimate political settlement in Europe may be, it can only be worse if it has
been preceded by years of hunger, misery, banditry and
ignorance.'

POLITICS VERSUS LITERATURE [*Polemic*, September 1946] In this
essay, sub-titled 'An Examination of *Gulliver's Travels*', Orwell
displays his lifelong admiration for Swift. '. . . he is one of the
writers I admire with least reserve, and *Gulliver's Travels* in
particular is a book which it seems impossible for me to grow
tired of.'

THE PREVENTION OF LITERATURE [*Polemic*, January 1946]
Orwell vigorously defends the concept of freedom of expression and discusses the impact of totalitarianism on literature:
'literature is doomed if liberty of thought perishes'.

THE PROLETARIAN WRITER [*Listener*, 19 December 1940] A discussion between Orwell and Desmond Hawkins which seeks
to define the phrase 'proletarian literature' and examines its
characteristics, language and achievements.

PROPAGANDA AND DEMOTIC SPEECH [*Persuasion*, Summer 1944]
An examination of the differences between written and spoken
English and of the meaningless slogans employed by politi-
cians. (Cf. 'Politics and the English Language' and his 'As I
Please' article of 17 March 1944.)

PROPHECIES OF FASCISM [*Tribune*, 12 July 1940] A discussion
and comparison of Jack London's *The Iron Heel*, H. G. Wells's
The Sleeper Awakes, Aldous Huxley's *Brave New World* and
Ernest Bramah's *The Secret of the League*. The essay is of par-
ticular interest in relation to his own anti-Utopia *Nineteen
Eighty-Four*.

THE QUESTION OF THE POUND AWARD [*Partisan Review*, May
1949] A short appraisal of Ezra Pound's stature as a writer.
Orwell is careful to draw a distinction between Pound as a
literary figure and his political opinions.

RAFFLES AND MISS BLANDISH [*Horizon*, October 1944] A comparison of the gentlemanly code of conduct in the 'Raffles'
stories by E. W. Hornung with the amorality of *No Orchids for
Miss Blandish*.

THE REDISCOVERY OF EUROPE [*Listener*, 19 March 1942] Orwell
discusses the literary giants of the early twentieth century and
argues that 'the basic fact about nearly all English writers of
that time is their complete unawareness of anything outside

the contemporary English scene'. He draws a contrast between James Joyce's *Ulysses* and Galsworthy's *The Forsyte Saga*,
arguing that, whilst both are intended to give a comprehensive
picture of society, Galsworthy's is inferior since it does not
move outside a comparatively narrow circle.

REFLECTIONS ON GANDHI [*Partisan Review*, January 1949] A
sympathetic appraisal of the life and work of Mahatma
Gandhi.

REVENGE IS SOUR [*Tribune*, 9 November 1945] Argues against
the idea of revenge and punishment of Nazi Germany: the
punitive peace settlement being forced on Germany was 'monstrous'.

RIDING DOWN FROM BANGOR [*Tribune*, 22 November 1946] A
discussion of *Helen's Babies* by John Habberton and of
stereotyped notions of America derived from childhood reading. (The title of the essay is taken from a student song which
the fourteen-year-old Eric Blair sang as his initiation on entering Eton College.)

THE ROAD TO WIGAN PIER A documentary account of a journey
to the coal mining areas of Lancashire and Yorkshire in 1936.
The book is of exceptional interest as an example of Orwell's
matured style of sociological reporting and for the autobiographical chapters describing his transition from a member of
the Indian Imperial Police to a chronicler of poverty. *The Road
to Wigan Pier* was an early selection of the Left Book Club,
founded by Victor Gollancz.

THE ROAD TO WIGAN PIER DIARY This typescript diary, found
among Orwell's papers after his death, covers the period 31
January–25 March 1936 and formed the basis for *The Road to
Wigan Pier*. Critical opinion is divided as to whether the diary
is (as it purports to be) a spontaneous notebook, or a literary
re-creation composed at a later date. Cf. Stansky and
Abrahams, *Orwell: The Transformation*, pp. 126–7, and Crick,
p. 182.

RUDYARD KIPLING [*Horizon*, February 1942] A review of T. S.
Eliot's anthology *A Choice of Kipling's Verse* and an examination
of Kipling's achievement as a poet and interpreter of his age.
Cf. 'On Kipling's Death'.

ST. ANDREWS DAY 1935 *See* LONDON PLEASURES.

SECOND THOUGHTS ON JAMES BURNHAM [*Polemic*, May 1946] A
lengthy discussion of James Burnham's *The Managerial Revo-*

lution, later reprinted as a pamphlet under the title 'James
Burnham and the Managerial Revolution'. The essay is significant for the insight it affords into Orwell's conceptions
of political theory *vis-à-vis Nineteen Eighty-Four*.

SHOOTING AN ELEPHANT [*New Writing*, Autumn 1936] One of his
most celebrated essays, 'Shooting an Elephant' describes the
execution of a tame beast which has run amok and Orwell's
simultaneous realisation of 'the hollowness, the futility of the
white man's dominion in the East'.

SHOOTING AN ELEPHANT AND OTHER ESSAYS An anthology published in 1950 containing the following essays:

Shooting an Elephant
A Hanging
How the Poor Die
Lear, Tolstoy and the Fool
Politics vs. Literature: An Examination of Gulliver's Travels
Politics and the English Language
Reflections on Gandhi
The Prevention of Literature
Second Thoughts on James Burnham
Confessions of a Book Reviewer
Books vs. Cigarettes
Good Bad Books
Nonsense Poetry
Riding Down from Bangor
The Sporting Spirit
Decline of the English Murder
Some Thoughts on the Common Toad
A Good Word for the Vicar of Bray

SOME THOUGHTS ON THE COMMON TOAD [*Tribune*, 12 April
1946] In this eulogy of the coming of spring Orwell reveals his
deep love of the countryside and his interest in the cycle of the
seasons. 'I mention the spawning of the toads because it is one
of the phenomena of spring which most deeply appeal to me,
and because the toad, unlike the skylark and the primrose, has
never had much of a boost from the poets.' Cf. his essay 'A
Good Word for the Vicar of Bray' and H. G. Wells's essay
'The Amateur Nature Lover'.

SOMETIMES IN THE MIDDLE AUTUMN DAYS [*Adelphi*, March

1933] A poem of eight verses on the theme of the transience of life and the duty of each individual to make the utmost of his opportunities.

THE SPIKE [*Adelphi*, April 1931] A description of a weekend's stay in a casual ward, later revised to form Chapters 27 and 35 of *Down and Out*. The essay should be compared with 'Clink' as an interesting early example of his documentary technique.

SPILLING THE SPANISH BEANS [*NEW*, 29 July and 2 September 1937] Written shortly after Orwell returned to Britain after having fought in the Spanish Civil War, this is a dispassionate attempt to disentangle for English readers the complexities of the conflict and a warning against distortions published in newspapers. (Cf. 'Notes on the Spanish Militias' and 'Looking Back on the Spanish War'.)

THE SPORTING SPIRIT [*Tribune*, 14 December 1945] Argues against international sporting activities on the grounds that 'sport is an unfailing cause of ill-will'.

SUCH, SUCH WERE THE JOYS [*Partisan Review*, September–October 1952] A lengthy account of his school days at St Cyprians, Eastbourne, where Blair had been a pupil from September 1911–December 1916. He forwarded the manuscript to his publisher in May 1947 but it appears to have been written much earlier, possibly *c*. 1940. Cf. Crick, pp. 410–12.

SUCH, SUCH WERE THE JOYS AND OTHER ESSAYS An anthology published in New York in 1953 containing the following essays:

Such, Such were the Joys
Why I Write
Writers and Leviathan
North and South
Notes on Nationalism
Anti-Semitism in Britain
Poetry and the Microphone
Inside the Whale
Marrakech
Looking Back on the Spanish War
England your England

('England your England' is a reprint of part of 'The Lion and the Unicorn'.)

THROUGH A GLASS ROSILY [*Tribune*, 23 November 1945] An examination of untruthful propaganda and of the dangers of suppressing information for fear that publication may cause offence.

TOBIAS SMOLLETT: SCOTLAND'S BEST NOVELIST [*Tribune*, 22 September 1944] A discussion of Smollett's achievement as a picaresque novelist, with particular reference to *Roderick Random* and *Peregrine Pickle*.

TOLSTOY AND SHAKESPEARE [*Listener*, 5 June 1941] An examination of Tolstoy's essay on Shakespeare. Orwell demonstrates that a critique of Shakespeare on philosophical grounds is necessarily irrelevant and that 'not only his reputation but the pleasure we take in him remain just the same as before'. Cf. 'Lear, Tolstoy and the Fool'.

TOWARD EUROPEAN UNITY [*Partisan Review*, July–August 1947] A discussion of the probable shape of human history in the nuclear age. 'The actual outlook, so far as I can calculate the probabilities, is very dark, and any serious thought should start out from that fact.'

W. B. YEATS [*Horizon*, January 1943] A review of *The Development of W. B. Yeats* by V. K. Menon and an appraisal of Yeats as a poet and thinker.

WAR-TIME DIARY Orwell maintained a detailed diary covering the period 28 May 1940 to 28 August 1941 and again from 14 March 1942 to 15 November 1942. The diary is reproduced almost in its entirety in *CEJL* vol. 2. It contains little information on his personal life and consists largely of commentary on the changing war situation as seen from London.

WELLS, HITLER AND THE WORLD STATE [*Horizon*, August 1941] An examination of Wells's strengths and weaknesses as a political thinker in which Orwell, whilst criticising Wells for his *naïveté* in the face of Hitler, pays warm tribute to him as a novelist and prophet.

WHAT IS SCIENCE? [*Tribune*, 26 October 1945] An attempt to define the words 'science' and 'scientist' and to contrast the scientific and non-scientific attitudes of mind.

WHO ARE THE WAR CRIMINALS? [*Tribune*, 22 October 1943] Reflections on the collapse of the Mussolini regime in Italy and on the unwisdom of a formal 'trial of war criminals'.

WHY I JOINED THE INDEPENDENT LABOUR PARTY [*New Leader*, 24 June 1938] A summary of the personal and ideological reasons which prompted Orwell to join the ILP. (He was a member from June 1938 until the outbreak of war in 1939; he resigned as he could no longer support the Party's pacifist line.)

WHY I WRITE [*Gangrel*, Summer 1946] In this, one of Orwell's most significant essays, he reviews his early literary interests and ambitions and the motives which led him to become a writer. 'Every line of serious work that I have written since 1936 has been written, directly or indirectly, *against* totalitarianism and *for* democratic Socialism, as I understand it . . . What I have most wanted to do throughout the past ten years is to make political writing into an art.'

WRITERS AND LEVIATHAN [*New Leader*, 19 June 1948] A discussion of the position of the writer in relation to the state. Orwell concludes that 'his writings, in so far as they have any value, will always be the product of the saner self that stands aside . . .' Cf. his essay 'Inside the Whale'.

YOU AND THE ATOM BOMB [*Tribune*, 19 October 1945] A discussion of atomic weapons and their implications for world peace. 'If, as seems to be the case, it [the atomic bomb] is a rare and costly object as difficult to produce as a battleship, it is likelier to put an end to large-scale wars at the cost of prolonging indefinitely a "peace that is no peace".'

YOUR QUESTIONS ANSWERED [2 December 1943] The text of a broadcast talk in which Orwell describes Wigan and the origin of the phrase 'Wigan Pier'. 'The landscape is mostly slag-heaps, looking like the mountains of the moon, and mud and soot and so forth.'

Part II

NOVELS AND DOCUMENTARIES

Down and Out in Paris and London

The first draft of the book which eventually became *Down and Out in Paris and London* was commenced early in 1930. The manuscript of this first version does not survive, but it was apparently cast in the form of a diary and described Orwell's experiences of poverty in Paris.[1] He worked steadily and enthusiastically on the draft through much of 1930, working partly at the home of his sister and her husband at Bramley near Leeds, and partly at his parents' home at Southwold. The manuscript was completed by October of that year, and on the advice of his friend Mabel Fierz he forwarded it to Jonathan Cape. Cape in due course rejected the book on the grounds that it was too short and fragmentary, but Orwell was sufficiently encouraged by their letter of rejection to feel that if he were to revise and lengthen the manuscript the publishers would be willing to reconsider it.

He set to work on a major revision and expansion of the book, casting it no longer as a diary but a continuous narrative, and adding his experiences of poverty in England. This new version (which is substantially the text as we know it today) was not completed until August 1931 and was again submitted to Cape, this time under the title *Days in London and Paris*. When in October the book was rejected by Cape for a second time Orwell was bitterly disappointed and his confidence in the work was totally undermined – not, it must be added, his determination to succeed as a writer, for within a few weeks he commenced work on the book we now know as *Burmese Days*. Disillusioned with his book on poverty, on which he had placed such high hopes, he accepted the advice of his friend Richard Rees to submit it to

79

T. S. Eliot, who was at that time a reader for the publishing house of Faber & Faber.

When Faber, after a delay of several months, also declined to publish the book Orwell's faith in his own creation diminished even further and he left the manuscript in the hands of Mabel Fierz, telling her to 'burn it and keep the clips'.[2] It is clear that he no longer had any hope that the book would be published. Mrs Fierz, however, was a woman of some determination (and not a little experience in literary matters) and, having read the manuscript, she was not so easily discouraged. Without consulting Orwell she took it personally to the literary agent Leonard Moore and extracted from him a promise that he would read it. Moore kept his promise, was impressed, and forwarded it to Victor Gollancz who, subject to minor alterations – the excision of some swear words and the alteration of one or two surnames – agreed to publish (July 1932). Orwell still hesitated over a title for the book and it was Gollancz who settled on its final title after rejecting several suggestions from the author, including *The Lady Poverty*, *In Praise of Poverty*, and *Confessions of a Dishwasher*. The book was eventually published in January 1933 and was thus in all three years in the making.

The publication of *Down and Out* marked the first book to appear under the pseudonym 'George Orwell' and was, in a real sense, the launching of his literary career. It was immediately accepted as a recommendation of the Book Society and was praised by a number of distinguished reviewers including J. B. Priestley, Compton Mackenzie and H. E. Bates. Writing in the London *Evening Standard* Priestley observed that *Down and Out* was 'uncommonly good reading and a social document of some value. It is, indeed, the best book of its kind I have read for a long time'. Mackenzie in the *Daily Mail* was equally enthusiastic, describing it as 'a genuine human document, which at the same time is written with so much artistic force that, in spite of the squalor and degradation thus unfolded, the result is curiously beautiful, with the beauty of an accomplished etching on copper'. Today Orwell's first book has achieved the status of a minor classic and has taken its place alongside Jack London's *The People of the Abyss* and Charles Booth's *Life and Labour of the People in London* as an unemotional chronicle of how the poor live.

Down and Out has been fairly described as 'a young writer's book, the book of a young man who was in many respects still unformed and inexperienced'.[3] Certainly it was the work of a young man: Orwell was twenty-nine when it was published, the same age as Rider Haggard and H. G. Wells respectively when *King Solomon's Mines* and *The Time Machine* were first published. What strikes one very forcibly on reading it today, despite the sombreness of its underlying theme, is the exuberance of the narrator and the complete absence of an *ideology*. Apart from one section (Chapter 36) in which Orwell sets down some general reflections on tramps and recommendations for the amelioration of their lot, the book is remarkably free of sociological comment. This may well be one reason why it has survived so vigorously and continues to be read fifty years after it first appeared. Had Orwell burdened it with chapters of commentary and advocacy the book would have 'dated' rapidly and lost much of that freshness which is its most appealing feature. The tone of the narrator throughout, despite the harrowing nature of his experiences, is one of predominant happiness and an engaging ability to describe people and incidents with the minimum of pretension and a perceptive eye for social nuances. The result is a book of extraordinary richness, a narrative which can be read, re-read and enjoyed in the same way that a novel is enjoyed and which will continue to be studied for its insight into poverty in two capital cities.

Any reader coming to the book for the first time has to bear one important qualification in mind. So skilful is Orwell's narrative power, so deceptively simple is his style, that it is all too easy to assume that *Down and Out* is merely what it purports to be: that is, a straightforward factual account of occurrences that befell him in Paris and London over a period of four or five months. The reality is rather more complicated. Orwell himself stated that 'nearly all the incidents described there actually happened, though they have been rearranged'.[4] The book is in fact a literary re-creation, a description of events which occurred in Paris during the last three months of 1929 and in London between the winter of 1928 and the summer of 1931, but re-arranged so as to achieve a consistent, symmetrical and ordered narrative. The events depicted in the book are true, but they did not necessarily occur in the order described, nor was there in real life such a neat balance between the length of time spent respectively in Paris and London. What Orwell has done – and done so skilfully that the transition is almost undetectable – is to take the raw material of his own experience and transform it into a coherent and utterly convincing work of art.

The opening chapters, with their vivid description of life in the Rue du Coq d'Or, Paris (in reality the Rue du Pot de Fer) are written with such intensity that they remain long in the mind and reinforce the impression that Orwell, coming fresh to Paris as a young man of twenty-four, immensely enjoyed his stay in the city and that subsequent visits never held for him the same fascination.[5] Again and again one is struck by the vividness of his descriptive powers and his ability to convey an animated word-picture with the maximum economy of language:

> Quarrels, and the desolate cries of street hawkers, and the shouts of children chasing orange-peel over the cobbles, and at night loud singing and the sour reek of the refuse-carts, made up the atmosphere of the street. It was a very narrow street – a ravine of tall, leprous houses, lurching towards one another in queer attitudes, as though they had all been frozen in the act of collapse.

These opening sequences form the backcloth to Orwell's first experiences of poverty. 'Poverty is what I am writing about,' he states, 'and I had my first contact with poverty in this slum.' It should be noticed that at no stage in the book does the narrator explain who or what he is, and how he came to be in Paris in the situation he describes. There is no introduction, no preliminary statement – as in *The People of the Abyss* – explaining the background to the book and the circumstances which led to the events described. Perhaps Orwell felt that such an introduction would weaken the effectiveness of the narrative, particularly if it became known that he was an Old Etonian and that the London experiences at least had been deliberately sought out on his part. Whatever the reason, the narrator does not introduce himself. He is simply 'I', the storyteller, an Englishman in Paris who has fallen on hard times because his money has been stolen.

The qualities which were to make Orwell's name a household word – the ability to write prose of crystal clarity, to produce vivid images in the simplest of English, to write in an apparently 'artless' style which conceals a literary technique of a high order, to make a telling point with a single memorable phrase – are abundantly in evidence in these early chapters. The whole of the third chapter, for example, which describes in detail the narrator's first contact with the world of poverty, and his reflections on having at last reached this state, could be regarded as a case-study in the art of writing an essay as Orwell conceived it. The language is so clear and direct, the writing so vigorous, that one cannot but admire him for the sheer literary prowess which is here in evidence. One has the impression that Orwell must have devoted considerable time and effort on the drafting of these sections in order to achieve the effect he desired. The result is all the more creditable when one reflects that while in Paris, he was engaged on a considerable amount of writing – novels, poetry and short stories – all, apparently, written in a florid and elaborate style totally different from the conversational manner he adopted in *Down and Out* and which he perfected in his later works of reportage.

The most memorable sequences among the Paris chapters are the descriptions of the life of a *plongeur* (dishwasher) at a large hotel which is named the Hotel X (actually the Lotti). The account of life behind the scenes in the hotel possess such energy and intrinsic interest that one returns to these chapters again and again for their abundant life and colour. Few writers have depicted the reality of a scullion's life with such honesty and good humour, or with such an eye for telling detail. Many critics have drawn attention to Orwell's weaknesses as a novelist – weaknesses of which he himself was not unaware[6] – but there can be no doubt that he possessed to an extraordinary degree the novelist's ability to see and describe the fascinating minutiae of living and to communicate this vividly to the reader. In his essay on Charles Dickens he observed:

> Much that he [Dickens] wrote is extremely factual, and in the power of evoking visual images he has probably never been equalled. When Dickens has once described something you see it for the rest of your life.

The same might be said of many of the episodes in *Down and Out*, so intensely drawn that they are etched indelibly on the mind. Consider, for example, the scenes in the French pawnshop, the description of life in the cafeterie of the Hotel X, the account of the kitchen at the Auberge de Jehan Cottard, the description of the lodging-house on the Waterloo Road, the tramps guying the religious service. Each is a vignette, complete in itself, written with total candour and with a fascinating recall of detail.

In order for the narrator to have adventures in both Paris and London, Orwell had to have some device for transporting him convincingly from France to England. He achieves this by the invention of a friend in London, 'B', who arranges to find a post for the narrator, caring for a congenital imbecile. 'B' pays his passage to England, but his experience of down and out life in London comes when he learns that his employers 'have gone abroad, patient and all', and is thus thrown upon his own resources for several weeks. This invention is perhaps a little contrived but it is so skilfully handled (the actual moment of transition from fact to fiction occurs early in Chapter 24) and is embedded so firmly in other experiences which are clearly factual, that the reader passes over the transition unaware that Orwell has for a moment departed from the truth.

Once in London the narrator plunges into a series of encounters with poverty which are at once fascinating and repugnant. There is a curious difference in atmosphere between the Paris chapters and those set in London, which strikes the reader immediately. The Parisian episodes are written with such enthusiasm and light-heartedness as to give the impression that Orwell was, on the whole, happy during his stay there. The London chapters, by contrast, are marked by a drabness and tedium which, despite the liveliness of the writing, suffuses the final portion of the book with a grey quality. Whatever the reason for this contrast – whether Orwell was repelled by his experience of poverty in England, or whether poverty in France is simply less squalid – there is an unmistakeable difference in tone between the two sections. To be without money in England in 1930 was a dispiriting, distressing situation and Orwell vividly conveys the hopelessness of it: 'The evil of poverty is not so much that it makes a man suffer, as that it rots him physically and spiritually . . . this is a dismal, demoralising way of life . . .'. In a series of starkly written chapters, the reader is introduced to the regions of penury which Gissing termed 'the nether world': the lodging-house, the casual ward, the shelter, the workhouse. Each episode is written with the clarity and animation of an engraving by Phiz. What makes these chapters so unforgettable is that at each stage of his experiences Orwell is not simply describing poverty in the abstract but is relating it to individual case-histories, those of himself and the characters he encounters in his wanderings – Paddy the Irish tramp, Bozo the pavement artist, Bill the moocher [beggar], and so on. The boredom and monotony of the life of a tramp is conveyed with an intensity which is far more effective than a dry factual report. 'Here,' says Orwell, 'is the world that awaits you if you are ever penniless.'

A number of critics have drawn attention to what is felt to be an inherent weakness in the book, that is that throughout the narrative poverty is described from the *outside*, that at no stage in his adventures was Orwell truly down and out. Had he really felt the need for money while in Paris he could undoubtedly have appealed for help to Nellie Limouzin Adam, his aunt, who was living in the city at the time; and in England his mother would certainly have been willing to assist him; in this sense there is some validity in the criticism. What makes his behaviour so remarkable, however, is that in both situations, knowing that he could as a last resort appeal to others for help, he deliberately chose not to do so. It was as if he felt impelled to taste the experience of penury for himself by deliberately doing without money. When his friend Brenda Salkeld asked him why he was living the life of a tramp he replied simply that he wished to know 'what it was like not to have anything'.[7] That he was intensely serious in his explorations of down and out life may be judged from the fact that his sojourns were frequently of long duration – the longest for which there is documentation extended over a period of six weeks – and that they continued even after work on the book was completed. His statement in *The Road to Wigan Pier* that his motive in submitting to this experience was a desire to expiate his guilt at having been an agent of imperialism in Burma may well be true, but it should be treated with a certain caution. *Wigan Pier* was written six years or more after his tramping experiences and when he was an established author becoming increasingly interested in social and political questions. Looking at his life in perspective it is entirely possible that there were other motives which, consciously or unconsciously, led him to follow the example of Jack London and immerse himself in the life of the poor. One was a recognition that if he was to achieve literary success this could only be as a result of writing about what he *knew*, i.e., that since his efforts to publish novels and short stories had come to nought, his wisest course would be to describe experiences which he had personally witnessed or participated in. Another motive, it seems clear, was curiosity: a genuine desire to understand the poor, to see how they lived and worked and thought, and to convey a picture of their world which others might read. 'Some day,' he observed on the final page, 'I want to explore that world more thoroughly . . . I should like to understand what really goes on in the souls of *plongeurs* and tramps and Embankment sleepers. At present I do not feel I have seen more than the fringe of poverty.' It seems fair to say that without this curiosity, both emotional and intellectual, there would have been no *Down and Out*: that what impelled him to undergo the life of an outcast was a wish to see for himself how the other half live – to share their misfortunes, to share their happinesses, to eat and sleep as they did.

One of Orwell's characteristics was his tendency to make sweeping generalisations as if they were statements of fact: a tendency which is evident throughout his career, not least in his early work. We learn, for example, that 'side whiskers . . . are the mark either of an apache or an intellectual'; that 'Roughly speaking, the more one pays for food, the more sweat and spittle one is obliged to eat with it'; that 'It is fear of a supposedly dangerous mob that makes nearly all intelligent people conservative in their opinions'; that 'It is a curious but well-known fact that bugs are much commoner in south than north London'. This tendency to generalise was inherent in his make-up and it is one of the qualities which gives to his writing such unusual directness and power. It would be unfair to cavil at these generalisations without at the same time drawing attention to the freshness of his writing and his ability to convey vivid word-pictures which remain long in the memory:

> When you went into the ice cupboard you dropped a hundred degrees of temperature at a single step; it used to remind me of the hymn about Greenland's icy mountains and India's coral strand.   (Chapter 11)

> Dirt is a great respecter of persons; it lets you alone when you are well dressed, but as soon as your collar is gone, it flies towards you from all directions.   (Chapter 24)

There are, indeed, many things in England that make you glad to get home; bathrooms, armchairs, mint sauce, new potatoes properly cooked, brown bread, marmalade, beer made with veritable hops – they are all splendid, if you can pay for them.   (Chapter 24)

It is this quality about *Down and Out*, this rare combination of vivid writing and freshness of approach, which helps to ensure a readership for it today, fifty years after it was written. Above all, what is so impressive about the book is its extraordinary *honesty*: Orwell's gift of writing about aspects of life which many readers would prefer to ignore, but doing so with a simplicity and direct- ness which compels attention. There is no attempt to gloss over unsavoury details or to conceal from the reader the bitter reality of poverty. Instead, Orwell's approach is to describe all that happened to him, however unpleasant, simply, unemotionally, and with the minimum of authorial comment.

When he first learned from his literary agent that there was a possibility of the book being published, he wrote: 'If by any chance you *do* get it accepted, will you please see that it is pub- lished pseudonymously, as I am not proud of it'.[8] The reasons why he was 'not proud of it' are not defined but it seems clear that it was the subject-matter of the book rather than any liter- ary defects which gave him cause for concern: apparently he felt that its descriptions of low life would cause offence, not least to his parents. These fears proved to be without foundation. The book, as we have seen, was well received and brought his name before a wide public. Moreover its inherent merits as a piece of writing are increasingly being recognised. After being out of print for many years it was republished in a new uniform edition in 1949 and has been continuously in print since that date. Although inevitably overshadowed by his later achievements it can be seen as the first full expression of that direct, unemo- tional, strikingly honest manner which came to be known as 'Orwellian'. It is moreover a remarkable piece of work in its own right and one which, though launched with unusual diffidence by an author who preferred to remain anonymous, deserves a place in literary history.

The *Manchester Guardian* in its review of *Down and Out* on 9 January 1933 observed that 'Mr. George Orwell tells of things which to most people are horrible in a quiet, level tone which enables him also to use a vocabulary suited to his subject'. This 'quiet, level tone' – which was to be used with masterly effect in *The Road to Wigan Pier* and *Homage to Catalonia* – was to be his greatest strength in the years to come.

Burmese Days

Burmese Days has been described as 'the most conventional of Orwell's novels, and as a novel the most successful'.[9] It was written during the years 1932–3 while he was working as a schoolmaster, first at The Hawthorns school, Hayes, and then at Frays College, Uxbridge. Much of the book had therefore to be written in the evenings after a full day of teaching and school activities, and successive drafts were typewritten as he sat in his lonely lodgings. The circumstances of his daily life at this time must have made the strangest contrast with the theme and atmosphere of the novel. Writing to his friend Eleanor Jaques from his lodgings at The Hawthorns, Station Road, Hayes he commented: 'The most disagreeable thing here is not the job . . . but Hayes itself, which is one of the most godforsaken places I have ever struck'.[10] The monotonous landscape of London suburbia can hardly have been a conducive environment from which to evoke the landscape of Upper Burma, and it says much for Orwell that despite his uninspiring surroundings and the lack of intellectual or imaginative stimuli he persevered with his novel. It also says much for him that he pressed on with it despite the fact that during much of its composition he had no expectation that *Down and Out in Paris and London* would find a publisher. He toiled away at his drafts determined that, come what may, he would sooner or later find a market for his work.

Burmese Days is such a mature and accomplished piece of work that it is difficult to appreciate that this was Orwell's first published novel. When living in Paris in 1928–9 it is known that he wrote two novels but later destroyed them when they were rejected. We know also that *Burmese Days* was conceived, if not actually begun, even before 1932: a fragment from an early draft, 'My Epitaph by John Flory'[11] appears to date from 1930 or even

89

before. The novel, then, is the culmination of a long and arduous literary apprenticeship, an apprenticeship in which he had had to learn the craft of the novelist – partly through his own reading (and here Somerset Maugham seems to have been the dominant influence), but above all through a laborious 'trial and error' process as he worked on a succession of novels and short stories from 1928 onwards.

The story can be fully understood only in relation to Orwell himself: his complex personality, his deeply ingrained sense of failure, his sense of alienation, his Anglo-Indian background. Each of these elements played a part in its making. The novel can be regarded, first, as a deliberate act of exorcism: an attempt to eradicate the Burmese experience from his mind. 'The landscapes of Burma,' he wrote, 'which, when I was among them, so appalled me as to assume the qualities of nightmare, afterwards stayed so hauntingly in my mind that I was obliged to write a novel about them to get rid of them.' Other writers have testified to the haunting quality of exotic climates – the preface by John Fowles to the revised edition of his novel *The Magus* is especially interesting in this connection – and there can be no doubt that for Orwell the experience left an indelible impression on his mind and outlook. Five years of living in the steamy, humid climate surrounded by strange sights, smells and impressions whilst still an impressionable young man made a permanent mark on his personality and philosophy. Sitting before his typewriter in the rainswept greyness of Hayes he sought to evoke for his readers the brilliantly coloured landscape of a tropical world.

The novel is memorable not least because of Orwell's extraordinary ability to evoke this vivid landscape in a series of intense images which remain long in the mind. Time and again one is struck by the vivid use of metaphor:

The sun circled low in the sky, and the nights and early mornings were bitterly cold, with white mists that poured through the valleys like the steam of enormous kettles.   (Chapter 5)

There were snipe in countless myriads, and wild geese in flocks that rose from the jeel with a roar like a goods train crossing an iron bridge.   (Chapter 5)

Sometimes a white pagoda rose from the plain like the breast
of a supine giantess.   (Chapter 7)

A naked child was crawling slowly about the floor like a large
yellow frog.   (Chapter 11)

The light lay thick, as though palpable, on everything, crust-
ing the earth and the rough bark of trees like some dazzling
salt, and every leaf seemed to bear a freight of solid light, like
snow.   (Chapter 15)

Writing to Henry Miller in 1936 he commented of the book:
'That is the only one of my books that I am pleased with – not
that it is any good qua novel, but the descriptions of scenery
aren't bad, only of course that is what the average reader skips'.[12]
The descriptions of scenery are indeed one of the greatest
strengths of the book, and it is these which haunt the imagination rather than the details of the plot.

The book was also an act of exorcism in the sense that it acted
as a catalyst for Orwell's attitudes; the writing of it helped him to
define and clarify his attitude to Burma and to the English.
Throughout his literary career he possessed the unusual ability –
unusual in an English writer that is – of seeing his country and
its institutions *from the outside* and of describing them with the
detachment of an expatriate. There can be no doubt that the
experience of living and working in Burma (followed by a period
of living and working in France) and the writing of *Burmese Days*
were decisive elements in the formation of his basic attitudes;
these experiences gave his writing a breadth and perception it
would otherwise have lacked.

To regard the book merely as an indictment of imperialism as
he had experienced it as a member of the Indian Imperial Police
is too simplistic. It is that, but only in part. It is much more a
distillation of the Burmese experience as a whole – an attempt to
summarise what he thought and felt about the Burmese land and
people and to convey this to the reader in the form of fiction.
That he felt a love–hate relationship for the country is clear from
many indications in the novel and in his other writings.[13]

It is entirely possible that he was not at all sure in his own
mind what exactly he felt about Burma, intellectually and emotionally, and that writing *Burmese Days* was his way of clarifying

his ideas and expressing his deep ambivalence towards the country and its people.

It is significant in this connection that when the central character, John Flory, has a chance of returning to England and the opportunity is withdrawn at the last moment he realises that he does not wish to return. 'This country which he hated was now his native country, his home. He had lived here ten years, and every particle of his body was compounded of Burmese soil ... He had sent deep roots, perhaps his deepest, into a foreign country.' Even more significant is that Orwell deliberately allowed several years to elapse before starting work on the novel. Instead of commencing it while in Burma, or immediately after arriving back in England – as would have seemed the natural course to follow – he chose instead the alien theme (to him) of poverty and embarked on *Down and Out in Paris and London*. It was not until three years after his return home that he began work on the book and even then the action of the story is deliberately placed backwards in time, in the year 1926. He clearly sensed that the experience of living and working in Burma for five years was too raw, too novel and altogether too traumatic to be assimilated at once and that he could only do justice to his theme by biding his time until some of the scars had healed and he had had an opportunity for mature reflection.

What strikes one forcibly on reading the novel today is that it is not so much an indictment of imperialism as a summation of his profound *disillusionment* with the imperial idea as he had observed it in practice. It has to be remembered that he had set out for Burma as a young man of nineteen filled with idealistic and essentially romantic notions of serving the Empire: *Kim* was one of the formative books of his youth, and he seems to have set out on the journey to Mandalay with little idea of the harsh realities of what lay before him. He was imbued instead with Kiplingesque ideas of taking up the white man's burden in a remote outpost of India as his father had done before him. The man who returned to his parents' home five years later was a totally different person: his health ruined, his illusions destroyed, his attitudes hardened by long exposure to cynicism and corruption. There remained with him a detestation of imperialism so deeply ingrained that he was unable to voice it for some time and a profound sense of the inherent dishonesty which lay at the heart of it:

It is a stifling, stultifying world in which to live. It is a world in which every word and every thought is censored. In England it is hard even to imagine such an atmosphere. Everyone is free in England; we sell our souls in public and buy them back in private, among our friends. But even friendship can hardly exist when every white man is a cog in the wheels of despotism. Free speech is unthinkable.[14]

It is possible to discern in passages such as this the germ of an idea which came eventually to dominate his life and which was the central theme of *Nineteen Eighty-Four*: the corrupting influence of despotism upon all who wield power within it. What Orwell is at such pains to describe is the insidious effect of undemocratic regimes, of whatever hue – the stifling of free speech inherent in such regimes, the impossibility of honest statement, the unqestioned sacrosanctity of the official code, the necessity to seek release in private, unspoken thoughts. It was a face of despotism he was to encounter again in Spain; and one not impossibly removed from the Thought Police.

The book can also be regarded as an extended parable on the theme of failure and rejection. Running through the novel as a leitmotiv is the birthmark which disfigures Flory. Flory is clearly ashamed of the birthmark which disfigures his face and constantly endeavours to hide it: 'at all times, when he was not alone, there was a sidelongness about his movements, as he manoeuvred constantly to keep the birthmark out of sight'. Elizabeth Lackersteen finds the mark repugnant and at the end of the story it is this which, in the last analysis, brings about his downfall:

He might have committed a thousand abominations and she could have forgiven him. But not after that shameful, squalid scene, and the devilish ugliness of his disfigured face in that moment. It was, finally, the birthmark that had damned him.

For Orwell the birthmark was clearly a powerful symbol; it was as if he felt that some men were branded by a stigma – whether of poverty, cowardice, guilt or failure – which clung to them all their days and could not be eradicated (Flory's birthmark only disappears with his own death). Deep in his make-up was a sense of failure, a feeling that whatever he attempted was fore-

doomed not to succeed. This sense of inadequacy was not overcome until he had enjoyed the assurance of some years of literary
success, but its importance as a shaping factor of his personality
may be judged from his essay about his schooldays, 'Such, Such
Were the Joys'[15] and particularly such passages as the following:

> All through my boyhood I had a profound conviction that I
> was no good, that I was wasting my time, wrecking my tal-
> ents, behaving with monstrous folly and wickedness and
> ingratitude – and all this, it seemed, was inescapable, because
> I lived among laws which were absolute, like the law of grav-
> ity, but which it was not possible for me to keep . . . Failure,
> failure, failure – failure behind me, failure ahead of me – that
> was by far the deepest conviction that I carried away.

At each stage in his life one is aware of this sense of inadequacy, a feeling of not belonging: as a schoolboy at St. Cyprian's
and at Eton, as a policeman in Burma, as a tramp (for he reveals
in *The Road to Wigan Pier* that when first embarking on his 'down
and out' guise he fears he will be recognised as a gentleman
beneath the rags and be set upon), and as a struggling author.
Flory is a failure in all he undertakes. Although he is accepted as
a member of the exclusive Club at Kyauktada the other members do not regard him as a true pukka sahib since he is friendly
with 'the natives', in particular with the Indian doctor Veraswami. When Elizabeth Lackersteen befriends him she quickly
perceives that he is not a true gentleman and at the end of the
novel rejects him utterly. Apart from his conversations with
Veraswami he is a loner, an outsider – there is a revealing passage in Chapter 4 in which he meditates on 'the bitterness of
being alone . . . If he had had one person, just one, to halve his
loneliness!' – seeking refuge in books and in his private thoughts.
After his death he is soon forgotten.

As a novel in the accepted sense *Burmese Days* must be counted as
one of Orwell's most satisfying achievements; with the possible
exception of *Coming Up For Air* it is his most polished and structurally harmonious work and the one on which he laboured
hardest to produce a coherent work of art.

The central figure, John Flory, is one of Orwell's most convincing and fully rounded characters in the sense that the reader is a participant not only in his actions but in his innermost thoughts. The character is not intended to be an autobiographical representation of Orwell himself although some commentators have regarded him as such. Christopher Hollis has observed in an illuminating aside: 'Flory was clearly to some extent Orwell as he imagined that he might have been if he had stayed in Burma'.[16] Certainly Flory embodies many of Orwell's opinions and attitudes, and it is not difficult to see in such passages as the following a direct commentary on his own life as he had experienced it in Burma in the years 1922–7:

> Time passed and each year Flory found himself less at home in the world of the sahibs, more liable to get into trouble when he talked seriously on any subject whatever. So he had learned to live inwardly, secretly, in books and secret thoughts that could not be uttered . . . But it is a corrupting thing to live one's real life in secret. One should live with the stream of life, not against it. It would be better to be the thickest-skulled pukka sahib who ever hiccuped over 'Forty years on,' than to live silent, alone, consoling oneself in secret, sterile worlds.

Yet Flory has an existence distinct from that of his creator and here, as with George Bowling in *Coming Up For Air*, Orwell does succeed in achieving a marked degree of authorial detachment. The relationship between Flory and Elizabeth Lackersteen is skilfully wrought and provides the novel with much of its underlying tension. Elizabeth and Flory are *each changed* as a result of their friendship – Elizabeth is brought into contact with the world of culture and ideas and into an awareness of the native people; Flory abandons his dissolute way of life and does his utmost to come up to her expectations of him. The description of the gradual process in which each impinges on the other calls for novelistic skills which Orwell had not previously had to employ and it is to his credit that these episodes are handled with such assurance.

It is a novel rich in memorable characters ranging from the wily magistrate U Po Kyin to the well-meaning Doctor Veraswami, from the scheming Ma Hla May to the xenophobic Ellis. These figures possess a solidity and conviction unusual in a first novel and rarely equalled in Orwell's later fiction. (Victor Gollancz, sensing that some of the characters were drawn from life, declined to publish the book at first for fear of libel but accepted it after it had been published in the United States.) Verrall, the Lieutenant with whom Elizabeth enjoys a brief flirtation, is also well drawn as a personification of a *type* whom Orwell clearly found detestable. At Eton, and possibly at St. Cyprian's also, he had encountered boys of the calibre of Verrall: boys who 'bore a charmed life' and carried all before them. The name itself may have been taken from Wells's novel *In the Days of the Comet*, in which one of the leading characters – who also attempts to seduce the heroine – is also named Verrall. Orwell does not hide the sense of discomfiture, tinged with envy, with which Flory regards Verrall's exploits at Kyauktada and it is with a sense of relief that the reader learns of his final departure from the town.

Burmese Days has a wealth of minor characters in addition to those mentioned and the entire work is interwoven with a sub-plot of some complexity. As an example of Orwell's skill in handling a scene which, though of minor importance to the plot is of exceptional literary interest, the whole of Chapter 11 – describing the visit of Flory and Elizabeth to the bazaar – is an exemplary case-study. The scene in which the couple enter the house of Li Yeik, the Chinese grocer, and are entertained to tea is particularly well handled. Orwell vividly conveys the sense of suspicion and distaste with which Elizabeth regards the Oriental household and Flory's determined attempts to interest her in Chinese ways. In this short scene, beautifully observed and sensitively described, is encapsulated a fundamental difference of attitude which lies at the heart of the novel: that Flory, with all his shortcomings, is genuinely interested in non-European peoples and seeks to understand their culture; Elizabeth, by contrast, has no such interest and is moreover incapable of the imaginative effort required to tolerate an alien civilisation. Throughout their relationship this divergence of view becomes more and more marked until finally it becomes unbridgeable. The bazaar sequence could be omitted in toto without impairing the coherence of the novel; but its presence adds appreciably to our understanding of the protagonists and of their respective personalities. Moreover it affords an excellent illustration of the manner in which Orwell achieves his chiaroscuro effects. The description of the bazaar with its strange smells, noises and colours is brilliantly done, and the entire scene is etched on the consciousness with the clarity of a Gaugin painting. Throughout the novel, not least in this sequence, Orwell is combining two different literary genres – the factual description he had already employed with considerable success in *Down and Out* and in his essay 'A Hanging' (1931), and the fictional structure of a realistic novel in the vein of Maugham or Conrad. It is doubtful if, even in the works of his maturity, he fused the two together with such artistry as in *Burmese Days*.

Structurally the novel has a strong narrative line which reveals his no mean prowess in the art of the storyteller. The hunting expedition and the attack upon the English Club at Kyauktada are both spirited pieces of writing which offer further evidence of his fondness for adventure stories. He never lost his early enthusiasm for such authors as Hornung and R. Austin Freeman[17] and the closing chapters of *Burmese Days*, as the story moves to its symbolic and actual climax, reveal his penchant for scenes of action and excitement. The exclusive English Club, with its members who are at pains to preserve it as a white domain, provides the novel with a point of reference – a 'commanding centre' in Henry James's phrase – which exerts an influence, directly or indirectly, on each character in turn. When the Club is directly attacked by a Burmese mob it emerges from the affray damaged but in all essentials unchanged. At the time of writing the novel Orwell clearly felt that British rule in India would continue indefinitely and he can have had no inkling that it would end during his lifetime.

Despite the occasional Orwellian generalisation (e.g., 'Painting is the only art that can be practised without either talent or hard work') and the overt criticism of the British Raj *Burmese Days* remains a novel and not a didactic tract. In the writing of it he may have been influenced by Forster's *A Passage to India* (1925) but in the last analysis only he could have produced such a characteristic amalgam of fiction and commentary. The novel occupies an important place in the canon of his work not simply as his first full-length work of fiction but as the first statement of themes which were increasingly to dominate his imagination. The conflict between the independent spirit and the rule of orthodoxy; the urge to renounce conventional values and opt out of society; the contrast between the man of ideas and the aesthete; the attempt to sublimate loneliness through emotional relationships; the rebel as a social outcast – these were to be his continuing concerns in the years ahead and the predominant topics of his fiction and essays alike.

A Clergyman's Daughter

Writing to his friend Brenda Salkeld in July 1934 Orwell gave vent to his feelings of frustration concerning the novel on which he had been working since the beginning of that year: 'I am so miserable, struggling in the entrails of that dreadful book and never getting any further, and loathing the sight of what I have done. *Never* start writing novels, if you wish to preserve your happiness.'[18] He had abandoned school teaching in December 1933 following a severe attack of pneumonia and was now able to devote himself wholly to writing. Living with his parents at their home at Southwold in Suffolk he worked steadily on *A Clergyman's Daughter* and submitted the completed work to his agent in October 1934. 'I am not at all pleased with it,' he wrote diffidently. 'It was a good idea, but I am afraid I have made a muck of it – however, it is as good as I can do for the present.'[19] Throughout the writing of the novel his letters to his friends indicate the difficulties he experienced during its composition. To Orwell the creation of a full-length work of fiction was always a time of travail but one has the impression that he found the writing of *A Clergyman's Daughter* an unusually difficult and laborious experience.

The opening chapter, a carefully written account of the town of Knype Hill and of the central character, Dorothy Hare – a chapter which must have caused him agonies of revision and self-doubt – is a detailed and convincing portrait of the life of a rector's daughter in a small East Anglian community. One is reminded of E. H. Young's *Miss Mole* (1930) and Dorothy Whipple's *High Wages* (1930) as comparable examples of the genre. Orwell excelled at the minutely circumstantial description of ordinary people's lives and surroundings, and he rarely bettered this evocation of a quiet English country town. The sharply observed description of Knype Hill is derived from his knowledge of Southwold (and also of life in the genteel hinterland of Hayes and Uxbridge) and is evoked with penetrating insight. The large and impoverished Rectory, the 'Olde Tea Shoppe' with its gossiping ladies, Mrs Semprill the town scandalmonger, Mrs Pither with her constant rheumatism and 'wormlike life of shuffling to and fro' – are all drawn with shrewdness and humour.

As a character, Dorothy Hare is drawn with care and compassion. At the time of writing the story Orwell's experience of women was limited, yet in creating the figure of the earnest and hard-working rector's daughter he does succeed to a remarkable degree in bringing to life a credible personality with an individuality of her own. At each stage of the narrative the reader is made aware of Dorothy's thought processes and emotions and identifies with her in her various experiences. The effect of this is that she gains the reader's sympathy at an early stage in the novel and holds it through the peregrinations of the story. However dissatisfied Orwell may have been with the book as a whole he had no reason to be discontented with his central figure. She is in many respects a more living figure than Elizabeth Lackersteen in *Burmese Days*. Although Dorothy as a person seems to have been wholly imaginary her background was one with which Orwell was closely familiar. He knew well the atmosphere of the church in small towns such as Southwold and supplemented this with the knowledge he had gained from long conversations with the curate at Hayes. The result is to give to the Knype Hill chapters a convincing air of solidity and realism which strengthens the novel as a totality. Moreover in creating Dorothy he revealed for the first time in his fiction an awareness of that repressed sexuality which Gissing, for example, had drawn so well in such novels as *The Odd Women*. Despite her sexual coldness she is not an unattractive woman and she possesses an energy and single-mindedness which make her one of Orwell's most memorable creations.

The Knype Hill sequence occupies the first third of the novel and is of about the same length as Lawrence's 'Daughters of the Vicar' or Arnold Bennett's 'The Death of Simon Fuge'. As it stands it could almost form a short story or novella in its own right: it is a complete picture of an imaginary world, written with conviction and understanding. Orwell realised, however, that the only way in which he could expand this fragment to the length of a full-scale narrative would be to incorporate episodes taken from his own experience – as a tramp, a hop-picker and a schoolteacher – and present them as Dorothy's. This he proceeded to do in the following chapters. The experiment might have succeeded had he been able to explain satisfactorily the transition from her life in the rectory to her experiences on the road and to connect the disparate episodes with a more convincing narrative framework. As it is, the description of Dorothy's loss of memory is handled assuredly enough yet there is an unexplained gap in her adventures. Between her last night in the rectory and her awakening in London in a confused state there is an interregnum of *eight days*: a gap in which she has not only travelled from Knype Hill to the New Kent Road but has been robbed of her clothes and possessions. What happened to her during this interval and how she came to be standing on a London street is not explained. Presumably this is the 'inherent fault of structure' of which Orwell was aware and which he felt 'could not be rectified in any way that I can think of'.[20]

Once this awkward moment is passed, however, and Dorothy encounters a number of characters who are manifestly drawn from life – Nobby in particular is surely a reflection of one of Orwell's tramping acquaintances[21] – the book regains verisimilitude and Dorothy's adventures amidst the lower fringes of life hold the reader's attention with renewed force.

The account of hop-picking in Chapter 2, so vividly written and extraordinarily evocative, is one of the most memorable sequences in the novel. In these passages he drew extensively on his own experience of hop-picking (at Wateringbury, Kent) in September 1931: an experience he recounted in his essay 'Hop-Picking' and which was clearly for him a time of great happiness although of wretched poverty. In describing Dorothy's recollections of the farm Orwell is giving expression to his own feelings of nostalgia:

Looking back, afterwards, upon her interlude of hop-picking, it was always the afternoons that Dorothy remembered. Those long, laborious hours in the strong sunlight, in the sound of forty voices singing, in the smell of hops and wood smoke, had a quality peculiar and unforgettable. As the afternoon wore on you grew almost too tired to stand . . . Yet you were happy,

with an unreasonable happiness. The work took hold of you
and absorbed you . . . when the weather was fine and the hops
were good you had the feeling that you could go on picking for
ever and for ever.

This simple, direct style – so reminiscent of the vivid narration
he had employed in describing the life of a hotel scullion in *Down
and Out* – contrasts sharply with the patently fictional elements in
the book which appear by comparison loose and contrived.
Determined to be a realistic novelist in the Maugham manner,
Orwell in 1934 was still feeling his way towards his true medium
and had not yet grasped that his real gift was for reportage
rather than the creation of imaginary characters and incidents.

Much criticism has been levelled at the school sequence and in
particular at the 'Ringwood House Academy for Girls' and its
Principal, Mrs Creevy, on grounds of their unreality. Orwell
commented at the time 'I am willing to admit that the part about
the school, which is what seems to have roused people's incredul-
ity, is overdrawn, but not nearly so much as people think'.[22] The
description of the school with its grasping headmistress and woe-
fully outdated tuition seems almost incredible today yet from
Orwell's standpoint it was probably not a wild exaggeration. In
writing it he seems to have drawn on his memories of some of the
more unpleasant aspects of St Cyprian's at Eastbourne which he
had attended from 1911–16 and, in the happier sequences (see
especially Chapter Four, 3) on his own experiences as a teacher
at Hayes and Uxbridge. Undoubtedly he found schoolteaching a
fascinating, and at the same time exhausting, profession and in
the 'Ringwood House' chapter he gave feeling expression to his
sense of the vocation he felt teaching should be and the travesty
of education represented by some of the less reputable private
schools of that time. Christopher Hollis found the description
'gorgeously comic'.[23] To a modern reader it seems not so much
comic as a caricature – in the same sense as Salem House in
David Copperfield is a caricature – and animated moreover with a
passionate desire to end the evils he is describing. Years later he
was to describe his schooling far more effectively in a lengthy
essay 'Such, Such were the Joys': an impassioned piece of writing which achieves its effects more bitingly for being cast in the
form of autobiography rather than fiction. In retrospect the
school sequence is the least successful portion of the novel for,

despite the author's sincerity, the description remains a distortion. The scenes which remain in the mind long after the novel has been read are those depicting backgrounds and situations which he *knew* – Knype Hill, the rectory, hop-picking, tramping – and described without exaggeration.

One of the most interesting aspects of the novel to the student of Orwell's thought is the sequence at its conclusion in which Dorothy meditates upon the nature of life and on her fundamental beliefs. It should be noted that although as a result of her experiences Dorothy loses her religious faith she does not abandon the church; on the contrary, she seems determined to spend the remainder of her days conforming (outwardly at least) to a life of duty and obedience. She takes comfort from the reflection that 'faith and no faith are very much the same provided that one is doing what is customary, useful and acceptable'. Writing some years later in his 'As I Please' column in *Tribune* Orwell commented:

> Western civilisation, unlike some oriental civilisations, was founded partly on the belief in individual immortality . . . I would say that the decay of the belief in personal immortality has been as important as the rise of machine civilisation . . . I do not want the belief in life after death to return, and in any case it is not likely to return. What I do point out is that its disappearance has left a big hole, and that we ought to take notice of that fact.[24]

He was undoubtedly perceptive in drawing attention to the vacuum caused by the decline in religious belief yet it is difficult to resist the conclusion that the tone of the closing pages of *A Clergyman's Daughter* is oddly passive, in sharp contrast to the anger and bitterness of *Keep the Aspidistra Flying*. The tone throughout is one of submission: that it is one's duty to conform to the codes, routines and formalities of life. In this sense it can be argued that the book is in essence a deeply conservative one which offers further evidence of that resistance to change which was an important strand in Orwell's make-up.

The ending, in which Dorothy relapses once again into the domesticity from which her loss of memory had released her, is curiously unsatisfying. The reader is conscious throughout that one of the most interesting aspects of the novel is its insight into the theme of metamorphosis which so clearly fascinated Orwell. In his own person he had transformed himself from Eric Blair the unknown Etonian to P. S. Burton the down and out with a Cockney accent, and from P. S. Burton to George Orwell the successful writer. Similarly Dorothy Hare the submissive rector's daughter from an obscure Suffolk town is transformed into a completely different persona, Ellen Millborough, a schoolteacher with ideas and a personality of her own. It is a great disappointment that at the conclusion of the story she not only rejects the offer of marriage which Warburton extends to her but opts to return to her former existence as an unpaid curate instead of launching into life on her own. The metamorphosis, in her case, has not completed itself: she has simply reverted to her former way of life.

This cyclic pattern, which Orwell was to repeat in *Coming Up For Air* – and which James Hilton had followed in *And Now Goodbye* (1932), a story bearing interesting similarities to *A Clergyman's Daughter* – provides the novel with a symmetrical structure yet leaves the reader with a vague sense of unease. It can be argued that each of Orwell's novels depicts a situation in which the central character attempts to escape from an oppressive normality and fails to do so. Yet Gordon Comstock and George Bowling (for example) do not meekly submit to their environment; each fails in his bid to liberate himself from convention but does so with deep resentment, never entirely abandoning the urge to break free. Dorothy, by contrast, simply submits to her fate: 'whatever happened, at the very best, she had got to face the destiny that is common to all lonely and penniless women'. It is this meekness, this deliberate refusal to seek any change in her environment, which seems out of character and which is finally unsettling.

A Clergyman's Daughter is generally acknowledged as the weakest of Orwell's novels. Certainly he himself was dissatisfied with it and gave instructions that it was not to be reprinted during his lifetime. In a letter to George Woodcock in 1946 he confessed:

> There are two or three books which I am ashamed of and have not allowed to be reprinted or translated, and that [*Keep the Aspidistra Flying*] is one of them. There is an even worse one

called *A Clergyman's Daughter*. This was written simply as an
exercise and I oughtn't to have published it, but I was desperate for money, ditto when I wrote *Keep the A*. At that time I
simply hadn't a book in me, but I was half starved and had to
turn out something to bring in £100 or so.[25]

It is clear from this and the letters written during its composition
that he was well aware of its shortcomings and made no attempt
to conceal these either from himself or his publisher. When for-
warding the novel to his agent Leonard Moore he added: 'There
are bits of it that I don't dislike, but I am afraid it is very
disconnected as a whole, and rather unreal'. In stressing its
episodic nature and its unreality he was drawing attention to two
of its most fundamental weaknesses: weaknesses which fracture
the novel and render it in the last analysis unsatisfactory as a
work of art. Continually one has the impression that he is using
the *wrong medium* for his material, that the book is an attempt to
fuse together several different genres in a continuous whole and
that the result is an uneasy compromise between factual reportage and imaginative storytelling.

These defects, real as they are, should not blind the reader to
its merits or to its importance as a watershed in Orwell's literary
apprenticeship. The book is important, firstly, because he
regarded it as an experiment and in the writing of it he explored
a number of techniques which were of value to him subsequently. The deliberate decision to write a novel in which the
principal character is a woman and to describe her *from the inside*,
as if the story was told in the first person, was a courageous step
and enabled him to handle the portrayal of character with
increasing subtlety and assurance. Moreover in describing the
Reverend Charles Hare and his milieu at Knype Hill he was
employing techniques of description and observation which later
came to full fruition in the description of Lower Binfield and the
Bowling family in *Coming Up For Air*. The experimental third
chapter, written consciously under the influence of James Joyce's
Ulysses, is cast in a dialogue form which he never repeated yet is
remarkable for its descriptive framework and sustained dramatic
power. For all these reasons *A Clergyman's Daughter* merits close
attention as a work of considerable intrinsic interest. Despite its
unevenness – it has been described as 'a chaotic mixture of
genuine fiction and the thinly disguised experiences and

opinions of the author' – its place in English literary history seems
assured. It will continue to be read for its finely observed portrait
of life in a small town between the wars, for its moving evocation
of hop-picking in Kent (a way of life now altogether vanished),
for its re-creation of the consuming passion of teaching. Above
all it will be studied by a new generation of readers for its insight
into poverty and deprivation: issues which came increasingly to
dominate Orwell's life and which ultimately turned his attention
from fiction to the social reportage which made his name.

Keep the Aspidistra Flying

From October 1934 to January 1936 Orwell worked as a part-time assistant at a secondhand bookshop, Booklovers' Corner, 1 South End Road, Hampstead. The pattern of his daily life at this time is summarised in a letter to Brenda Salkeld in which he described his working routine:

> I am living a busy life at present. My time-table is as follows: 7.a.m. get up, dress etc., cook & eat breakfast. 8.45 go down & open the shop, & I am usually kept there till about 9.45. Then come home, [a furnished room close to the bookshop] do out my room, light the fire etc. 10.30.a.m.–1.p.m. I do some writing. 1.p.m. get lunch & eat it. 2.p.m.–6.30.p.m. I am at the shop. Then I come home, get my supper, do the washing up & after that sometimes do about an hour's work. In spite of all this, I have got more work done in the last few days than during weeks before when I was being harried all day long.[26]

The novel on which he toiled for about three hours a day throughout most of his time at Booklovers' Corner and which he was determined should be 'a work of art'[27] was *Keep the Aspidistra Flying*, an angry, splenetic work in the strangest contrast to *A Clergyman's Daughter*. In its pages he gave vent to the smouldering resentment he felt at the values of moneyed society and the frustration and bitterness he had experienced as a literary apprentice in Paris and London.

Keep the Aspidistra Flying is a work of unusual intensity. It is dominated by the image of the aspidistra as a symbol of respectability – 'There will be no revolution in England while there are aspidistras in the windows' – and by the notion that money and the possession of money are inherently evil. Its central character,

Gordon Comstock, an angry, embittered young man who deliberately abandons a well-paid post in an advertising agency in
order to opt out of 'the money-trap', is obsessed by the idea that
to lead a life of respectability – marriage and a suburban home –
is to sell one's soul to 'the money-god', and that the only alternative is to cut oneself loose from conventional society altogether.
The novel tells the story of his half-hearted attempts to achieve
an alternative way of living, first by writing poetry and then by
consciously accepting a post calling for the minimum of effort
and aspiration.

It is unlike any other Orwell novel – with the exception of his
last work, *Nineteen Eighty-Four*, written during the unhappy years
of his final illness – in that it is written throughout in a tone of
acrimony and ill-humour of almost morbid intensity.

There is moreover a curious ambiguity about the tone of the
book which makes the entire novel an extremely interesting case
study of Orwell's ambivalence as a creative writer. Although the
novel is not written in the first person the events and incidents
described are seen almost exclusively from Gordon's point of
view. Yet it is never clear whether the narrator is speaking with
Gordon's voice or Orwell's own. On a careful re-reading it is this
ambiguity, this awareness that at each crucial stage of the story
there is a blurring of focus, which is arguably the book's most
serious weakness. On the other hand it is a novel of extraordinary power which, despite the obsessive nature of its theme,
merits close attention as a seminal work whose preoccupations
tell us much concerning its author's attitudes in the mid-1930s.

Although it is a much slighter novel than *Burmese Days* or *A
Clergyman's Daughter* – the actual range of incidents described is
surprisingly small – it marks a distinct advance on its predecessors in the depth of its characterisation and the skill with which
Orwell integrates his disparate materials into a cohesive whole.
Reviewing George Moore's *Esther Waters* a year later, he wrote:
'It was written by a man whose fingers were all thumbs and who
had not learned some of the most elementary tricks of the novelist, for instance, how to introduce a new character, but the
book's fundamental sincerity makes its surface faults almost neg-
ligible'.[28] *Keep the Aspidistra Flying* is a much tauter, more well-
knit book than his previous novels; it was written moreover by a
man whose fingers were *not* all thumbs, a man with a growing
literary self-confidence.

The characterisation is assured and workman-like. In addition to a diverse range of well-drawn minor characters – Julia Comstock, Gordon's hard-working sister; Mrs Wisbeach, the incurably inquisitive landlady; Flaxman, the fat and well-meaning lodger at Willowbed Road (a preliminary sketch for George Bowling in *Coming Up For Air*) – there are three characters who dominate the story and whose lives interact: Gordon Comstock, his girl-friend Rosemary, and the wealthy editor Ravelston. Their personalities and the manner of their presentation throw an interesting light on Orwell's attitudes at the time of writing.

Gordon himself is a figure of some complexity. Although he shares many of Orwell's attitudes (including his prejudice against Scotland and Scottish writers)[29] he is an individual in his own right rather than a self-portrait. The fact that he too works as a bookshop assistant has led many an unwary reader to assume that Orwell and Comstock are one and the same; this is not so. (That the account of the bookshop in the first chapter of the novel is exaggerated may be seen by comparing the much more balanced account in his essay 'Bookshop Memories'.) Gordon, in common with John Flory, is a fantasia on the Eric Blair who might have been: the penurious author of unpublished novels and poems, a dweller in a twilight world of sordid necessity, a man with a grudge against society.

There is no question that the *idea* of poverty exercised for Orwell a powerful emotional attraction. In *Down and Out in Paris and London* he had written:

And there is another feeling that is a great consolation in poverty. I believe everyone who has been hard up has experienced it. It is a feeling of relief, almost of pleasure, at knowing yourself at last genuinely down and out. You have talked so often of going to the dogs – and well, here are the dogs, and you have reached them, and you can stand it. It takes off a lot of anxiety.

Something of the same attitude returns to Gordon Comstock in the closing pages of *Keep the Aspidistra Flying* when he appears to be sinking into a life of squalor:

In this place he could have been happy if only people would

let him alone. It was a place where you *could* be happy, in a sluttish way. To spend your days in meaningless mechanical work, work that could be slovened through in a sort of coma . . . to sit over a squalid meal of bacon, bread-and-marg and tea, cooked over the gas-ring; to lie on the frowzy bed, reading a thriller or doing the Brain Brighteners in *Tit Bits* until the small hours; it was the kind of life he wanted. All his habits had deteriorated rapidly.

Two points should be noted concerning this and similar passages in the novel. First, although *Keep the Aspidistra* is partly autobiographical the description of Gordon's circumstances cannot be interpreted as a picture of Orwell's background at this time; his own circumstances in 1935, whilst certainly not affluent, were far more comfortable and happy than the drabness and anger of the novel would suggest. In writing it he was drawing on his memories of an earlier period; on his experiences of poverty and sordid living in Paris during 1929 and the frustration and sense of failure he had known in the years 1929–32: years in which he must have undergone moods of despair as his literary aspirations seemed further and further from realisation. Second, Gordon himself is not so much a self-projection of Orwell as a portrait of the embittered and slovenly failure he felt he might have become (and so nearly *did* become during the difficult years between his return from Burma and the publication of *Down and Out*). From this standpoint the writing of *Keep the Aspidistra* can be seen as an act of exorcism, as a kind of therapeutic renunciation of the life of failure. In writing this angry, vitriolic book – George Woodcock commented perceptively that 'no doubt Orwell was deliberately evoking a paranoiac mood'[30] he was laying the ghost of Eric Blair, failed poet and aesthete, and bringing to an end a chapter of frustration and lack of direction in his life.

Rosemary Waterlow, the gentle, submissive young woman who befriends Gordon and ultimately consents to marry him is, for the first time in Orwell's fiction, a wholly credible female character. She is not based upon any particular individual but is rather a composite of several young women Orwell knew at this time. There is the sharpest contrast between her personality – so level-headed, sensible and outgoing – and Gordon's temperament, which seems by contrast irascible, peevish and self-centred. Where Gordon is immersed in self-pity and bitterness,

Rosemary is concerned only for his wellbeing and responds to his tantrums with tolerance and understanding. Indeed the selfishness of the central character is so marked, and long before the end of the novel has become so obsessive, as to militate against any sympathy the reader may otherwise feel for him. Whereas Flory in *Burmese Days* and Dorothy Hare in *A Clergyman's Daughter* arouse the reader's interest and compassion, Gordon forfeits this because of his self-centredness and irresponsibility. Rosemary, on the other hand, is a warm and sympathetic character whose attitude to life is totally at variance with that of her lover. Her outgoing, kindly personality mitigates his inwardness and ultimately triumphs over it.

Philip Ravelston, editor of the magazine *Antichrist* and a man who seeks to encourage Gordon's literary ambitions, is sympathetically presented and seems to embody attitudes and manners which Orwell found desirable. He is a man of wealth, influential in literary circles, and a professed socialist. Even his clothes bear an unmistakeable Orwell flavour:

> He wore the uniform of the moneyed intelligentsia; an old tweed coat . . . very loose grey flannel bags, a grey pullover, much-worn brown shoes. He made a point of going everywhere, even to fashionable houses and expensive restaurants, in these clothes, just to show his contempt for upper-class conventions; he did not fully realise that it is only the upper classes who can do these things.

We know from the testimony of his friends that this was the style of dress favoured by Orwell himself throughout the last twenty years of his life, and indeed it is not difficult to discern in the portrayal of Ravelston a reflection of a range of qualities which Orwell found attractive: financial security, ease of manner, contempt for convention, literary and political self-confidence. In a sense Ravelston and Comstock are two aspects of himself: the man of success, easy, assured and generous; and the man of failure, embittered, poor and outcast. The relationship between the two men and the manner in which Ravelston attempts to draw his friend out of his life of drabness provides the novel with much of its interest, and is a counterbalance to the troubled friendship between Comstock and Rosemary.

The ending of the novel, in which Gordon agrees to marry

Rosemary and return to his post in an advertising agency (thus abandoning the principles he has fiercely defended up to this point) is perhaps the least satisfactory element in the story. Gordon's sudden rejection of all that he has stood for and his willingness to embrace a life of suburban respectability lacks conviction. The reader simply does not believe it – any more than he believes that Mr Micawber in *David Copperfield* would become a successful magistrate, or that Lewisham in H. G. Wells's *Love and Mr. Lewisham* would abandon his ambitions and subside into domesticity. Moreover this conclusion reinforces rather than weakens the reader's uneasy awareness of the novel's ambiguity. It is not clear, for example, whether we are meant to approve or disapprove of Gordon's final reconciliation with Rosemary and his decision henceforth to lead a life of conventionality. Nor is it at all clear whether Orwell himself approves of his hero's behaviour. We are simply left to draw our own conclusions. Gordon's eager relapse into domesticity is rendered more inexplicable by his specific renunciation of it at an earlier stage in the narrative:

That was what it meant to worship the money-god! To settle down, to Make Good, to sell your soul for a villa and an aspidistra! To turn into the typical little bowler-hatted sneak – Strube's 'little man' – the little docile cit who slips home by the six-fifteen to a supper of cottage pie and stewed tinned pears, half an hour's listening-in to the B.B.C. Symphony Concert, and then perhaps a spot of licit sexual intercourse if his wife 'feels in the mood'! What a fate! No, it isn't like that that one was meant to live.

Gordon condemns this way of life yet has no satisfactory alternative with which to replace it and ends by embracing whole heartedly the ethos he professes to despise.

What impresses the reader even more forcibly in the light of Orwell's subsequent development is the complete absence of political awareness or even of social conscience on the part of the central figure. Considering that the book was written against a background of widespread poverty and unemployment this seems with hindsight a strange omission. (At one point Gordon actually declares 'If the whole of England was starving except myself and the people I care about, I wouldn't give a damn'.)

Orwell's deep commitment to socialism as a political philosophy did not come until 1936 with the journey to the north of England[31] – a journey which resulted in *The Road to Wigan Pier* and which was followed almost immediately by his involvement in the Spanish Civil War – prior to that date he displayed little interest in political questions despite his obvious fascination with poverty and with the lives of humble people. The ambivalence of such works as *Down and Out in Paris and London* and *Keep the Aspidistra Flying* seem almost incongruous today and yet it is this very factor, this sharp contrast between the 'political' writings of 1936 onwards and the 'non-political' works which preceded them, which is fundamental to an understanding of Orwell as man and writer.

Keep the Aspidistra Flying belongs firmly in the English tradition of Gissing and Wells. As an example of a novel concerned predominantly with poverty it invites comparison with such works as Gissing's *New Grub Street*, Wells's *Love and Mr. Lewisham* and Robert Tressell's *The Ragged Trousered Philanthropists*. In its obsessive concern with the minutiae of poverty, its atmosphere of drabness and its unrelieved emphasis on futility and boredom it is entirely characteristic of the genre. It is not only a novel of poverty, however, but is in a deeper sense a novel of alienation. Gordon Comstock, one feels, is a man at odds with the world: a man who will not adapt himself to the accepted norms of society and who is determined not to do so. One is reminded of another Gissing hero, Henry Ryecroft, commenting ruefully on his own alienation:

> The truth is that I have never learnt to regard myself as a 'member of society'. For me, there have always been two entities – myself and the world, and the normal relation between these two has been hostile. Am I not still a lonely man, as far as ever from forming part of the social order?[32]

Comstock is in fact a rebel, a forerunner of the 'angry young men' who were to feature so prominently in the novels and plays of twenty years later. But in the final analysis the reader does not identify with his protest, for Comstock's dissatisfaction with his lot is largely of his own making. Moreover, although he rejects the 'money-world' and the values on which it is based he finally embraces this world by becoming part of it. And he does so not through any conscious decision of his own but because Rosemary is expecting his child: a trite conclusion to an otherwise memorable work.

Richard Rees, a close friend of Orwell's upon whom the character 'Ravelston' is said to be modelled, described the novel as having 'marked the end of the first period of Orwell's writing'.[33] That it marks a watershed in his work there can be no doubt. In its political *naïveté*, its self-pity, its introspection and its mood of unreasonable anger it represents the last of his apolitical novels and the end of a phase in his career during which he was feeling his way, slowly and laboriously, towards a style and a purpose of his own. Years later, in his seminal essay 'Why I Write', he observed: 'And looking back through my work, I see that it is invariably where I lacked a *political* purpose that I wrote lifeless books and was betrayed into purple passages, sentences without meaning, decorative adjectives and humbug generally'.

In this observation he was doing less than justice to himself. *Keep the Aspidistra Flying* is very far from being a 'lifeless' book: it pulsates with a raw energy which infuses certain episodes (the whole of Chapter 7, for example, in which Rosemary and Gordon go out into the country together) with vitality.

Yet it is clearly different in kind from all that followed it. The 'purple passages' of his prentice literary achievements lay behind him. Ahead of him lay *The Road to Wigan Pier*, *Homage to Catalonia* and a distinguished career as iconoclast and polemicist. Eric Blair, Etonian and novelist manqué had been exorcised; George Orwell, social critic, essayist and prophet was henceforth in the ascendant.

The Road to Wigan Pier

In January 1936 Orwell was commissioned by Victor Gollancz to make a study of unemployment in the depressed areas of the north of England and to write about what he had seen. The understanding was that the book resulting from the journey would not only be published by Gollancz but would also be considered as a selection of the Left Book Club, which the publisher was planning to form in the spring of that year. Orwell accepted the commission at once and embarked on a tour of the Black Country, Lancashire and Yorkshire which occupied the period 31 January to 25 March 1936, returning to London at the end of March. Travelling partly on foot and partly by public transport his journey took him to Coventry, Birmingham, Wolverhampton, the Potteries, Macclesfield, Manchester (where he stayed five days), Wigan (two weeks), Liverpool (one week), Sheffield (four days), Leeds (one week), and Barnsley (two weeks). Throughout this time he met with miners, trade union officials, officials of the NUWM – National Unemployed Workers' Movement – and others in an attempt to study housing conditions and to see for himself the effects of poverty, malnutrition and unemployment on the lives of ordinary people. He recorded his impressions in a diary which was found among his papers after his death and subsequently published in the *Collected Essays, Journalism and Letters*.[34] This diary – unselfconscious, vivid, and moving in its sincerity – formed the basis of the book which became *The Road to Wigan Pier*. The two need to be read in conjunction in order to appreciate the manner in which Orwell transformed his immediate day-to-day impressions into a social document of enduring worth: a piece of reportage which is now acknowledged as a classic of the genre and as one of the seminal works of the inter-war years.

Orwell's knowledge of the north of England prior to this journey had been limited to occasional visits to his sister and her
family in Leeds, but at those times he had been hard at work on
Down and Out in Paris and London and had had little time or
inclination for travelling outside his immediate circle. This journey was therefore his first real contact with the northern industrial towns and his first extended experience of manual workers.
Both encounters came to him as a revelation. It is largely
because he is describing scenes and conditions which to him are
so novel – he had, after all, rarely travelled in England beyond
the southern counties and for five of the most impressionable
years of his life he had been outside England altogether – that
the book has such a strong sense of immediacy. He came to
Wigan, Sheffield and Barnsley as a stranger, describing what he
saw and felt with a freshness which could not otherwise have
been achieved and which accounts in large measure for the distinctive tone of this remarkable book. It is the work of a man who
was seeing a landscape and a people from a completely fresh
standpoint, without inside knowledge and without prejudices.
The result is a work of passionate, almost painful honesty.

The Road to Wigan Pier was published as a Left Book Club
selection in March 1937 in an edition of 40 000 copies. It says
much for the integrity of Gollancz and of his fellow-members on
the selection committee, Harold Laski and John Strachey, that
the book was chosen and commended despite the fact that it
cannot have been at all the kind of document Gollancz envisaged
when Orwell was commissioned. The publisher had had in mind
a 'Condition of England' book: a work of documentary reportage
after the manner of Engels's *The Condition of the Working Classes in
England in 1844* or Charles Booth's *Life and Labour of the People in
London*. The manuscript which Orwell delivered complied with
his original terms of reference only in part. In form the book is a
collection of disparate essays, divided into two parts almost
equal in length. The first part, which resembles most nearly
Gollancz's commission, is a series of essays describing social
conditions amongst the miners and the unemployed of Lancashire and Yorkshire. The second part, which Gollancz had not
asked for at all and which must have taken him aback when he
first read it, is a long autobiographical statement of Orwell's
approach to socialism, his attitudes to the socialist movement,
and his views on the vexed question of class. The contentious

nature of these chapters is such that Gollancz felt obliged to preface the Left Book Club edition with a lengthy introduction in which he dissented from many of Orwell's conclusions. He recognised at once, however, that the book as a whole was a work of impressive power. 'It is a long time,' he wrote, 'since I have read so *living* a book, or one so full of a burning indignation against poverty and oppression.'[35] He sensed that the first part in its entirety was a document of quite exceptional interest, and indeed decided later to issue Part One as a separate pamphlet, at a price of one shilling. In this form it had a very wide circulation and earned for Orwell a considerable reputation as a writer on social questions.

The opening chapter is written in a very different style from the remainder of the book: in tone it more nearly resembles the opening section of a novel than a work of sociology. There is no preface or introductory statement explaining the origins of the book. Instead, the reader is plunged immediately into a northern industrial milieu:

> The first sound in the mornings was the clumping of the mill-girls' clogs down the cobbled street. Earlier than that, I suppose, there were factory whistles which I was never awake to hear.

At once one is struck by Orwell's extraordinary reticence: there is no attempt on the part of the narrator to introduce himself or to explain how he came to be in this environment; he is simply 'I', the anonymous lodger in an overcrowded bedroom, describing with pitiless clarity the sordidness of his surroundings. This detailed description of his lodgings [on Darlington Road, Wigan][36] is remarkable for its Dickensian accumulation of detail and for the extraordinary vividness of its impressions. Here, for example, is the description of the kitchen table at which the family and the lodgers ate their meals:

> I never saw this table completely uncovered, but I saw its various wrappings at different times. At the bottom there was a layer of old newspaper stained by Worcester Sauce; above that a sheet of sticky white oil-cloth; above that a green serge cloth; above that a coarse linen cloth, never changed and seldom taken off. Generally the crumbs from breakfast were

still on the table at supper. I used to get to know individual
crumbs by sight and watch their progress up and down the
table from day to day.

No one reading this chapter can ever forget the Brookers and
their dreary lodging-house above the tripe-shop. What affronts
Orwell is not so much the squalor of his surroundings, the mean
food and unsavoury smells, but 'the feeling of stagnant meaningless decay, of having got down into some subterranean place
where people go creeping round and round, just like blackbeetles, in an endless muddle of slovened jobs and mean grievances'. It is, he adds characteristically, 'a kind of duty to see
and smell such places now and again, especially smell them, lest
you should forget that they exist'. The word *duty* in this context is
interesting and serves to illustrate once again an aspect of Orwell
we have already noted in discussing *Down and Out*. It would have
been entirely possible for him to have found more comfortable
lodgings elsewhere in Wigan, but had he done so he would have
failed to make contact with people like the Brookers: people
whom he felt it was his duty to mix with, even live with, in order
to understand their way of life. To one as fastidious as Orwell,
with his acute sense of smell and distaste for uncleanliness the
experience must have been unpleasant in the extreme, yet he felt
he had to undergo it if he was to describe what he had seen with
conviction. *Wigan Pier* is such a vital and memorable book not
least because one has a sense of participation. Orwell did not
merely visit miners' homes, he actually *lived* in them; he did not
merely gain information concerning housing and nutrition, he
experienced these things at first hand. It is this quality which
illuminates the Wigan chapters with such a strong sense of
immediacy.

Whether he had originally intended to cast the whole book in
this form (the style is strongly reminiscent of the Paris chapters
in *Down and Out*) is not clear. What is noticeable is that in the
remaining six sections of Part One the tone is much more
serious; the chapters are still cast in the first-person but are much
more 'documentary' in approach. It is as if he intended this first
chapter to stand on its own as a backcloth to the sections which
follow: a prose picture which, in a series of memorable vignettes,
sets the scene for his exploration of the 'two nations'. This exploration, whilst documentary in form, is nowhere clinical or dis-

passionate. Whilst superficially it has the appearance of a series of fragmented essays, the book as a whole has a unity by virtue of Orwell's distinctive voice. He is not merely studying working-class life in a northern industrial town but is describing *his own reactions to it*: the reactions of an acutely sympathetic observer who was still feeling his way towards a political faith and a medium of writing he could make his own.

The second chapter, describing a descent into a coal-mine, has become justly famous in its own right and was later reprinted as an essay under the title 'Down the Mine'.[37] It is a remarkable piece of writing, executed with a kind of unemotional honesty which he rarely equalled and which conveys vividly to the reader the physical experience involved: *this*, one feels, is what a coal-mine is like. Orwell visited three mines – one at Wigan and two at Barnsley – but it was the impact of the Wigan experience (Crippen's mine, where he remained underground for three traumatic hours) which he found so memorable and which provided the basis for his essay. Orwell's technique is to describe as simply and matter-of-factly as possible the experience of journeying into the mine *as it happened to him*, and to do so with a detachment which belies the deep emotion he must have felt and yet seems entirely appropriate to his subject. In a series of striking images he evokes the descent in the cage, the painful walking to the coal face, the heat and noise, the sheer physical drudgery in cramped and dangerous conditions. What makes this chapter such an impressive literary achievement is the forcefulness and vigour of the writing: the manner in which the *feel* of the mine is ineradicably communicated. It is this quality which infuses so much of his writing with a clarity and animation that are quite unforgettable and which makes the reading of his work both an emotional and a literary experience. One thinks of the description of early morning in the Rue du Coq d'Or and of the life of a dishwasher in *Down and Out in Paris and London*; of the riot sequence in *Burmese Days*; of hop-picking in *A Clergyman's Daughter*. All these passages are written with an unusual intensity: an intensity achieved not by the use of mannered or exaggerated language but through prose of compelling honesty and power.

To these Orwell now added an impressive range of scenes which testify not only to his descriptive powers but to his increasing mastery of words and his evident determination to achieve a prose style combining the utmost simplicity and precision with an ability to inform and arouse his readers. Few who have read 'Down the Mine' can ever erase the description of 'the line of bowed, kneeling figures, sooty black all over, driving their huge shovels under the coal with stupendous force and speed', or the real sense of humility with which he regards the miners and their immense physical stamina.

There follows a series of chapters concerning housing, malnutrition and social conditions in the depressed areas. Throughout these chapters Orwell is not content merely to *describe* poverty, mining and the social consequences of unemployment and poor housing, but seeks at each stage of his exposition to arouse the anger and engage the emotions of his readers. He is saying in effect: this state of affairs is intolerable, it cannot be allowed to continue. Moreover, his approach throughout is one of compassion and a deep sense of outrage at the affront to human decency represented by squalid housing, poverty and malnutrition:

> Words are such feeble things. What is the use of a brief phrase like 'roof leaks' or 'four beds for eight people'? It is the kind of thing your eye slides over, registering nothing. And yet what a wealth of misery it can cover!

The awareness of this misery is communicated to the reader through an adroit combination of statistics and text, handled throughout with a penetrating eye for detail and a dexterity in the presentation of unpalatable facts. In the chapter on housing conditions, for example, there is an unforgettable description of the caravan dwellings inhabited by many thousands of families in the northern towns during the years of the depression. He remarks at one point that one caravan he inspected had seven people in it – 'seven people in about 450 cubic feet of space', adding immediately afterwards: 'which is to say that each person had for his entire dwelling a space a *good deal* smaller than one compartment of a public lavatory'. The effect of the amplification is to heighten immeasurably the readers' sense of the squalor and overcrowding Orwell is describing. The wretched caravan dwellings are depicted in prose of almost unbearable clarity; it is almost as if the reader is *there*, sharing with him his revulsion at such unendurable conditions.

One sentence may be selected as an example of his distinctive approach:

Along the banks of Wigan's miry canal are patches of waste
ground on which the caravans have been dumped like rubbish
shot out of a bucket.

Notice that the sentence would lose much of its effect if the word
miry was subtracted. Consider also how much less effective the
statement would be if Orwell had simply said 'Along the banks
of Wigan's miry canal are patches of waste ground on which
estates of caravans have proliferated'. His phrase 'dumped like
rubbish shot out of a bucket' is at once memorable and descriptive; it sticks in the mind as a vivid simile and conveys unforgettably the sense of congestion and filth which Orwell intends.

The first part of the book, then, is notable for its *literary* qualities. Again and again one is impressed by Orwell's eye for the
unusual, his gift for the vivid metaphor and the striking phrase:

I never saw anyone who could peel potatoes with quite such
an air of brooding resentment. You could see the hatred of this
'bloody woman's work', as he called it, fermenting inside him,
a kind of bitter juice. He was one of those people who can
chew their grievances like a cud.   (Chapter 1)

At night, when you cannot see the hideous shapes of the
houses and the blackness of everything, a town like Sheffield
assumes a kind of sinister magnificence. Sometimes the drifts
of smoke are rosy with sulphur, and serrated flames, like circular saws, squeeze themselves out from beneath the cowls of the
foundry chimneys. Through the open doors of foundries you
see fiery serpents of iron being hauled to and fro by redlit boys,
and you hear the whizz and thump of steam hammers and the
scream of the iron under the blow.   (Chapter 7)

The canal path was a mixture of cinders and frozen mud,
criss-crossed by the imprints of innumerable clogs, and all
round, as far as the slag-heaps in the distance, stretched the
'flashes' – pools of stagnant water that had seeped into the
hollows caused by the subsidence of ancient pits. It was horribly cold. The 'flashes' were covered with ice the colour of raw
umber, the bargemen were muffled to the eyes in sacks, the
lock gates wore beards of ice. It seemed a world from which

vegetation had been banished; nothing existed except smoke, shale, ice, mud, ashes, and foul water.   (Chapter 7)

Always it is the unusual detail which is noted, the vivid simile, the telling phrase: 'chew their grievances like a cud', 'sinister magnificence', 'serrated flames like circular saws', 'fiery serpents of iron', 'the lock gates wore beards of ice'. At his best Orwell had an eye for detail and a gift of expression almost worthy of Dickens. He possessed moreover the ability to convey striking and intense mental images which linger in the mind long after the book has been laid aside. The description of the Brookers ménage, of the descent into a coal-mine, of the caravan-dwellings in the northern towns, of the unemployed men and women 'scrambling for coal' on the slag heaps – all are depicted with indelible clarity and with an accumulation of circumstantiality impressive in its power. *The Road to Wigan Pier* could so easily have been a mere catalogue of facts and statistics, an indictment of local and national government for its apparent indifference in the face of such widespread squalor. Instead, whilst skilful use is made of statistics in their place, the whole of Part One is an extraordinarily *human* document.

In an interesting passage Orwell reveals his affection, almost nostalgia, for the wholesome warmth and companionship of a working-class home:

> I have often been struck by the peculiar easy completeness, the perfect symmetry as it were, of a working-class interior at its best. Especially on winter evenings after tea, when the fire glows in the open range and dances mirrored in the steel fender, when Father, in shirt-sleeves, sits in the rocking chair at one side of the fire reading the racing finals, and Mother sits on the other with her sewing, and the children are happy with a pennorth of mint humbugs, and the dog lolls roasting himself on the rag mat – it is a good place to be in, provided that you can be not only in it but sufficiently *of* it to be taken for granted.

Notice that in this passage he is not describing a working-class interior he had seen in Wigan but is looking back to a memory of many years earlier, to homes 'as I sometimes saw them in my childhood before the war [the First World War] when England was still prosperous'. It is essentially a nostalgic image: there is a coal fire, a steel fender, a rocking chair and a rag mat. Clearly the vision of this homelike interior held a strong appeal for Orwell. Critics of the book have seized on passages such as this and accused him of having sentimentalised the working-classes; the reality is more complex. He is not so much sentimentalising as giving vent to that conservatism which formed such an inerad-icable strand in his make-up. This was a man who delighted in the ways of the countryside and was fascinated by the life of the common toad,[38] who had an intense dislike for the noise and artificiality of twentieth-century life, and who, whilst *The Road to Wigan Pier* was being written, was running a village shop and a smallholding in a remote part of rural Hertfordshire.

The passage is also revealing as an indication of the powerful attraction which the camaraderie of the working-class held for him. In a perceptive study of Orwell, Jenni Calder has observed that he 'found a more decent, vital and attractive kind of human-ity amongst working-class people than he ever did amongst the class to which he belonged'.[39] What appealed to Orwell about the homely interior by the fireside was that within it 'you breathe a warm, decent, deeply human atmosphere which it is not so easy to find elsewhere'. It is interesting to compare this reaction with his evident liking for the communal lodging-house kitchen in *Down and Out in Paris and London* and his enthusiasm for the comradeship of the Lenin Barracks in Barcelona.[40] He clearly felt at home in this environment and sensed moreover that its warmth was genuine, not artificial; he responded at once to its implicit invitation: he felt, despite his Etonian background, that he *belonged*, or at least ought to belong.

It should be noted finally that his description is written *from the outside looking in*: 'it is a good place to be in, provided that you can be not only in it but sufficiently *of* it to be taken for granted'. In the diary in which he recorded his impressions of his travels he noted: 'All the men at the N.U.W.M. very friendly . . . I cannot get them to treat me precisely as an equal, however. They call me either "Sir" or "Comrade".' Orwell clearly felt a strong desire to be accepted by manual workers on equal terms but, with rare exceptions – as a *plongeur* in Paris, as a down and out, as a member of the militia in Spain – he failed to achieve this and could only write about them as a sympathetic observer. His writing about manual workers in *The Road to Wigan Pier* and elsewhere is almost invariably well-informed and suffused with understanding and insight, yet it remains the work of an acutely intelligent onlooker describing men who are different from himself. He was aware of this and sought consciously to diminish the invisible barrier which separated him from working-class men, yet paradoxically this very distance proved to be one of his greatest strengths. It enabled him to write about coal-miners, for example, with an objectivity and compassion which is wholly admirable and which at once engages the attention of the reader. When he confides frankly that 'the miner's job would be as much beyond my power as it would be to perform on the flying trapeze or to win the Grand National' the effect is to compel admiration for his honesty and at the same time to cause the reader to reflect anew on the exhausting drudgery involved in the hewing of coal.

The second part, a series of highly idiosyncratic essays on socialism and social class, is by common consent far less successful than Part One. These final six chapters lack the intrinsic interest of the descriptive essays and are marred moreover by innumerable contentious statements – e.g., 'A generation ago every intelligent person was in some sense a revolutionary', 'No human being ever wants to do anything in a more cumbrous way than is necessary' – which are advanced without qualification and with a finality which suggests that these propositions are beyond argument. It is the polemical nature of Part Two, the *hardness* of so many of Orwell's statements, his apparent unwillingness to concede the existence of other points of view, which antagonised so many readers in 1937 and which still causes raised eyebrows today. What is of enduring value in these chapters is the essential decency and morality of his conception of socialism and the patent honesty of his attempts to understand its opponents.

For Orwell, socialism was not an economic creed but a philosophy of life which meant that poverty, injustice and deprivation must be replaced with a fuller and richer way of living. Throughout his exposition of socialism words such as 'justice', 'liberty', and 'decency' abound. His conception of socialism was clearly a deeply humanitarian vision, undoctrinaire and compassionate. It has much more in common with William Morris than Marx. His essential thesis was that socialists were alienating large numbers of potential adherents by their apparent advocacy of machine-civilisation, by their remoteness from the world of manual workers, and by their failure to present an attractive vision of socialism in practice. Unless the socialist movement could remedy these deficiencies, he argued, the struggle with fascism would be lost (the Spanish Civil War had broken out whilst the book was in draft) and large numbers of the intelligentsia would defect to totalitarian ideologies.

Nowhere in *The Road to Wigan Pier* is there any definition of socialism *per se*, nor any attempt to define how socialism could be achieved: an omission which many critics, including Gollancz himself, were not slow to point out. Instead, Orwell devotes considerable attention to a discussion of the *image* of socialism (from the standpoint of non-socialists), and to a résumé of the aspects of the movement which prospective sympathisers found distasteful. What impresses the reader when returning to these essays today is Orwell's salutary frankness in facing issues such as class and snobbery, and his willingness to discuss them even when his admissions place himself in an unfavourable light. 'When I was fourteen or fifteen,' he confesses disarmingly, 'I was an odious little snob.' There can be few English writers of this century who have exposed their innermost traits with such candour.[41]

To a student of Orwell's life and art the most fascinating section of Part Two, and an essay which stands on its own merits as an intriguing exercise in autobiography, is the ninth chapter. In this chapter he describes with frankness and an engaging modesty his transition from 'an odious little snob' as a public schoolboy to his involvement with tramps and beggars after his return to England from Burma in 1927. The chapter should be studied closely by all who seek to understand Orwell – or more explicitly the transformation from Blair to Orwell – but at the same time it should be borne in mind that, in common with *Down and Out*, it is a literary re-creation of events which cannot in practice have taken such an orderly form as is here described. What he is doing is imposing a rationalisation upon events which had occurred ten years earlier.

We may illustrate this point by the passage in which he describes his motives in descending into the abyss of poverty:

When I thought of poverty I thought of it in terms of brute starvation. Therefore my mind turned immediately towards the extreme cases, the social outcasts: tramps, beggars, criminals, prostitutes. These were 'the lowest of the low,' and these were the people with whom I wanted to get in contact . . . at least I could go among these people, see what their lives were like and feel myself temporarily part of their world. Once I had been among them and accepted by them, I should have touched bottom, and – this is what I felt: I was aware even then that it was irrational – part of my guilt would drop from me.

The reality, as we now know, was rather more complex than this passage would suggest. It is doubtful if Blair in 1927 had reasoned out his motives quite so rationally as this; he displayed at that time little or no interest in politics and social questions and it was not until some years later – years of mature reflection and experience – that he had fully digested his involvement with imperialism in Burma and grasped all that it had meant to him. Moreover, in seeking to immerse himself in the world of social outcasts there were other motivations at work which Orwell does not mention. Principal among these was surely his overriding ambition to become a writer, and his realisation that to live on terms of equality with down and outs and then to describe what he had seen, as Jack London had done before him, would be a possible and distinctive theme for a book. Orwell does not in fact mention his five years in the literary wilderness, nor the interval he spent living in Paris – it is simply ignored. Instead, there is a smooth transition from his return from Burma to the writing of *Down and Out in Paris and London*, as if the one followed immediately and logically from the other. Chapter 9, then, needs to be read with caution before it is accepted as a straightforward autobiographical account.[42] Always when reading his autobiographical statements one needs to be conscious that there is a selective process at work. He was such a modest and reticent person that it is only now, thirty years and more after his death, that we are in a position to assess this most quixotic of men and to view his life and work as a totality.

Writing apropos *The Road to Wigan Pier* to his friend Jack Common, Orwell commented: 'It is not a novel this time but a sort of book of essays', adding with characteristic diffidence 'but I am afraid I have made rather a muck of parts of it'. Despite its unevenness and its intensely idiosyncratic approach to the prob-

lems it addresses, the book has taken its place as one of the most
significant social documents of the 1930s and as one of those
works of reportage which is destined to outlive the immediate
economic conditions which are its theme. Clearly such a work
would not be in such continuous demand – it has been frequently
reprinted since its reappearance in paperback form in 1962 –
were it not for certain intrinsic qualities: qualities which infuse it
with a richness and life that compel one to return to it as one of
the key works of its time. It is interesting to identify these elements and to relate them to Orwell's ongoing concerns as a
writer.

There is, first, the distinctive voice which speaks directly to
the reader throughout: anonymously in Part One and more
obtrusively in Part Two. It is the voice of a man who is acutely
interested in all he sees and hears, a man who, because of his
unusual background, is witnessing for the first time in his life the
living and working conditions of manual workers, and a man
possessed of an unusual gift for describing what he sees with
penetrating honesty. It is not in any way the voice of an orthodox
socialist, but of a man who, amidst the defilement of the industrial north, digresses to observe the courtship ritual of rooks;[43] a
man who confesses that it is not the triumphs of modern technology but 'the memory of working class interiors' which reminds
him that 'our age has not been altogether a bad one to live in'; a
man who takes the trouble to pause in the middle of Sheffield
and count the number of factory chimneys he can see. It is this
voice, at once shrewd and naïve, which speaks through all his
writings, fiction and reportage alike, and which reaches its
height in the works of his maturity.

Secondly, the work is notable for the evidence it affords of
Orwell's growing mastery of language. For all its structural
defects and occasional inconsistencies, the book as a whole is
unforgettable: and it is so by virtue of its language. It is the work
of a writer who is seeking to convey as vividly and straightforwardly as possible a series of shocking truths. He achieves his
effects by deliberately adopting a simple and direct style, even
when writing of matters which are by their nature extraordinary.
'Good prose is like a window pane,' he wrote in one of his most
celebrated essays.[44] Certainly in his account of his odyssey to the
north of England at the height of the depression he achieved
such prose, prose which cannot fail to move the reader by its

cumulative force. A small example will suffice to illustrate the point:

> One woman's face stays by me, a worn skull-like face on which was a look of intolerable misery and degradation. I gathered that in that dreadful pigsty, struggling to keep her large brood of children clean, she felt as I should feel if I were coated all over with dung.

It is impossible to erase such a passage from the memory. Long after the book has been completed and when many of the details of house rents and unemployment benefits have been forgotten, what remains persistently in the mind are images such as this: the 'skull-like face on which was a look of intolerable misery and degradation', striving to maintain a sense of human decency amidst surroundings of inconceivable squalor.

Finally, the book is of crucial importance to the development of Orwell as a politically conscious writer. There is a world of difference between the apolitical inwardness of *Keep the Aspidistra Flying* and the compassionate anger of *The Road to Wigan Pier*. He became politically aware by witnessing poverty, malnutrition and squalor for himself, and this awareness was to be transformed into a burning idealism by the traumatic experience of Spain. The 'I' of *Down and Out* is a different person from the 'I' of *Wigan Pier*: in both the narrator, the shaping presence, is a deeply idiosyncratic personality, but from 1936 onwards the personality becomes much more overtly political. In his essay 'Why I Write' he made this quite explicit: 'Every line of serious work that I have written since 1936 has been written, directly or indirectly, *against* totalitarianism and *for* democratic socialism, as I understand it'. The fact that in *Wigan Pier* Orwell simply takes his own conversion for granted – he remarks casually 'This [the journey to the north] was necessary to me as part of my approach to socialism' – should not blind the reader to the decisive importance of the experience for him or to the dichotomy between the works preceding this journey to the coal areas and those which came after it. Both are written by an invented personality, 'George Orwell', but after what he had seen and experienced in Lancashire and Yorkshire he was no longer politically indifferent: he was a writer with a mission and a philosophy which coloured all his subsequent actions. For all these reasons *The Road to Wigan Pier* marks a watershed in Orwell's intellectual and emotional pilgrimage.

Critical opinion remains deeply divided over its significance: Tom Hopkinson dismisses it roundly as 'Orwell's worst book', and Laurence Brander as 'his most disappointing performance'.[45] On a dispassionate appraisal it can be seen that, whilst the book has many imperfections, it remains readable and relevant to our times despite the vast changes which have taken place since its conception. In common with Dickens's *Hard Times* it will continue to be read for its indictment of *laissez-faire*, its moving portrayal of the lives and homes of ordinary people, its power to stir the conscience of a nation. George Woodcock said of it: 'In a decade of documentary reportage, Orwell was in fact the only writer who gave permanence to what is normally the most ephemeral of literary crafts'.[46]

Homage to Catalonia

The Spanish Civil War began in July 1936 when a group of military commanders led by General Franco, resentful of the growing socialist and anti-clerical tendencies of the Republican Government, organised a revolt against it. Spain at once became an ideological battleground for fascists and socialists from many different nations, with the USSR supporting the Republic and Germany and Italy supporting the insurgents. Opponents of fascism organised an International Brigade to defend the Republic and this was involved in heavy fighting throughout the war.

It is important to understand at the outset that the Civil War was not only a conflict between Republican (socialist) forces and Nationalist (anti-socialist) forces but also between the socialists themselves. The various socialist and communist parties in Spain were deeply divided over fundamental questions of policy, and were themselves torn by internal dissensions of Marxist and Trotskyist theory. Thus, whilst the war in its early stages must have appeared to many Englishmen, including Orwell, as a simple struggle between socialism and Fascism, it was in reality a much more complicated imbroglio than it seemed.

As soon as he had completed work on *The Road to Wigan Pier* Orwell determined to journey to Spain in order to see the situation for himself. It was not possible to enter the country without accreditation of some kind, so he made an initial approach to the Communist Party in the hope that they would issue him with the necessary papers. Harry Pollitt, the General Secretary at that time, declined to assist him however when he learned that he would make no commitment to join the International Brigade: Orwell, not unnaturally, preferred not to commit himself until he had seen the situation at first hand and had had an opportunity to form his own judgements. He then approached the ILP (Independent Labour Party). Although he was not then a member of the ILP he was slightly familiar with its work through his *Adelphi* connections and he had attended one of their annual summer conferences. In the event the ILP was willing to provide him with the necessary accreditation and he was also issued with a letter of introduction to their representative in Barcelona, John McNair.

Orwell arrived in Barcelona in late December 1936, ostensibly as a correspondent for the *New Leader*, the journal of the ILP. With characteristic diffidence he remarks in the opening chapter of *Homage*: 'I had come to Spain with some notion of writing newspaper articles, but I had joined the militia almost immediately, because at that time and in that atmosphere it seemed the only conceivable thing to do'. These militias were loosely organised armed groups sponsored by political parties and trade unions. Because he was carrying ILP papers he was automatically assigned to the militia of the POUM – (Partido Obrero de Unificacion Marxista: Worker Party of Marxist Unification) – which was the ILP's sister party in Spain. To Orwell, whose political beliefs then and later were completely undoctrinaire, it did not seem to matter which militia he joined so long as he was fighting for the Republic. In his innocence he had not realised that Spanish Civil War politics were a minefield of conflicting ideologies, that each militia had its own ideological 'position', and that unwittingly the POUM was increasingly being caught up in an internal power struggle between Anarchists, Socialists and Marxists who disagreed violently over the future course the revolution should take. At first sight it seems odd that Orwell, a non-Marxist and a man whose conception of a just society was moral rather than economic, should have joined a militia organised by a tiny Marxist splinter-group. But to him at the time this course seemed perfectly natural. It was not until much later in the war that the full significance of this step was brought home to him. Had he joined the International Brigade instead of the POUM militia – as did many thousands of Englishmen – his experience of the war would have been entirely different. As it was, his involvement with the POUM and his witnessing of their subsequent persecution was to be one of the decisive experiences of his life, affecting his fundamental political attitudes and generating the apocalyptic vision which led in time to *Animal Farm* and *Nineteen Eighty-Four*.

Before turning to a discussion of *Homage to Catalonia* a word of explanation is necessary regarding the geography of Spain: essential to an understanding of the course of the war and of the book itself. Catalonia is a province on the north-eastern coast of Spain, adjoining its frontier with France: Barcelona is its principal city. Its neighbouring provinces are Aragon (of which the principal city is Saragossa) and Valencia. At the outbreak of the war the Republican Government remained in control of Madrid, Barcelona, Bilbao, and Valencia; Cadiz, Saragossa, Seville and Burgos were under the control of the insurgents. Catalonia played a crucial role throughout the Civil War; it was Franco's offensive against Catalonia in December 1938 which led to the collapse of the republican front and the final surrender of Barcelona to his forces. To Orwell, Catalonia with its revolutionary traditions and gentle, innately decent people was synonymous with the Spanish people at their best and with the values he was fighting for.

The province was also deeply attractive to him because it was there that the process of socialisation had been carried out furthest. The resistance to General Franco had been accompanied in many areas by a spontaneous outbreak of revolution: land had been seized by the peasants, trade unions had assumed control of factories, churches had been destroyed. Simultaneously there was an attempt to inaugurate the crude beginnings of a system of government through local committees of workers and trade unions. The war therefore was more than a simple struggle between Democracy and Fascism; it was a triangular conflict between those who wished to restore the status quo, those who wished Franco to succeed, and those who were determined that the revolution should be maintained and intensified. Once Orwell grasped the situation he threw himself wholeheartedly on the side of the revolutionaries. His book, then, is an act of homage both to the people of Catalonia and to the experiment in socialism he had briefly witnessed there. The six months he spent in the region were an interlude which he looked back upon for the remainder of his life with affection and nostalgia. 'This period,' he wrote, 'which then seemed so futile and eventless is now of great importance to me. It is so different from the rest of

my life that already it has taken on the magic quality which, as a
rule, belongs only to memories that are years old.'[47]

Homage to Catalonia, the memoir of his war experiences which he
wrote on his return to England (the book was written at his
home at Wallington between July 1937 and January 1938) is an
unforgettable book: unforgettable because of its passionate
honesty and its moving evocation of a stricken nation, divided
against itself, struggling against impossible odds to achieve a
more egalitarian society. The book is cast in the form of a series
of documentary essays relating in chronological order his experiences as they befell him: Chapter 1 describes his enlistment in
the Lenin Barracks in Barcelona, Chapters 2–4 and 6–8 describe
his adventures as a soldier on the Aragon front, Chapters 9–10
contain a detailed and vivid account of the street fighting he
witnessed whilst on leave in Barcelona, Chapter 12 describes his
return to the front and his nearly fatal throat wound, and 13–14
narrate his return to Barcelona, the nightmare events surrounding the suppression of the POUM, and his eventual return to
England. There are two sections of analysis interspersed with the
narrative: Chapter 5, which is a summary of the internal political situation at the commencement of the war, and Chapter 11, a
résumé of the larger issues behind the street fighting and an
attempt to disentangle the truth from the widespread distortions
circulating at the time in the Spanish and English press. These
sections, which have been much criticised on the grounds that
they allegedly mar a work of considerable literary merit, should
be carefully studied (despite Orwell's explicit invitation to the
reader to 'skip' them) for they are written with care and testify to
his determination to present a balanced appraisal of the war and
to correct what he saw as a misleading impression of events in
the English and Spanish press.

The book as a whole is so vividly written and has such a
powerful sense of immediacy that it is difficult to believe that it
was not written contemporaneously with the events it describes.
There are many excellent war memoirs in the English language –
one thinks of such compelling documents as Sassoon's *Memoirs of
an Infantry Officer* and Gristwood's *The Somme* – but there are few
books in the genre which convey the reality of modern warfare
with such veracity and readability as *Homage to Catalonia*. Orwell
achieves his effects through the use of simple, direct language

even when describing the most extraordinary or horrifying events; by communicating to the reader a strong sense of participation which adds conviction to the narrative; and, dominating all else, by the overwhelming impression of honesty which breathes through the entire work. The tendency to make sweeping generalisations and intolerant judgements – a tendency which mars passages of his earlier works – is altogether absent here. Instead, the overriding impression one receives from a reading of *Homage* is that of a deeply honest man, powerfully moved by all that he has seen and participated in, who is determined to tell the truth at all costs.

The opening chapter, with its moving description of revolutionary Barcelona, depicts a scene which must have seemed in the completest contrast to England at the height of the depression:

> To anyone who had been there since the beginning it probably seemed even in December or January that the revolutionary period was ending; but when one came straight from England the aspect of Barcelona was something startling and overwhelming. It was the first time that I had ever been in a town where the working class was in the saddle . . . All this was queer and moving. There was much in it that I did not understand, in some ways I did not even like it, but I recognised it immediately as a state of affairs worth fighting for.

To Orwell, with his sojourn with the Yorkshire and Lancashire miners still fresh in his memory and with his conceptions of social class rooted firmly in an essentially English background, those few days he spent in Barcelona must have been a revelation. The workers had seized all buildings of importance and draped them with revolutionary flags; all shops and cafeterias had been collectivised (i.e., were under common ownership); tipping was forbidden by law; extremes of poverty and wealth seemed to have disappeared. It was, superficially at least, a classless society. He had devoted much space in *The Road to Wigan Pier* to a discussion of whether 'a classless society' was merely an empty phrase or whether it was capable of realisation. Now, for the first time in his life, he was witnessing such a community in being. During the months which followed he was to have a much more extensive experience of classlessness as a

militiaman – he wrote later that 'I had dropped more or less by
chance into the only community of any size in Western Europe
where political consciousness and disbelief in capitalism were
more normal than their opposites'[48] – which affected him even
more profoundly. This foretaste of a social revolution in action
made an impact on Orwell as a man and as a writer which it
would be impossible to exaggerate.

Because of his practical experience as a policeman in Burma
and as a member of the OTC at Eton he was made a corporal as
soon as the militia reached the front, and was in command of a
guard of twelve men. He remained at the front – at Alcubierre in
the Aragon province – for a total of 115 days before returning to
Barcelona on leave. The phrase 'at the front' suggests a picture
of intense military activity: the reality for Orwell was very different. The Aragon front at that time was in a state of lull.
Although there was some fighting (and it has to be said in fairness to Orwell that he did not avoid participating in actual
combat whenever the opportunity occurred) the conflict in this
particular sector soon settled down into the inconclusiveness of
trench warfare. The substance of his war experience was one of
sentry duty, volunteering for patrols, gathering fuel, trying to
keep warm in the intense cold, and keeping the enemy positions
under constant surveillance. It is the boredom and frustration of
this life, the mundaneness and comradeship of life in the
trenches, which are vividly portrayed in the opening chapters.

At the time the experience seemed to him 'one of the most
futile of my whole life'[49] but in retrospect his months in the
Aragon hills seemed to him of cardinal importance: an interregnum he looked back upon with nostalgia, as if it was a period in
his life he wished to recapture. It is partly for this reason that the
book is so much more than a conventional war memoir; in its
pages he sought to distil a complex of emotions and experiences
and at the same time to create a work which would have enduring value as a record of its time. The romanticised idea of Spain
which dwelt in his imagination, the camaraderie of the trenches,
the unhurried Spanish people, the nobility and baseness unleashed by the war, the vivid realisation of human potentialities
– all these are expressed in a volume which can be read and
re-read with genuine pleasure. Orwell makes no attempt to conceal the sordid reality of war fought with shells and machine-
guns. He was well aware that war means death and suffering as
well as fellowship and momentary happiness; his concern is to

tell it as it happened, making no attempt to conceal unpleasant facts from his readers. The lice, the dirt, the smells, the privation: all is here, depicted in prose of transparent clarity. Above all one has a sense of the intense misery of trench conditions in the cold and wet:

> We were between two and three thousand feet above sea-level, it was mid winter and the cold was unspeakable . . . Sometimes there were shrieking winds that tore your cap off and twisted your hair in all directions, sometimes there were mists that poured into the trench like a liquid and seemed to penetrate your bones; frequently it rained, and even a quarter of an hour's rain was enough to make conditions intolerable. The thin skin of earth over the limestone turned promptly into a slippery grease, and as you were always walking on a slope it was impossible to keep your footing . . . For days together clothes, boots, blankets and rifles were more or less coated with mud.

What this must have meant to Orwell, who admitted that he was 'unusually sensitive to cold', can only be imagined. The sojourn in the trenches provides yet one more example of an interesting facet of his character: the deliberate and repeated subjection of himself to unpleasant and unrewarding situations. One would normally have expected an Etonian with literary ambitions to seek an entrée into the world of letters via editorship or publishing. But Orwell was by no means a conventional aspiring author. Instead, he chose a succession of unusual occupations: a member of the Indian Imperial Police, a hotel scullion, a tramp, a teacher in an impoverished private school, a village shopkeeper. To these he now added the experience of serving as a poorly paid militiaman during a particularly bloody civil war. It is possible to argue that each of these occupations was unnecessary; that there was no need for him to humiliate himself in this way and that by doing so he was making a martyr of himself to no avail. The converse view is that Orwell showed considerable courage in adopting the course that he did, that there was something virtuous in his make-up which compelled him towards these situations, and that he could have gathered the raw material for his novels in no other way. Certainly *Homage to Catalonia* would have been an infinitely poorer book had it not

1. 36 High Street, Southwold, the home of Orwell's parents from 1932 to 1939. Orwell stayed here frequently whilst still an unknown writer, using Southwold as the setting for *A Clergyman's Daughter*.

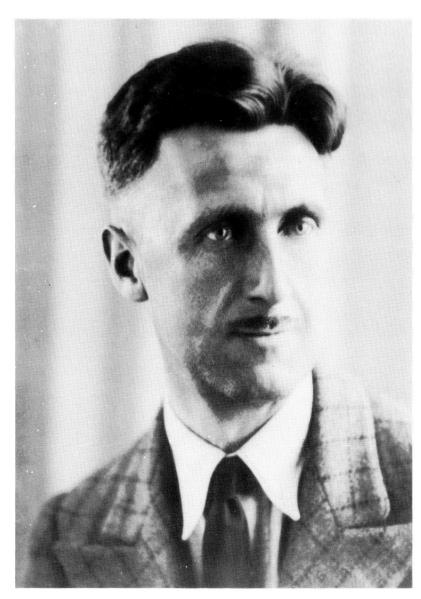

2. Orwell in the early 1930s, a young man on the brink of his literary career. The publication of *Down and Out in Paris and London* in 1933, when Orwell was thirty, marked the beginning of his career as novelist, essayist and author of works of reportage.

3. Plaque marking the site of Booklovers' Corner, 1 South End Road, Hampstead, where Orwell worked as an assistant from October 1934 to January 1936.

4. Colin Blakely (left) as George Bowling in the BBC television production of *Coming Up For Air.*

5. Anne Stalleybrass as Rosemary and Alfred Lynch as Gordon Comstock in the BBC television production of *Keep the Aspidistra Flying*.

6. Housing conditions in Wigan in the 1930s. Early in 1936 Orwell made a close study of housing and unemployment in Lancashire and Yorkshire, a study which formed the basis of *The Road to Wigan Pier*.

7. Orwell at the BBC microphone in 1943. He worked as a Talks Assistant, later becoming a Talks Producer, in the Indian section of the BBC Eastern Service.

8. Mass-produced paperback editions of Orwell's works have brought his name before a readership of millions. His reputation became world-wide with the publication of *Animal Farm* and *Nineteen Eighty-Four*.

Animal Farm

been written by a man who was actually a participant in all that he describes. The first person narrative, the continual use of such phrases as 'I remember', 'It was an extraordinary life that we were living', 'I crept up to the barbed wire to listen', give to the whole book an immediacy and sense of action reminiscent of Buchan. Continually one has a sense of *participation*, of a narrator who does not simply describe his adventures as they unfold but is physically and intimately involved with all that he relates. Through some alchemy of language he communicates not only the sounds, sights and smells of war but the nature of the experience itself; the reader sees the trenches in his imagination and, beyond this, becomes part of the narration. Orwell's skill as a writer is such that the reader shares with him the *feel* of warfare. To read the first eight chapters of *Homage to Catalonia* is to relive in an extraordinarily striking manner the experience of serving as a militiaman among the Aragon mountains at the height of the civil war.

The book owes its distinctive flavour not only to its documentary qualities but to the highly individual character of Orwell as a narrator. One detects at once that, as in all his books told in the first person, the 'I' is a personality with a quirkiness and independence all his own. Years later Orwell wrote:

> I could not do the work of writing a book, or even a long magazine article, if it were not also an aesthetic experience. Anyone who cares to examine my work will see that even when it is downright propaganda it contains much that a full-time politician would consider irrelevant.[50]

How valid this is may be seen by an examination of *Homage*. Intermingled with the nightmarish descriptions of warfare are the reflections and observations of an acutely idiosyncratic personality: a man who notices the absence of birds, rhapsodises on the beauty of the dawn among the mountains, watches the peasants hunting quails ('apparently only male quails were caught, which struck me as unfair'), muses over a primitive harrow, patiently watches a man making goatskin water-bottles and notes the curious pattern of swallows' nests on the cornices of ruined buildings. It is these observations, embedded amidst the matter of fact portrayal of violence and privation, which render the book not only a moving account of one man's testimony of

war but also 'an aesthetic experience'. The overwhelming impression one receives from a reading of *Homage* is of a deeply sensitive man, fascinated by Spain and its history, outraged by the
affront to human decency symbolised by the Fascist uprising and
determined to play his part in ensuring the defeat of the
insurgents. It is, however, much more than this: running behind
and through the surface narrative there is a continual interplay
of comment and scrutiny. One is aware of a strongly individual
voice, the voice of a man who is keenly observant of wild life and
the passing of the seasons, a man with an eye for the poignancies
and ironies of life.

It is the voice of a writer possessed of a vivid sense of imagery:

> The trench-mortars, small though they were, made the most
> evil sound of all. Their shells are really a kind of winged
> torpedo, shaped like the darts thrown in public-houses and
> about the size of a quart bottle; they go off with a devilish
> metallic crash, as of some monstrous globe of brittle steel
> being shattered on an anvil.

In passages such as this Orwell reveals his growing mastery of
language and his ability to achieve memorable prose through the
use of contrast and hyperbole. The homely metaphor 'shaped
like the darts thrown in public-houses' contrasts sharply with the
simile of the 'monstrous globe . . . being shattered on an anvil'
and heightens the effect he is seeking to create. Moreover the
deliberate use of such adjectives as 'evil', 'devilish' and 'monstrous' emphasises the sinister and destructive aspects of war:
aspects to which he was at pains to alert his English readers, for
many of whom (particularly of his own generation) war was a
new and unknown experience.

Orwell conveys unforgettably the horror and desolation of the
sodden battlefields:

> Along the line for miles around a ragged meaningless fire was
> thundering, like the rain that goes on raining after a storm. I
> remember the desolate look of everything, the morasses of
> mud, the weeping poplar trees, the yellow water in the
> trench-bottoms; and men's exhausted faces, unshaven,
> streaked with mud, and blackened to the eyes with smoke.

Again there is the skilful deployment of graphic adjectives: the *ragged* rifle-fire, the *weeping* trees, the *yellow* water, the *blackened* faces. It is as if the description is painted on canvas or recalled from a coloured photograph. And it is entirely characteristic of Orwell that when he himself was almost mortally wounded – he was hit in the throat by a Fascist sniper – he proceeds to describe the occurrence with a dispassionate regard for the truth: 'The whole experience of being hit by a bullet is very interesting and I think it is worth describing in detail . . .'

The voice which speaks through *Homage* is also that of a man who, even at the height of battle, does not lose his sense of humour:

> . . . I had gone out on patrol in the mist and had carefully warned the guard commander beforehand. But in coming back I stumbled against a bush, the startled sentry called out that the Fascists were coming, and I had the pleasure of hearing the guard commander order everyone to open rapid fire in my direction.

It is this ability to detect the humorous side of potentially frightening situations, to observe both the comedy and the pathos of war, which makes the book at once saddening and pleasurable. Always he is at pains to point out the *human* aspects of the war: the woeful standards of Spanish marksmanship, the endless confusion of telegrams which do not arrive and trains which never leave on time, the comic appearance of soldiers wrapped up against the cold, the misunderstandings caused by language difficulties.

The chapters describing his return on leave to Barcelona and his participation in the street-fighting there are extremely significant in the light of his subsequent development as a novelist. On his return from the front he found the city a seething cauldron of internecine warfare, hatred and persecution. It was basically a power struggle between those who wished the revolution to succeed and those who wished to suppress it; throughout the city there was an evil atmosphere of fear and suspicion:

> It is not easy to convey the nightmare atmosphere of that time – the peculiar uneasiness produced by rumours that were always changing, by censored newspapers, and the constant

presence of armed men. It is not easy to convey it because, at the moment, the thing essential to such an atmosphere does not exist in England. In England political intolerance is not yet taken for granted.

The traumatic events in Barcelona in May 1937 were a revelation to Orwell. The POUM was now a suppressed organisation: as a small, dissident Marxist party it made a convenient scapegoat and was outlawed. Known POUM sympathisers were arrested and imprisoned without trial; many were executed. In place of the revolutionary fervour he had witnessed six months earlier there was now, in total contrast, an insidious atmosphere of treachery, duplicity, violence and recrimination. The effect of this upon him, with his public-school background of fair play and his innate sense of honesty and decency, can well be imagined. To Orwell the atmosphere of lies and vilification was both repugnant and frightening; it made an ineradicable impression on him and determined the shape of his primary concerns, both political and artistic, for years to come. Here, in Spain, can be traced the germ of the ideas which came to full realisation in the Thought Police of *Nineteen Eighty-Four*.

The closing pages mount to an intensely moving climax as the narrative rises towards a sense of culmination he rarely recaptured. It is difficult to read without emotion the account of his final days in Catalonia, his desperate attempts to assist his friend Georges Kopp (commander of the POUM militia) who had been summarily imprisoned, his growing disillusionment at the realisation that the ideas he and many others had fought for were being cynically betrayed. It is with a deep sense of relief that the reader follows him to England. At last, in a passage which anticipates the nostalgia of *Coming Up For Air*, he returns to the familiar sleepiness of a countryside in which violence seems remote:

Down here it was still the England I had known in my childhood: the railway-cuttings smothered in wild flowers, the deep meadows where the great shining horses browse and meditate, the slow-moving streams bordered by willows, the green bosoms of the elms, the larkspurs in the cottage gardens . . . all sleeping the deep, deep sleep of England, from which I some-

times fear that we shall never wake till we are jerked out of it
by the roar of bombs.

The book ends on this characteristically ambivalent note: on the
one hand a deep affection for the unchanging pastoral scenes he
had known as a child, on the other hand a growing sense of
foreboding at the intolerance and erosion of fundamental values
symbolised by the rise of fascism. The English, he felt, were too
insular, too trusting, and altogether too innocent to appreciate
the real nature of totalitarian political creeds. It was partly for
this reason – as an exposé of the forces of persecution and violence then rapidly growing in strength – that the book was written.

Homage to Catalonia did not receive the widespread attention
which Orwell had hoped for. Unlike *The Road to Wigan Pier* it was
not a selection of the Left Book Club (indeed Gollancz had
declined to publish it on political grounds) and it had therefore
no guaranteed sale. From its publication in 1938 to his death in
1950 it sold only nine hundred copies, and it was not until its
appearance in paperback form in 1962 that the book became
widely known. The book received few contemporary reviews and
these were for the most part highly critical. This indifferent
reception, combined with the immense popular success of *Animal
Farm* and *Nineteen Eighty-Four*, has served to obscure the very real
literary standing of *Homage* and its importance as a turning point
in his emotional pilgrimage.

George Woodcock remarked of it: 'The great virtue of *Homage
to Catalonia* is not merely that it brings the period back to life in
one's mind, but that it does so with such exceptional radiance'.[51]
That it is such a radiant book is due in large measure to Orwell's
own enthusiasm: despite the violence and duplicity which he
portrays it is on the whole a happy book, and one cannot resist
the conclusion that on the whole he valued the experience and
would not have done without it. As he himself wrote: 'It was
beastly while it was happening, but it is a good patch for my
mind to browse upon'.[52] He had, after all, just missed the First
World War (he was fifteen in 1918) and there were elements in
his make-up for which the excitement and glamour of war held a
strong appeal. Its qualities as a war memoir are due in equal

measure to the literary skill with which he organises his materials and communicates his effects to the reader. In his essay 'Why I Write' he observed with characteristic modesty: 'in the main it is written with a certain detachment and regard for form. I did try very hard in it to tell the whole truth without violating my literary instincts'. As a documentary it is an improvement on those which preceded it since it lacks the defects of construction which are occasionally evident in *Down and Out* and the intolerance which mars the second half of *The Road to Wigan Pier*. One has the feeling that here at last Orwell had achieved a mature and accomplished style and that in doing so he had found himself as a creative artist. That simple, direct, honest style – a form of writing which later generations were to characterise as 'Orwellian' – was brought to perfection in *Homage to Catalonia*. It is the style in which all his finest descriptive essays are written (the reader is referred especially in this connection to 'Shooting an Elephant', 'Marrakech', 'Looking Back on the Spanish War' and 'How the Poor Die') and by which he is best remembered as a literary figure. One thinks, for example, of the unforgettable picture of the trenches on the Aragon front and the manner in which Orwell conveys the sights, sounds and smells of warfare; of the vivid descriptions of battle (Chapter 7 is an excellent example of the technique) which seem to owe so much to his boyhood enthusiasm for tales of adventure; of the horrifying description of street fighting, so evocative that one senses the evil atmosphere brooding over the city and the constant crackle of rifle fire; of the final, eloquent pages recounting his flight from Spain to France and then on to England, a beautiful piece of writing which has the quality of a coda in a symphony and which brings the entire work to a satisfying conclusion. Regarded purely as a literary achievement *Homage* should rank highly in the canon of his work. It will take its place alongside Hemingway's *For Whom the Bell Tolls* and Koestler's *Spanish Testament* as a true and moving account of one man's involvement in the Spanish Civil War.

The book is also significant in that it marks a crucial stage in Orwell's political development: first, because it marks the beginning of his concern for objective historical truth – a concern which came increasingly to dominate his life; and second, because it records the transformation of his socialism from a theoretical belief to a positive faith.

There are numerous instances in *Homage to Catalonia* and in the essay 'Looking Back on the Spanish War' (1943) in which he records his disillusionment that the whole concept of objective truth was not merely being challenged but blatantly denied. In Spain he had witnessed censored newspapers, press reports that bore no relation to reality, accounts of battles which had not taken place, soldiers denounced as 'fascist spies' whom a few months previously had been hailed as heroes. In short, he had learned the validity of the aphorism that 'in war, the first casualty is truth'. What so distressed him was the deliberate manufacture of false statements, even to the extent of asserting that a particular event in the past *had not happened*:

> I am willing to believe that history is for the most part inaccurate and biased, but what is peculiar to our own age is the abandonment of the idea that history *could* be truthfully written . . . It is just this common basis of agreement, with its implication that human beings are all one species of animal, that totalitarianism destroys . . . This prospect frightens me much more than bombs – and after our experiences of the last few years that is not a frivolous statement.[53]

His concern for the truth and care in the use of language can be seen at a number of points in his earlier writings – in the distaste with which Flory in *Burmese Days*, for example, describes an atmosphere in which it was not possible to speak one's mind, and in the repugnance with which Gordon Comstock in *Keep the Aspidistra Flying* regards the world of advertising. But Spain convinced him that the real threat confronting civilisation was not Fascism as such but totalitarianism with its concomitant denial of verifiable truth. The civil war, coupled with the Moscow Trials of 1936–7, was in this sense a deeply saddening experience for Orwell. This personal observation of the cynical manner in which truth could be manipulated in the interests of party doctrine marks the onset of that passionate concern for objective statement which reaches its culmination in the satire of Doublethink and the Ministry of Truth.

In Catalonia during the winter of 1936–7 Orwell was for the first and only time in his life a member of a completely egalitarian society. Throughout his previous experience – as a schoolboy at Eton, a member of the Indian Imperial Police, a down and out in Paris and London, a shop assistant, a writer among the Wigan miners – he had been subject in greater or lesser degree to the nuances and heirarchies of social class. Now, briefly, he was a member of 'a sort of microcosm of a classless society. In that community where no one was on the make, where there was a shortage of everything but no privilege and no boot-licking, one got, perhaps, a crude forecast of what the open-ing stages of socialism might be like. And, after all, instead of disillusioning me it deeply attracted me.'[54] It is difficult to appreciate the impact this must have made upon him, coming as he did from a quintessentially English and Anglo-Indian back-ground. In Wells's novel *Tono-Bungay* there is a memorable pic-ture of the rigidities of the class system in the Victorian era:

> In that English countryside of my boyhood every human being had a 'place'. It belonged to you from your birth like the colour of your eyes, it was inextricably your destiny. Above you were your betters, below you were your inferiors, and there were even an unstable questionable few, cases so disput-able that you might, for the rough purposes of every day at least, regard them as your equals.[55]

The young Eric Blair, growing up in the sedate English com-munity in Bengal and in Edwardian Henley-on-Thames, had spent the most impressionable years of his life against precisely that background. Even as a dishwasher in Paris he had not been free of it for he found that the hotel staffs had a hierarchy of their own, and in the depressed areas of the north of England the miners would not accept him as an equal because of his public school accent. Now, at the age of thirty-three, he found himself at last part of an egalitarian community: it was an experience he was never to forget. Above all, he had not only participated in 'a crude forecast of what the opening stages of Socialism might be like', but he had witnessed its destruction. The suppression of the POUM, the dismantling of the militias and the victory of the anti-revolutionary forces in Catalonia and elsewhere meant that the fragile experiment in creating a classless society came to an end. These two events – the spontaneous construction of a social revolution, and its systematic dismemberment – made a deep impression upon him. Paradoxically they did not lead to the abandonment of his belief in socialism nor to the dilution of his ideals. His idealism remained undimmed and, if anything, enhanced as a result of his experiences. The fundamental difference between the Orwell of pre-1936 and the Orwell of post-1936 was this: that until he arrived in Spain his advocacy of socialism was entirely theoretical, based upon a passionate concern for social justice. To say this is not to question in any way the genuineness of his beliefs but merely to point out that he was much more clear what he was fighting *against* than the concept he was fighting *for*. Catalonia, on the other hand, provided him with a practical experience of socialism in action: an experience which, though of brief duration, was of incalculable significance to his development as a novelist. In the deeply moving concluding passages of *Homage* he gives eloquent testimony to the reaffirmation of his faith:

When you have had a glimpse of such a disaster as this – and however it ends the Spanish War will turn out to have been an appalling disaster, quite apart from the slaughter and physical suffering – the result is not necessarily disillusionment and cynicism. Curiously enough the whole experience has left me with not less but more belief in the decency of human beings.

Coming Up For Air

Coming Up For Air was written between September 1938 and
March 1939 at Marrakech, Morocco. Orwell's doctors had
advised him to spend the winter in a warm climate (his lungs
were tubercular and it was felt that the warm air would have a
beneficial effect on his health). His financial circumstances were
such that it would not have been possible for him to accept this
advice, but L. H. Myers the novelist, who greatly admired his
work, anonymously gave him £300 to enable him to do so.
Orwell gratefully accepted this on the understanding that it was
to be regarded as a loan and spent the winter of 1938–9 in North
Africa, working steadily on the novel. The book was published in
June 1939, three months before the outbreak of the Second
World War.

The entire story is pervaded with the atmosphere of uncertainty which affected England and the English during the year
preceding the outbreak of the war. Fear of invasion, uncertainty
regarding Hitler's actions and intentions, ominous indications of
a more regimented society: all are writ large in *Coming Up For
Air*. Writing to his friend Jack Common in the spring of 1938 he
remarked apropos his projected novel:

> It's a bore not being able either to work or to get home & try
> & salvage what is left of the garden after this bloody weather,
> but undoubtedly the rest has done me good & incidentally has
> made me keen to get started with my next novel, though when
> I came here [Preston Hall, a sanatorium at Aylesford, Kent]
> I had been thinking that what with Hitler, Stalin & the rest of
> them the day of novel-writing was over. As it is if I start it in
> August I daresay I'll have to finish it in the concentration
> camp.[56]

One of the most interesting aspects of *Coming Up For Air* in the light of Orwell's subsequent literary achievement is the extraordinary manner in which many of the themes of *Nineteen Eighty-Four* are prefigured in the earlier novel. There is a remarkable passage (in Part Three, I) in which George Bowling anticipates the nightmare, regimented world which he is convinced will follow in the wake of war:

> War! I started thinking about it again. It's coming soon, that's certain. But who's afraid of war? That's to say, who's afraid of the bombs and the machine-guns? 'You are,' you say. Yes, I am, and so's anybody who's ever seen them. But it isn't the war that matters, it's the after-war. The world we're going down into, the kind of hate-world, slogan-world. The coloured shirts, the barbed wire, the rubber truncheons. The secret cells where the electric light burns night and day, and the detectives watching you while you sleep. And the processions and the posters with enormous faces, and the crowds of a million people all cheering for the Leader till they deafen themselves into thinking that they really worship him, and all the time, underneath, they hate him so that they want to puke. It's all going to happen.

The duplicity, torture, and suppression of free speech which Orwell had witnessed at first hand in Spain clearly filled him with foreboding for the future of civilisation and in the story of the life and disillusionment of George Bowling he gave expression to his deepest fears for the future of mankind. Although this betrays him at times into exaggeration (the scene in which a British aeroplane bombs Lower Binfield in error seems a contrived piece of writing, and for this reason lacks conviction) there is no question of his utter sincerity in giving vent to his anxieties: anxieties which he wished to communicate to his readers and which he wanted them to share. The much quoted final paragraph of *Homage to Catalonia* in which he had referred to the peacefulness of the Kentish countryside 'all sleeping the deep, deep sleep of England, from which I sometimes fear that we shall never wake till we are jerked out of it by the roar of bombs' was no mere rhetorical peroration. What he had witnessed in Spain had convinced him that violence, cruelty and destruction were features of twentieth-century life which were escalating at an alarming rate. Writing to Cyril Connolly whilst the novel was in progress he observed: 'everything one writes now is over-shadowed by this ghastly feeling that we are rushing towards a precipice and, though we shan't actually prevent ourselves or anyone else from going over, must put up some sort of fight'.[57]

The disillusioning experience of Barcelona, which was fresh in his memory, had convinced him that the English were still polit-ically innocent. England had, after all, known no armed invasion since 1066. The insidious forces which were endemic in Europe – intolerance, lies, persecution, propaganda, torture – had been unknown in his own country for centuries. What he sought to do therefore in *Coming Up For Air* was to present in the form of a novel a warning of the dangerous forces being unleashed by totalitarian ideologies, and to bring the message indelibly home to English readers by placing the story firmly in a recognisable and familiar setting.

This sense of impending catastrophe pervades the book with a curious *fin de siècle* atmosphere: an atmosphere strongly reminis-cent of a number of late nineteenth-century novels which pre-dicted the end of an age. There is, for example, a striking passage in Wells's *The War of the Worlds* (1898) in which an artilleryman on Putney Hill speaks of

> all those damn little clerks that used to live down *that* way . . .
> They just used to skedaddle off to work – I've seen hundreds of
> 'em, bit of breakfast in hand, running wild and shining to
> catch their little season-ticket train, for fear they'd get dismis-
> sed if they didn't; working at businesses they were afraid to
> take the trouble to understand; skedaddling back for fear they
> wouldn't be in time for dinner; keeping indoors after dinner
> for fear of the back-streets; and sleeping with the wives they
> married, not because they wanted them, but because they had
> a bit of money that would make for safety in their one little
> miserable skedaddle through the world.[58]

The entire passage is a vivid anticipation of Bowling's strictures against the inhabitants of West Bletchley, 'the poor little five-to-ten-pound-a-weekers' who live in mortal fear of the boss, the wife, the sack. Deliberately writing in a terse, documentary, col-loquial style, Orwell consciously set out to convey to his readers the uncertainty and confusion prevailing in the aftermath of

Munich: a period in which the English people went about their daily affairs with an outward calmness but with inward feelings of trepidation and doubt.

It is an apocalyptic novel in the sense that Orwell clearly foresaw the imminence not only of world war but of the collapse of civilised values and the emergence of totalitarian regimes based on hatred and violence. Seen in this light it is a bridge between *Homage to Catalonia* with its moving affirmation of human decency and the pessimism of *Nineteen Eighty-Four*. It occupies an important place in the corpus of his work for it is not only a transition between the concerns of his early writings and those of his last but is an extended essay on a theme which, explicitly or otherwise, underlay all his life: the tension between his professed desire for social change and a passionate longing to return to a world in which time stood still.

As *Coming Up For Air* was the last conventional novel which Orwell wrote, and the only one written in the first person, it is interesting to examine the techniques employed by the author in presenting the character of the narrator, George Bowling.

Replying to Julian Symons, who had criticised some aspects of his technique, he wrote: 'Of course you are perfectly right about my own character constantly intruding on that of the narrator. I am not a real novelist anyway, and that particular vice is inherent in writing a novel in the first person, which one should never do.'[59] In fact Orwell does succeed to a remarkable extent in giving his narrator a personality of his own, even in such details as Bowling being a plump man whereas Orwell himself was exceptionally tall and gaunt. H. G. Wells remarked apropos his own novel *The World of William Clissold*: 'How can one imagine and invent the whole interior world of an uncongenial type? Every author must write of the reactions he knows; he must be near enough to them to *feel* them sympathetically.'[60] One feels that Orwell would have unhesitatingly endorsed this point of view, yet in presenting George Bowling as his narrator and central character he created a more complex figure than is generally acknowledged. Bowling is in fact a curious amalgam of attitudes – some of them Orwell's own and others invented. The author succeeds to an extraordinary extent in creating a completely *imaginary* character with a background and outlook different in many respects from his own. The description of Bowling's home background and of his mother and father are totally different from what we know of his own: indeed there could hardly be a sharper contrast than that between the sedate Anglo-Indian background of Eric Blair as a boy and the boyhood of George Bowling in the seed-merchant's shop. It is arguable that the description of Bowling's home milieu is in reality an idealisation of the kind of childhood background Orwell would have wished to have had; what is certain is that in these chapters he is not simply drawing on his own memories (as he had done for much of *A Clergyman's Daughter* and *Keep the Aspidistra Flying*) but evoking, in an essentially creative way, a complex pattern of impressions and sensations. From this standpoint the novel marks a considerable advance on all that has gone before: despite his claim that 'I am not a real novelist' *Coming Up For Air* can justly claim to be a coherent work of art in the sense that, more fully than in any of the preceding novels, there is unmistakeable evidence of those imaginative gifts which transform journalism into literature. It is not simply that Orwell is a skilful technician, although he is certainly that. It is that, in assembling the materials of his novel – the boyhood of George Bowling, his experiences during the First World War, his marriage to Hilda, his humdrum life in suburbia – he fuses these elements together through a *literary* process to achieve an artistically satisfying whole. The result is a book of extraordinary richness, a story which, though pervaded with the mental atmosphere of the 1930s, possesses those timeless qualities which enable the reader to turn to it time and again with enjoyment.

Orwell deliberately places Bowling *backwards* in time – he himself was born in 1903, but Bowling is born ten years earlier, in 1893. The effect of this is that Bowling has certain memories – for example, the outbreak of the Boer War – which Orwell himself cannot have had. The effect is also to give a sense of distance to the childhood chapters which they would not otherwise possess.[61] (In adopting this device Orwell was following in a distinguished literary tradition: Dickens, in both *The Pickwick Papers* and *Great Expectations*, consciously places his opening scenes in an earlier decade in order to achieve the effect of distance.) With considerable skill the childhood world of George Bowling is evoked: the shop, the High Street, his mother and father, his elder brother, the sights and smells of a pre-1914 boyhood in a small country town.

Orwell shared with a number of other radical English novelists, most notably H. G. Wells, a nostalgia for the unchanging rural order he had known and loved as a child. This affection for the peaceful, timeless countryside he remembered from his childhood at Henley-on-Thames (and the neighbouring village of Shiplake) during the years 1907–17 is evident from numerous passages in his writings and becomes a major theme in *Coming Up For Air*:

> It was a wonderful June morning. The buttercups were up to my knees. There was a breath of wind just stirring the tops of the elms, and the great green clouds of leaves were sort of soft and rich like silk. And it was nine in the morning and I was eight years old, and all round me it was early summer, with great tangled hedges where the wild roses were still in bloom, and bits of soft white cloud drifting overhead, and in the distance the low hills and the dim blue masses of the woods round Upper Binfield.[62]

In such passages as this, and throughout the boyhood reminiscences of George Bowling, Orwell is drawing upon his memories of carefree school holidays spent in fishing, shooting rabbits and exploring the unspoilt countryside around Henley: holidays which are described with charm and affection in Jacintha Buddicom's *Eric and Us: A Remembrance of George Orwell*. It is clear that both Orwell in his own person and his fictional creation George Bowling looked back with nostalgia to their childhood: a childhood which possessed a security and continuity irrevocably destroyed by the holocaust of 1914–18. With considerable skill the *peacefulness* of pre-1914 England is evoked:

> And then the cool of the evening outside, the smell of night-stocks and pipe-tobacco in the lane behind the allotments, the soft dust underfoot, and the nightjars hawking after the cockchafers . . . What's the use of saying that one oughtn't to be sentimental about 'before the war'? I *am* sentimental about it. So are you if you remember it.[63]

Orwell is, in fact, an extremely interesting case-study of the presence within one and the same person of radical and conservative attitudes. It is abundantly clear from his writings (particularly those after the Spanish Civil War) that he was a professed socialist; it is equally clear that many of his attitudes and preferences were those of a conservative English gentleman. In an autobiographical fragment he prepared in 1940[64] he made it clear that his list of 'likes' included 'coal fires, candlelight and comfortable chairs', and his dislikes included 'big towns, noise, motor cars, the radio, tinned food, central heating and "modern" furniture'. It is significant that the aspects of life which he despised were all twentieth-century in origin; those he found congenial belonged to an earlier age. And in an article on his favourite public house, given the imaginary name 'The Moon under Water', he specified that 'its whole architecture and fittings are uncompromisingly Victorian'.[65] In his distaste for many aspects of modern society and his affection for those of a past era he is strongly reminiscent of George Gissing, a writer whom he greatly admired. Indeed Gissing's volume of essays *The Private Papers of Henry Ryecroft*, with its deep affection for rural England and its attachment to nineteenth-century values needs to be read as a companion piece to *Coming Up For Air*: both reveal the longing of the expatriate for the cherished England of their memories. (The word 'expatriate' here is literally true since both works were written whilst their authors were in exile.)

Although Orwell uses the word 'sentimental' to describe Bowling's attitude towards Edwardian England it is clear that in looking back to his boyhood he is recalling not simply its surface pleasures but the sense of *permanence* which those years embodied. The young Bowling and those before him are not frightened about the future, they have no inkling that their way of life will not continue, their values are stable values which show no sign of dissolution: it is these elements which, looking back in 1938, he finds so appealing and which he seeks to recall. By contrast with the world of his childhood, life on the eve of the Second World War seems totally lacking in stability: it is a world in which there are no enduring components, no certainty, no continuity, no peace of mind. Seeking to recapture the sense of peace he had known in that vanished world he determines to revisit Lower Binfield in an attempt to savour once again the quietness and freedom from worry he recalls so sharply.

The lyrical descriptions of fishing, which years later Orwell confessed he had 'passionately' wished to write about,[66] are revealing not only for their insight into his attitudes towards the pastime – for him it was an essentially *peaceful* hobby, 'the opposite of war' – but for the description of the hidden pool which Bowling discovers in the grounds of Binfield House:

> ... and then suddenly there was a clearing and I came to another pool which I had never known existed. It was a small pool not more than twenty yards wide, and rather dark because of the boughs that overhung it. But it was very clear water and immensely deep ... At some time this pool had been connected with the other, and then the stream had dried up and the woods had closed round the small pool and it had just been forgotten.[67]

It is not too fanciful to see in this secret pool – which George considers of immense importance and which he revisits years later, only to find that it has been drained of water and used as a tip – a symbol of Orwell's romantic yearning for a pastoral life, or more specifically of the *sense of loss* which is communicated by so much of his work. The physical details of the pool may well be derived from his memories of fishing at Henley (or at Ticklerton, Shropshire, the home of the Buddicom's grandfather, where he once spent an idyllic Bevis-like holiday, shooting, fishing and exploring the countryside) but symbolically it seems clear that the hidden pool has its origins in his secret imaginings. Again and again in his life and work we find evidence of a desire to free himself from the trappings of urban civilisation and return to a simpler, rural, less hurried past. This can be seen, for example, in his decision to move from London to Hertfordshire in 1936 and to live in a small cottage with no modern conveniences. It can be seen in his quixotic determination in the closing years of his life to live on the island of Jura in the Hebrides, where conditions were primitive in the extreme. And above all it can be seen in the frequent references in his writings to nature – see his delightful essay 'Some Thoughts on the Common Toad' and the numerous comments on wildlife in his 'As I Please' column – which reveal a marked interest in the countryside and in the passing of the seasons. This was more than the romantic sentimentalising of the city-dweller for the imagined benefits of living in the country; this was a deeply felt longing to return to the unspoilt, simple, pastoral life he had glimpsed in his boyhood and adolescence and which he sought throughout his life to regain. In this sense *Coming Up For Air* is the most characteristic of his works, for in contrasting the world of the present with life as it might be Orwell does not look forward to an imaginary utopia but *backward* to life as it was in the early years of the century.

The evocation of Bowling's childhood is, then, the most memorable section of the novel – certainly it is these chapters which remain in the mind most vividly after the book has been lain aside – but the story contains much else of abiding value. The courtship between Bowling and Elsie Waters, his love of reading, the description of the Vincent family and their Anglo-Indian milieu: these are sketched with a lucid pen and with an apparent simplicity, an apparent artlessness which conceals a very real literary talent. Orwell is on record as stating that 'I believe the modern writer who has influenced me most is Somerset Maugham, whom I admire immensely for his power of telling a story straightforwardly and without frills'.[68] Certainly in *Coming Up For Air* he brought to perfection the art of narrating a memorable story in the simplest possible language, and in doing so captured the mood of the times in a way which no other novel of the period has equalled.

Maugham's influence on the story is evident at a number of points, most strikingly in the section describing Bowling's return to Lower Binfield after a lapse of twenty-five years. This is so reminiscent of the scene in *Cakes and Ale* (1930) in which Ashenden returns to Blackstable, the small seaside town in which he had lived as a young man, that it is difficult to resist the conclusion that *Cakes and Ale* may have been in his mind during the writing of this passage. There is the same disillusioning arrival at the hotel, the same chagrin at finding that one's surname is not recognised, the same disappointment on seeing fields transformed into housing estates, the same sadness at the realisation that the familiar scenes of childhood have been altered out of recognition. Orwell adds, however, an element of *anger* which is altogether missing from Maugham's account: 'And they'd filled my pool up with tin cans. God rot them and bust them! . . . Not that there's anything one can do about it, except to wish them the pox in their guts.' He undoubtedly felt deeply about the erosion of rural England and in *Coming Up For Air* gave expression to his strong distaste for the artificiality and ugliness of modern life.

The intensity of Bowling's search for his past is such as to pose the question whether or not *Coming Up For Air* is basically a conservative novel. In the sense that it looks back with nostalgia it is a conservative, indeed a reactionary, novel; yet it is precisely the element of anger which marks it as the work of a twentieth-century writer. In Spain Orwell had seen for himself that the past could be distorted for political ends. Bowling, in returning to the scenes of his childhood, sees that the past can be taken away: it is as if the simple, unspoilt life he remembered had never been. It is this realisation which lies at the heart of Bowling's invective, an awareness that the values which had shaped the lives of his ancestors – honesty, decency, contentment, concern for the land – were being altogether destroyed by social and technological forces over which he had no control. This feeling of *helplessness* in the face of overwhelmingly powerful and destructive forces is the dominant impression of the novel.

Despite the anger of the narrator, *Coming Up For Air* is a markedly passive novel by comparison with its predecessors and particularly *Keep the Aspidistra Flying*. There is nothing comparable to Gordon Comstock's rebellion against society. At the conclusion of the story Bowling concedes defeat, by his marriage and by life as a whole, and returns to an existence he finds detestable. The dynamic Orwell is altogether absent. It is interesting in this connection to note that, immediately before his involvement in the Spanish Civil War, he had met the novelist Henry Miller and had been much struck by Miller's attitude that a Second World War was inevitable and that any resistance to it was futile. Whilst disagreeing with this attitude Orwell clearly reflected on it very seriously and acknowledged its intellectual force. In creating the character of George Bowling and giving his creation considerable freedom to comment and digress he is in effect thinking aloud about the problems of peace and war. Bowling's passivity seems odd when compared with the vigour and participation of *The Road to Wigan Pier* and *Homage to Catalonia* yet he undoubtedly expressed the fears and uncertainties of many thousands of readers in 1939. Passivity, however, was not a stance Orwell could have maintained for long. With the onset of war within months of the book's publication he abandoned the hostility to 'imperialist' war he had maintained since June 1938 (when he had joined the Independent Labour Party) and sought actively for an opportunity to serve his country. The time for inertia was over.

Writing to a friend in 1948 Orwell remarked: 'Of course the book was bound to suggest Wells watered down. I have a great admiration for Wells, i.e. as a writer, and he was a very early influence on me.'[69] The reference to 'Wells watered down' is of course to *The History of Mr. Polly*, a novel which had a marked impact upon him and which is referred to specifically in *Coming Up For Air* (Part Two, 8). A comparison between the two novels tells us much about Wells and Orwell and also about the differences in mental attitudes between 1910 and 1938. On the surface there are many resemblances between them. In both the central character is an imaginative figure prone to romantic longings derived from his reading and reminiscences; in both he looks back upon a childhood which was on the whole happy; in both he finds the routines of his daily life intolerable (Bowling after eighteen years as an insurance salesman, and Polly after fifteen years as a draper) and seeks to escape from the limitations of his environment. Moreover the *structure* of the two stories reveals interesting similarities: both begin with the protagonist in middle-age reflecting on his situation; this is followed by a lengthy section tracing the story of his life up to the point at which the book begins; then follows a final section recounting the experiences of the hero from this point onwards. Consciously or unconsciously, then, *Mr. Polly* would appear to be one of the formative literary sources which helped to determine the shape and atmosphere of *Coming Up For Air*. The differences between the two stories are, however, most striking. Whereas Mr Polly succeeds in escaping from a wife and an existence which have become anathema to him and eventually finds lasting happiness in the rural haven of the Potwell Inn, George Bowling finds no such release. His attempt to recapture the peace and security of his childhood ends in complete disillusionment and he returns to the lifeless routines of his marriage, convinced that another world war is imminent and that all attempts to opt out of the coming holocaust are futile. Orwell's vision, then, is profoundly more pessimistic than Wells's. Whereas *Mr. Polly* could be described as an allegory on the theme of paradise regained, *Coming Up For Air* is a fantasia on the theme of paradise destroyed. It is significant that in his quest to find traces of the country town he had loved George Bowling fails utterly: almost every aspect of Lower Binfield has been changed – either removed altogether, urbanised, or so altered as to be almost unrecognisable. 'The old life's finished,' he acknowledges bitterly, 'and to go about looking for it is just waste of time. There's no way back to Lower Binfield, you can't put Jonah back into the whale.'

Coming Up For Air is a picture of a world in process of disintegration: a world which is visibly crumbling while the events are being described. It is in a real sense a 'Condition of England' novel – a portrait of England at a particular point in time, in process of decay. Today its place in literary history seems secure. (It is a measure of the changes in literary fashion that today *Coming Up For Air* is readily available in a variety of editions, but when it was reprinted by Secker & Warburg in 1948 as the first volume in a uniform edition the book was so completely out of print that a copy had to be stolen from a public library in order to provide a text from which it could be reset.) It will take its place beside other 'Condition of England' novels – *Sybil*, *North and South*, *Tono-Bungay* – as an acutely perceptive commentary on its age and as a picture of one man's attempt to come to terms with his past.

Animal Farm

Between the publication of *Coming Up For Air* in June 1939 and the commencement of *Animal Farm* in November 1943 a gap of four years intervened: years of intense creative activity for Orwell but also of considerable frustration. Rejected by the armed forces on the grounds of his health, he sought to serve his country by joining the Home Guard, where he was soon promoted to the rank of sergeant. From August 1941 to November 1943 he was on the staff of the British Broadcasting Corporation as a Talks Assistant (later a Talks Producer) in the Indian section of its Eastern Service. There are several reasons why Orwell felt unable or unwilling to attempt another novel during this period. One was that, with his growing ill-health and tendency towards overwork, he felt the need for a complete rest from novel writing. He confided to his friend Geoffrey Gorer: 'I want to lay off writing for a bit, I feel I have written myself out & ought to lie fallow'.[70] He had published eight books in eight years and not unnaturally wanted a break from what he regarded as the 'horrible, exhausting struggle'[71] of writing another one. A further reason was that the unsettled, frenzied atmosphere of the early war years was not conducive to the writing of novels. He had for some time been contemplating a long family saga in several volumes but found it impossible to settle down to the writing of this whilst war was raging in the background (he remained living in London throughout the blitz). During this period, however, he produced a considerable amount of writing. To these years belong his important essays 'Charles Dickens', 'Inside the Whale', 'The Lion and the Unicorn' and 'Rudyard Kipling', as well as prolific journalism and book reviewing for *Tribune*, *Horizon*, the *New Statesman* and other journals: all this in addition to

his full-time work at the BBC and his Home Guard duties, both
of which he carried out conscientiously.

By November 1943 he had resigned from both the Home
Guard and the BBC and embarked at once on *Animal Farm*, the
idea for which had come to him some years earlier. In his preface
to the Ukrainian edition (published in 1947) he summarised the
genesis of the story in these terms:

> And so for the past ten years [i.e., since the Spanish Civil War
> and the purges in the USSR] I have been convinced that the
> destruction of the Soviet myth was essential if we wanted a
> revival of the Socialist movement. On my return from Spain I
> thought of exposing the Soviet myth in a story that could be
> easily understood by almost anyone and which could be easily
> translated into other languages. However the actual details of
> the story did not come to me for some time until one day (I
> was then living in a small village) I saw a little boy, perhaps
> ten years old, driving a huge cart-horse along a narrow path,
> whipping it whenever it tried to turn. It struck me that if only
> such animals became aware of their strength we should have
> no power over them, and that men exploit animals in much
> the same way as the rich exploit the proletariat.[72]

The idea of expressing his disillusionment with Stalinism – and,
in a wider sense, with totalitarian regimes in general – in the
form of an animal fable was thus simmering in his mind for a
long time before he found the opportunity to write it. In the end
it took him just four months to produce the finished manuscript,
yet the writing of it cannot have been easy; he confessed later
that he had 'sweated' over its preparation.[73] We know that
Orwell was a painstaking craftsman who revised and polished
his manuscripts with great care until he was satisfied. *Animal
Farm* is surely no exception, for it bears all the hallmarks of a
work which has been most carefully written. This, above all his
other writings, has been wrought with the utmost attention to
language, style and construction.

On its completion in the spring of 1944 he cast about for a
publisher. He must have realised, however, that the climate was
highly unfavourable to the publication of a book which would be
construed as an anti-Soviet satire. Since the German invasion of
1941 the Soviet Union had been regarded as an ally, and now

that Russian troops were fighting with great gallantry on the Eastern front many publishers looked askance at the idea of issuing a fable which, whilst described as 'a fairy story', would be widely interpreted as an attack on the USSR and on Stalin in particular. In the event the book was rejected on political grounds by three publishing houses – Gollancz, Jonathan Cape, and Faber & Faber – before being accepted (in August 1944) by Secker & Warburg. Orwell had to wait until August 1945 before the book was actually published. The twelve-month delay was due to a combination of factors including the acute shortage of paper necessitated by the war effort and legal complications arising from the fact that he was still under contract with Gollancz. At last, however, these difficulties were resolved. *Animal Farm* was published on 17 August 1945, in an edition of 4500 copies and at once began to sell at a pace which must have gratified both author and publisher. The first edition sold out in a matter of days and a second impression was put in hand. It speedily became clear that the book was enjoying a wider sale than any of his previous works. It was widely reviewed and brought his name for the first time to the attention of a world audience. Since its original publication *Animal Farm* has sold upwards of ten million copies in hardback and paperback editions in Britain and the United States and has in addition been translated into many foreign languages. Fredric Warburg, his friend and publisher, has commented: 'In the quarter-century since it was published, this little book has shown a vitality in terms of sales which to me is conclusive proof that it will remain for generations a classic of English and world literature'.[74]

The book is totally different in style and conception from anything Orwell had previously written. Written in a simple and fluent manner, it is cast in the form of a short narrative describing a group of animals on a farm who, inspired by the teachings of a wise old boar, rebel against the farmer and assume control for themselves. Leadership devolves upon the pigs who direct and supervise the others in the running of the enterprise. At first the animals are guided in their activities by Seven Commandments which 'form an unalterable law by which all the animals on Animal Farm must live for ever after'. Gradually, however, these Commandments are altered or diluted by the pigs to suit their own convenience until they bear little relation to the original tenets. The pigs become increasingly dictatorial and in time arrogate to themselves the privileges previously exercised by humans. One by one the principles which inspired the original rebellion are abandoned until at last there remains a single Commandment: ALL ANIMALS ARE EQUAL BUT SOME ANIMALS ARE MORE EQUAL THAN OTHERS. By the end of the story the pigs have assumed so many human attributes that they resemble human beings in appearance. The book ends on a note of discord as the pigs invite the neighbouring farmers to a conference and quarrel whilst playing cards:

> Twelve voices were shouting in anger, and they were all alike. No question, now, what had happened to the faces of the pigs. The creatures outside looked from pig to man, and from man to pig, and from pig to man again; but already it was impossible to say which was which.

Critical discussion of *Animal Farm* has tended to concentrate largely on its satirical and allegorical elements. Certainly there are close parallels between the plot of the book and the history of the USSR between 1917 and 1943, and the book should be examined carefully for such parallels. The numerous symbolisms may be expressed in tabular form, as follows:

Mr Jones	Tsar Nicholas II
Major	Marx
Boxer	The Proletariat
Napoleon	Stalin
Snowball	Trotsky
Squealer	*Pravda*
Minimus	Mayakovsky
The Pigs	The Bolsheviks
Moses	The Russian Orthodox Church
Mollie	The White Russians
Pilkington	Britain
Frederick	Germany
The farmhouse	The Kremlin
The Rebellion	The Russian Revolution
The Battle of the Cowshed	The allied invasion of 1918–19
The Battle of the Windmill	The German invasion of 1941
The windmill	The Five-Year Plans
'Beasts of England'	'L'Internationale'

The symbolism of the book is remarkably detailed and reveals an impressive knowledge of Soviet history and Marxist theory. The principal events in the history of the USSR are followed in detail and include, for example, the sailors' uprising of 1921 (the revolt of the hens), the collectivisation of 1929–33 (the failure of the crops), the Moscow Trials of 1936–8 (the confession of the pigs), and the Teheran Conference of 1943 (the final conference of pigs and humans). So gentle is the satire, however, that the allegory which provides the story with its *raison d'être* is not obtrusive. It would be entirely possible for a reader unaware of its nuances to approach the narrative simply as an animal fable. Indeed it is on record that one publisher declined to accept the book on the grounds that 'it was impossible to sell animal stories in the U.S.A.'.[75]

Yet it would be too simplistic to interpret *Animal Farm* solely in terms of a satire on the Soviet Union. It is clear from many indications that Orwell had wider aims in mind. In a letter to his agent Leonard Moore he stated that the book 'is intended as a satire on dictatorship in general',[76] and indeed a careful reading of the story reveals a number of pointers to a more generalised interpretation. There is, first, the fact that the ruling pig is named 'Napoleon': a reminder that there have been many dictatorships in history apart from that of Stalin. Then there are a number of characters which are difficult to place in a strict equation with Russian history: Benjamin the donkey, for example, who clearly has a wider relevance than his minor role in the story would immediately suggest. Most significant of all is that the story is not presented as a simple apposition between the pigs and the other animals; all the animals *including the pigs* are deceived by the neighbouring farmers Frederick and Pilkington, whom Napoleon and his followers come more and more to resemble. The regimes of Frederick and Pilkington, then, are no less cynical and debased than that of Napoleon. It is not Communism as such which corrupts Napoleon as much as the relentless accumulation of power. Totalitarianism *per se*, whatever form it may take, is the enemy Orwell had learned to fear and detest and which *Animal Farm* sought to expose.

It is significant that he chose to do this in the form of an animal fable – a literary genre which can be traced back at least to *Aesop's Fables* of the sixth century BC – rather than a conventional novel or political treatise. If the book was no more than a satirical allegory told in the form of a parable it is doubtful if it would have achieved the extraordinary success it has enjoyed since 1945.[77] Clearly it must possess some intrinsic literary qualities which have encouraged readers to return to it again and again as a story which can be read for enjoyment and not simply for instruction. It is now acknowledged as his most perfectly constructed work, a work of admirable symmetry and unusual imaginative power. How was it done?

Its strength lies, I suggest, in two aspects: first, its incomparable success as a beast fable and second, the extremely skilful manner in which language is deployed to achieve the effects the author is striving for.

There is no doubt that animals had a deep appeal for Orwell. In an essay written towards the end of his life, 'Such, Such were the Joys', he wrote: 'Most of the good memories of my childhood and up to the age of about twenty are in some way connected with animals'.[78] As a boy he was very fond of Beatrix Potter's *The Tale of Pigling Bland* and he and a friend would take it in turns to read it aloud. That he was fascinated by animals and their characteristics may be seen from the unusual amount of animal imagery in his novels. To give only four examples: Ma Hla May in *Burmese Days* is described as having 'rather nice teeth, like the teeth of a kitten'; we are told that the expression on the face of Mrs Creevy in *A Clergyman's Daughter* 'sullen and ill-shaped with the lower lip turned down, recalled that of a toad'; Julia Comstock in *Keep the Aspidistra Flying* was 'one of those girls who even at their most youthful remind one irresistibly of a goose'; and Hilda Vincent in *Coming Up For Air* bore 'a distinct resemblance to a hare'.[79] This tendency to attribute non-human characteristics to human beings had its counterpart in an ability to endow farm creatures with human emotions. Much of the appeal of *Animal Farm* stems from the fact that such characters as Boxer, Clover, Benjamin and Mollie are not simply caricatures but wholly believable individuals.

His childhood friend Jacintha Buddicom wrote:

The only book by George Orwell I had ever seen was *Animal Farm*, but it had impressed me more than anything I had read for years. Of course, once you knew, it was obvious that it could only have been written by Eric. It was so exactly like him, so exactly the book he would have loved to read if someone else had written it when he was a boy. It is a *beautiful* book.[80]

Throughout his life Orwell loved animals. While living at Wallington he kept goats and hens, and he and his wife invented humorous names for them and related to each other imaginary stories in which the farmyard animals had amusing adventures. The idea of writing a beast fable would also have had a strong appeal for him in view of his deep admiration for such allegorical works as *Gulliver's Travels*. What is so remarkable about *Animal Farm* is the skilful manner in which animal characteristics are portrayed; the animals are not merely symbols but each possesses the traits of its species:

> At the last moment Mollie, the foolish, pretty white mare who drew Mr. Jones's trap, came mincing daintily in, chewing at a lump of sugar. She took a place near the front and began flirting her white mane, hoping to draw attention to the red ribbons it was plaited with. Last of all came the cat, who looked round, as usual, for the warmest place, and finally squeezed herself in between Boxer and Clover; there she purred contentedly throughout Major's speech without listening to a word of what he was saying.

It is a book which could only have been written by an author who liked animals and understood their ways and foibles. Orwell clearly sympathises with the animals at each stage of their experiences: this empathy, this ability to reach inside their minds and describe their thoughts and emotions *as if from the inside* is one of the most attractive features of the story and is one of many reasons why the satire is so successful. A story in which the animals were merely caricatures without individual traits would not have been nearly so effective.

The advantage of the beast fable is that it enables a simple message to be conveyed without the distraction of psychological considerations and the subtleties of plot and atmosphere normally inseparable from a novel. It enables an oversimplified picture to be presented, divorced from complex human personalities, which in a satire of this kind would have no place. Since Orwell's strengths were those of an essayist and satirist

rather than those of a novelist in the accepted sense the fable
provided him with an ideal medium for the presentation of his
theme. (It should be noted, however, that simplicity does not
necessarily mean unambiguity. *Animal Farm* was interpreted by
some critics as an indication that he had abandoned his socialist
beliefs: this was not his intention.)

The tone of the book is on the whole benevolent; it is a *good
natured* satire, free of rancour or invective. Ridicule and sarcasm
are certainly present, but the story is told with such detachment
and humour that the serious intention underlying the work tends
to be masked. Nevertheless there are a number of crucial points
when the affectionate tone is deliberately and abruptly changed.
One such moment occurs at the conclusion of the scene in which
the pigs, hens and sheep confess to crimes instigated by Snowball:

> And so the tale of confessions and executions went on, until
> there was a pile of corpses lying before Napoleon's feet and the
> air was heavy with the smell of blood, which had been
> unknown there since the expulsion of Jones. When it was all
> over, the remaining animals, except for the pigs and dogs,
> crept away in a body. They were shaken and miserable. They
> did not know which was more shocking – the treachery of the
> animals who had leagued themselves with Snowball, or the
> cruel retribution they had just witnessed.

This horrifying scene, the beginning of the reign of terror initi-
ated by Napoleon (and corresponding to the Stalin purge trials)
marks a departure from all that has preceded it. Although there
has been violence before, most notably in the Battle of the
Cowshed, this has been of a faintly comic character – e.g., 'All
the pigeons, to the number of thirty-five, flew to and fro over the
men's heads and muted upon them from mid-air; and while the
men were dealing with this, the geese, who had been hiding
behind the hedge, rushed out and pecked viciously at the calves
of their legs'. Even during the Battle no one is killed: a stable-lad
who is struck on the head by Boxer's iron-shod hoofs is thought
to be dead but turns out to be only stunned. The confession of
the animals in Chapter 7 is of a very different character. Orwell
clearly intends his readers to share his deep sense of revulsion at
the treachery and ruthlessness of Napoleon; this revulsion is

signalled not merely by a change of style but by a significant transformation of *language*. Hence the sudden transition from the composed, even tone of the first six chapters to the emotive, painful atmosphere of the confession scene. Phrases such as 'the tale of confessions and executions', 'pile of corpses', 'the smell of blood', 'cruel retribution' are clustered together in a single paragraph of great emotional power. When we learn that the animals were 'shaken and miserable' and that they 'huddled about Clover, not speaking', it is possible to share something of their horror and unease at the savagery of Napoleon's punishment and their unspoken awareness that the ideals with which the revolution began have been betrayed. As Clover reflects on these things the reader identifies fully with her unhappiness:

> As Clover looked down the hillside her eyes filled with tears. If she could have spoken her thoughts, it would have been to say that this was not what they had aimed at when they had set themselves years ago to work for the overthrow of the human race. These scenes of terror and slaughter were not what they had looked forward to on that night when old Major first stirred them to rebellion. If she herself had had any picture of the future, it had been of a society of animals set free from hunger and the whip, all equal, each working according to his capacity, the strong protecting the weak, as she had protected the lost brood of ducklings with her foreleg on the night of Major's speech.

In passages such as this Orwell demonstrates his mastery of the beast fable as a literary genre. The horse is a dumb animal and cannot therefore express its thoughts in words: this adds appreciably to the pathos of the scene. Clover, however, is not merely an anonymous horse but is an individual with a personality of her own; the homely detail 'as she had protected the lost brood of ducklings with her foreleg' underlines her essential kindliness and motherly instincts. The phrase 'her eyes filled with tears' has an irresistible appeal, imbuing her with human characteristics of sorrow and tenderness. These two passages taken in conjunction – the confession and execution of the alleged traitors, followed by the sadness and disquiet of the remaining animals – surely represent one of the most crucial sequences in the story. In writing these paragraphs Orwell exhibits once again those qualities which transcend journalism and which have ensured a place for *Animal Farm* as one of the most potent myths of our time: the ability to use language in such a way that the reading of a particular passage becomes both an emotional and a literary experience; the alteration of style and tone to indicate a crucial shift of key; the power of entering into the personality of his creations and participating imaginatively in their responses; the gift of communicating complex human feelings in prose of the utmost simplicity and precision.

'*Animal Farm*,' wrote Orwell, 'was the first book in which I tried, with full consciousness of what I was doing, to fuse political purpose and artistic purpose into one whole.'[81] It is widely regarded as one of his finest works and seems destined to earn for him a posthumous reputation far exceeding any renown he enjoyed during his lifetime. It has taken its place alongside *Candide* and the talking horses of *Gulliver's Travels* as one of those parables which embody permanent truths: a myth that will long outlast the particular historical events which form its background. Now that it is possible to view the work in context, freed of the emotional circumstances surrounding its publication, we can recognise it for what it is: a dystopia, a satirical commentary upon human societies which vividly recalls Swift's *A Tale of a Tub*.

It is unique among Orwell's full-length works in that he himself as narrator or *alter ego* is absent. Elsewhere he is either the narrator in a story told in the first person (e.g., *Down and Out in Paris and London*) or one of the principal characters (for example, Gordon Comstock in *Keep the Aspidistra Flying*) or is present in the sense that he comments upon the thoughts and behaviour of his protagonists. *Animal Farm* however, is written throughout in a plain, dispassionate, almost neutral style which admirably suits its theme and in which his distinctive voice is not felt. The result is a gain in impersonality which strengthens the satirical elements in the work and at the same time enhances its ability to stimulate thought and disturb the emotions. Orwell as commentator and interpreter is missing; as a shaping presence, organising and fashioning his material, he is there. It is this which gives the book its distinctive flavour: it is 'Orwellian' in the sense that it deals with themes characteristic of its author and in language of the utmost simplicity; only he could have written it. Yet the 'I' of the previous works, the idiosyncratic presence who combined passionate socialist beliefs with a desire to conserve the past, remains outside the frame he has created.

The essential thesis of the book, then, is that all human revolutions fail to achieve the lofty expectations of their originators; that with the passage of time the ideals and precepts which inspired the revolution become more and more diluted; that revolutions, whilst professing democracy and equality, tend to produce a ruling élite which concentrates power in its own hands; that the blame for the failure of policies is placed firmly on external factors and not on internal leadership; that the ruling élite becomes corrupted by the growth of its own power until at last it is responsible to no one but itself and ruthlessly destroys any opposition. Tyranny is by definition evil, regardless of its political complexion.

Seen in these terms *Animal Farm* has a relevance to twentieth-century history far wider than a strictly literal interpretation would suggest. Indeed, the satire continues to have relevance despite the fact that the events which inspired it are now a matter of history. One of the reasons why the book has such a wide appeal today is that it possesses those timeless qualities which enable readers of different generations and different cultures to apply its lessons to their own circumstances. One commentator has shrewdly observed: 'There have been, are, and always will be pigs in every society, Orwell states, and they will always grab power. Even more cruel is the conclusion that *everyone* in the society, wittingly or unwittingly, contributes to the pigs' tyranny.'[82] The book is then a profoundly pessimistic fable, a parable which owes its origins to the betrayed idealism of *Homage to Catalonia* and which anticipates the hopelessness and regimentation of *Nineteen Eighty-Four*.

Nineteen Eighty-Four

At the end of May 1947 Orwell wrote to his publisher, Fredric Warburg, apropos his new novel:

> I have made a fairly good start on the book and I think I must have written nearly a third of the rough draft . . . Of course the rough draft is always a ghastly mess having very little relation to the finished result, but all the same it is the main part of the job. So if I do finish the rough draft by October I might get the book done fairly early in 1948, barring illnesses. I don't like talking about books before they are written, but I will tell you now that this is a novel about the future – that is, it is in a sense a fantasy, but in the form of a naturalistic novel. That is what makes it a difficult job – of course as a book of anticipations it would be comparatively simple to write.[83]

A year previously, in May 1946, he had rented a house on Jura which he intended to make his permanent home. Weary of the constant demands upon his time in London he hoped that in Jura he would find some respite from the pressures of journalism – he had been writing regularly for *Tribune*, the *Observer*, and the *Manchester Evening News* – and find the peace and leisure to embark on a novel once again. Here in August 1946 he commenced work in earnest on *Nineteen Eighty-Four* (as early as 1943 he had prepared a detailed outline for the book under the title *The Last Man in Europe*), completing the first draft by October 1947. Throughout the autumn of 1947 however his health was markedly deteriorating. The chest ailment from which he had suffered for many years was now diagnosed as tuberculosis of the left lung, and on specialist advice he was obliged to adopt an increasingly sedentary way of life. The preparation of the final draft – a task which occupied him almost continuously from May to November 1948 – had therefore to be carried out against a background of rapidly declining health. On completing the novel he typed out the finished version himself, an incredible achievement for a man who was by that time confined to his bed and seriously ill with tuberculosis. The book was published in June 1949 and was at once chosen as a selection of the American Book of the Month Club. *Nineteen Eighty-Four* was recognised at once as a work of impressive and haunting imaginative power. Today it is acknowledged as one of the seminal works of the twentieth century, a novel which ranks with Camus's *The Plague* and Koestler's *Darkness at Noon* as a searching commentary upon our times and which, had Orwell written nothing else, will ensure him a permanent place in literary history.

The novel is divided into three parts of roughly equal length. Part One describes the central character, Winston Smith, and places him in context against the background of the regimented, oppressive world of 1984; the second part describes his friendship and love affair with a young woman, Julia, and the transformation of his life through the happiness the relationship brings; Part Three depicts his imprisonment and torture at the hands of the Thought Police and the final abandonment of his intellectual integrity. What is so remarkable about the book is its coherence and solidity as a picture of a wholly imaginary world. Orwell's skill as a storyteller is such that the reader enters imaginatively into the nightmare world he has created. It is a world in which there is virtually no privacy; in which the omnipresent Party has absolute control of the press, communication and propaganda; where to question the Party's rule or to rebel against it is to incur imprisonment, torture or liquidation; where language, history, and even thought are controlled in the interests of the state. Every detail in his vision ministers to the terrible logic of the police state: the telescreen in each room, the Two Minutes Hate, the posters proclaiming BIG BROTHER IS WATCHING YOU, the slogans, Newspeak, the universal drabness. It is a world of three giant powers, Oceania, Eurasia and Eastasia, perpetually at war amongst themselves, each conducting a never-ending propaganda campaign of hatred against its opponents. Above all it is a world in which the individual has no place, a society where every aspect of life is subordinated to the state.

The fact that Orwell reviewed Zamyatin's satirical dystopia *We* (1924) shortly before embarking on *Nineteen Eighty-Four* – his review was published in *Tribune* on 4 January 1946 – and that there are many superficial resemblances between the two works has led some commentators to assume that Orwell's vision of a regimented society derives directly from that depicted in *We*. The reality is rather more complex. It is not so much that *Nineteen Eighty-Four* is based upon *We* as that both are derived from a common ancestor: H. G. Wells's anti-Utopian satire *When the Sleeper Wakes* (1899).

It is certain that Orwell and Zamyatin were both familiar with Wells's work. Yevgeny Zamyatin was well versed in English and American literature and had not only translated Wells's scientific romances into Russian but had also written critical studies of them. In one such essay he remarked perceptively:

Wells used this form [the fantasia of the future] almost exclusively in order to reveal the defects of the existing social structure and not in order to construct some paradise of the future ... in his novels of socio-fantasy Wells created a new and entirely original species of literary form.[84]

Orwell had certainly read *When the Sleeper Wakes* and discussed it – comparing it interestingly with Jack London's *The Iron Heel* (1907) and Aldous Huxley's *Brave New World* (1932) – in an article written in 1940. It was, he said, 'a vision of a glittering sinister world in which society has hardened into a caste system and the workers are permanently enslaved'.[85] Wells's novel is an imaginary description of London in the year 2100. It depicts a society in which humanity is concentrated in giant glass-enclosed cities ruled by tyrants and in which all manual work is carried out by an identically clad proletariat, the drudges of the Labour Company. The significance of the book to the student of Orwell is that many of the ideas matured in *Brave New World*, *We* and *Nineteen Eighty-Four* are present in embryo form within it. There is, for example, an emphasis on greatly distended centres of population (there are only five cities in the whole of Britain); on the dissemination of lying propaganda – the phrase 'the world-wide falsehoods of the news-tellers' actually occurs – by the telephonic machines which have replaced newspapers; on the regimentation and standardisation of the common life; on the presence of a massive labouring population 'helpless in the hands of demagogue and organiser, individually cowardly, individually swayed by appetite, collectively incalculable'. Moreover there are interesting similarities between the shape of all four stories: each tells the story of an individual who rebels against the established order and fails – Graham in *When the Sleeper Wakes*, D-503 in *We*, the Savage in *Brave New World*, and Winston Smith in *Nineteen Eighty-Four*. Above all the atmosphere of the novels is so akin – an atmosphere of regimented, soulless uniformity – as to render irresistible the conclusion that Wells's far-seeing work was the progenitor of those which followed.[86]

It should be noted that whilst all four are ostensibly descriptions of the future they are in fact critiques of the *present*: what each author has done is to deliberately exaggerate a number of contemporary tendencies in order to satirise them in the form of fiction. Orwell makes this quite explicit in a letter to an American correspondent in June 1949:

> I do not believe that the kind of society I describe necessarily *will* arrive, but I believe (allowing of course for the fact that the book is a satire) that something resembling it *could* arrive. I believe also that totalitarian ideas have taken root in the minds of intellectuals everywhere, and I have tried to draw these ideas out to their logical consequences.[87]

The phrase 'draw these ideas out to their logical consequences' is interesting. What Orwell has done in *Nineteen Eighty-Four* is to take a number of aspects of life in the 1940s – rationing, food shortages, the black market, stereotyped meals, uniformity, patriotic propaganda, rocket bombs – and extrapolate them in the form of a satirical fantasy. In doing so he depicts a world in which all those aspects of twentieth-century life which he despised are writ large: indeed the book has been described as 'the culmination of all the tendencies which he deplored in his own time'.[88] The ubiquitous radio sets, the increasing invasion of privacy, the corruption of language, the drabness and regimentation of wartime England: all are here. Superimposed on these elements is an elaborate political framework derived from his experiences in Spain: the one-party state, the denial of objective truth, the manipulation of the past, imprisonment without trial, torture, indifference to human suffering. A satire must by its very nature exaggerate. Nevertheless many readers in 1949 must have baulked at the idea that a totalitarian government could establish itself in Britain. Orwell replied to such hesitations by stating that 'The scene of the book is laid in Britain in order to emphasise that the English-speaking races are not innately better than anyone else and that totalitarianism, *if not fought against*, could triumph anywhere'.[89] To see the book as a warning against totalitarian tendencies and attitudes is to recognise that it is not simply an anti-Communist treatise: the society described is an amalgam of the worst features of both Communist and Nazi regimes. As with *Animal Farm* it is not any particular form of dictatorship which is being satirised but dictatorship in general; what is being attacked is not an ideology but the insidious effects of concentrating power in the hands of an unscrupulous élite.

The book is then a homily on the destruction of all those aspects of life which Orwell valued: beauty, truth, honesty, liberty, peacefulness, affection, privacy and human decency. The overwhelming impression of the book is of a sense of loss, a feeling of regret that beauty and a regard for beautiful things – indeed all the finer emotions and values – now belong to the past. This is symbolised for Winston Smith in the image of the paperweight, a work of craftsmanship belonging to a vanished age:

> What appealed to him about it was not so much its beauty as the air it seemed to possess of belonging to an age quite different from the present one. The soft, rain-watery glass was not like any glass that he had ever seen . . . It was a queer thing, even a compromising thing, for a Party member to have in his possession. Anything old, and for that matter anything beautiful, was always vaguely suspect.

Winston becomes increasingly fascinated by the paperweight until at last it encapsulates for him the fragile impermanence of his love for Julia:

> He had the feeling that he could get inside it, and that in fact he was inside it, along with the mahogany bed and the gateleg table, and the clock and the steel engraving and the paper-

weight itself. The paperweight was the room he was in, and the coral was Julia's life and his own, fixed in a sort of eternity at the heart of the crystal.

When their refuge above the antique shop is raided by the Thought Police the first act of the police is to smash the paperweight: a symbolic act, destroying both the object itself and the peace which it represents. An artefact so fragile, so redolent of the past, clearly has no place in the world of 1984.

It is significant also that the words of nursery rhymes such as 'Oranges and Lemons' have been forgotten and have to be lovingly reconstructed from the memories of elderly people. But it is in the descriptions of natural beauty, particularly of the unspoiled countryside, that Orwell reveals most poignantly his emotional attachment to the past. The lyrical descriptions of landscapes (in Part One, 3, and again in Part Two, 2) and his reference to 'a landscape I've seen sometimes in a dream' vividly recalls the nostalgia of *Coming Up For Air* and reminds us once again of his deep love of the land and, conversely, his detestation of many aspects of urban living. Life in London during and immediately after the war *was* drab and depressing, and it is not surprising that he felt the urge to cut loose from it altogether and move to the unspoilt landscapes of the Hebrides. Here, surrounded by the sea and the open hills, remote from the telephone and all that reminded him of the pressures of modern living, he was free to write the novel he had contemplated for so long.

The fact that *Nineteen Eighty-Four* was the last book Orwell wrote before he died has led many readers to regard it as a valediction or last testament comparable to H. G. Wells's *Mind at the End of its Tether*. To do so is misleading. It is a last testament in the sense that, aware of his own grave illness, he was determined to complete the book and see it through publication before his health deteriorated irreparably, but after its completion he was actively planning other works. In the last months of his life he was planning a collected edition of his essays (this was the volume published posthumously in 1950 under the title *Shooting an Elephant*) and a novella, the idea for which had been in his head 'for years'.[90] Had he lived he would undoubtedly have continued to write novels, and these would probably have been quite different in nature from *Nineteen Eighty-Four*.

There is a sense, however, in which the book marks a culmination of his creative achievement – at least of his achievement up to that time – and Orwell himself seems to have been aware of this. This can be seen in the repeated use of images and scenes from his previous novels. There is, for example, the woman 'with lined face and wispy hair, fiddling helplessly with a blocked waste-pipe', an image taken directly from *The Road to Wigan Pier*; a bombing raid resulting in a severed human limb, a scene which also occurs in *Coming Up For Air*; a seduction scene during a country walk, an episode which strongly recalls one of the central incidents in *Keep the Aspidistra Flying*. There are also many similarities between *Nineteen Eighty-Four* and *Animal Farm*, since Trotsky is caricatured in both works (as Goldstein and Snowball respectively) and there is the same emphasis on an enemy suddenly transformed into an ally and vice versa. It is as if Orwell is consciously attempting a summation of themes and ideas which had appeared in his writings from 1934 onwards. In this, his most ambitious and influential novel, can be found the obsession with the distortion of language which so exercised Gordon Comstock, the revulsion against the artificiality of life and the affection for rural England which are so characteristic of George Bowling, the exposure of duplicity and propaganda which is a leitmotif of *Homage to Catalonia*, the sombre warning of the abuse of power which is the dominant theme of *Animal Farm*. And permeating the novel is the atmosphere of inward revolt which had so repelled John Flory in *Burmese Days*: 'It is a stifling, stultifying world in which to live. It is a world in which every word and every thought is censored . . . In the end the secrecy of your revolt poisons you like a secret disease. Your whole life is a life of lies.'

If *Nineteen Eighty-Four* is treated as a warning rather than a prophecy, as a satire on present tendencies rather than a forecast of the future, it can be seen that its effect has been wholly salutary. Today such terms as 'doublethink', 'newspeak' and 'thoughtcrime' have passed into accepted usage and for a generation of readers the book has come to be regarded as a standard treatise on the growth and influence of totalitarian trends. As a critique of the corrupting effects of the accumulation of power in the hands of the state the book is unrivalled in this century: indeed one suspects that future generations will rank it with Hobbes's *Leviathan* and Machiavelli's *The Prince* as one of the cardinal works of political theory. Its value as a warning of the corruption of language, the abuse of power, the invasion of privacy and the regimentation of society has been inestimable and for these reasons alone the book merits an honoured place in the history of our times.

In a deeper sense, however, it is a flawed masterpiece: a courageous achievement marred by its overwhelming tone of despair. To read it is a painful experience; to read *Homage to Catalonia* (for example) is a moving one; therein lies the difference. It is the difference between a work dominated by hopelessness and one animated by idealism, between a work written in a mood of deepening pessimism and one executed in anger but with a basic faith in humankind still intact.

The pessimism rises to a crescendo in the final section describing the torture and humiliation of Winston Smith in the dreaded 'Room 101', a scene which has been much criticised on the grounds of its sadism. Certainly this sequence is acutely painful to read. By piling horror upon horror in an attempt to shock the reader Orwell alienates his audience and forfeits much of the critical understanding gained in the earlier sections. The technique adopted by Poe in 'The Pit and the Pendulum' in carefully building up an atmosphere of controlled suspense would have been far more effective than the accumulation of gratuitous violence which has the opposite effect from that he is seeking to achieve. In his essay 'Raffles and Miss Blandish' (1944) he strongly criticised novels which 'take for granted the most complete corruption and self-seeking as the norm of human behaviour' and in which the 'whole theme is the struggle for power and the triumph of the strong over the weak'.[91]

The final pages of *Nineteen Eighty-Four*, however, display precisely the attitude he had earlier deplored and reveal a relish in sadistic violence frightening in its totality. There is a denial of integrity, of truth, of all finer human feelings. Before his arrest and torture Winston had reflected that

> They could not alter your feelings: for that matter you could not alter them yourself, even if you wanted to. They could lay bare in the utmost detail everything that you had done or said or thought; but the inner heart, whose workings were mysterious even to yourself, remained impregnable.

The explicit denial of this impregnability in the Room 101 sequence is in the last analysis unconvincing and in its total denial of humanity tells us much about Orwell's state of mind at the time. Writing to Julian Symons in June 1949 he commented: 'You are of course right about the vulgarity of the "Room 101" business. I was aware of this while writing it, but I didn't know another way of getting somewhere near the effect I wanted.'[92] Some critics, most notably Anthony West, have seen in these pages evidence of a 'hidden wound' in Orwell's make-up and have asserted that, consciously or otherwise, in describing the world of 1984 he was depicting St. Cyprian's writ large.[93] Whatever the truth of this assertion it is unquestionable that there was an element of sadism in his character and it is at least arguable that in the closing years of his life this – combined with the deep-rooted pessimism which was never far from the surface of his mind – came to the fore in a bitter cry of despair. To state this is not to deny that torturers such as O'Brien exist – we know from the experience of Belsen and Dachau that they do – but to reject the implication that they are, or can be, invincible.

What seemed then – and seems today – so alien to English readers is the utter hopelessness of the book, a mood in the sharpest contrast to the gentle irony of *Animal Farm*. One has only to compare the satire of *Nineteen Eighty-Four* with that of the Circumlocution Office in *Little Dorrit*, for example, to recognise at once a significant difference in tone. Whereas Dickens's critique is good-natured (but none the less effective for that) Orwell's is sombre, despairing, almost unrelievedly pessimistic. It is the work of a man who has lost hope, not merely in politicians and causes but in mankind itself. Despite the undeniable power and vividness of the novel – it is one of those books which, once read, is never forgotten – one closes the work with a sense of unease which, whilst difficult to analyse, is none the less real. This sense of dissatisfaction stems, I suggest, from a basic structural weakness in *Nineteen Eighty-Four* which fractures it as a work of art.

Orwell must have been aware from his own experience in Spain and from his reading of history that tyrannies are invariably opposed by those who are subjected to them. The regime of Nazi Germany, for example – possibly the most despotic and ruthless in modern times – was violently opposed from both within and without and lasted twelve years from beginning to end. When the Low Countries, France and Norway were invaded by Nazi forces the occupying regimes were subject to persistent and well-organised resistance from citizens who were determined at all costs to rid their country of tyranny. This resistance continued despite vindictive and merciless reprisals, including considerable loss of life.

In a book review written in May 1946 criticising James Burnham's *The Managerial Revolution* for having posited the development of giant autocratic states motivated solely by the pursuit of power Orwell wrote:

> Burnham, therefore, was unable to see that the crimes and follies of the Nazi regime *must* lead by one route or another to disaster. So also with his new-found admiration for Stalinism. It is too early to say in just what way the Russian regime will destroy itself . . . But at any rate, the Russian regime will either democratise itself, or it will perish. The huge, invincible, everlasting slave empire of which Burnham appears to dream will not be established, or, if established, will not endure, because slavery is no longer a stable basis for human society.[94]

Despite his recognition that 'slavery is no longer a stable basis for human society' he postulates in *Nineteen Eighty-Four* a totally static community, a society in which there is no possibility of change. It is a world in which the mass of the people, 'the proles', submit to their totalitarian rulers with a mindless, uncomplaining apathy and make no attempt at protest. Winston and Julia, we are asked to believe, are the only two individuals to whom it occurs to resist and even their dissent is doomed to failure. It is a vision altogether too extreme. The reader senses that no totalitarian regime, however powerful and autocratic, could be as invincible as that depicted here. Granted that the book is intended as a warning and not as a prophecy, the effectiveness of the warning is diminished by its total pessimism. To assert this is not to deny Orwell's achievement – *Nineteen Eighty-Four* is by any standards a work of immense power – but to argue that the force of the satire is vitiated by the absence of hope.

It would be entirely possible to contend that the pessimism which suffuses the novel is itself a pose, and that the despair of the hero is no more to be attributed to Orwell personally than the nostalgia of George Bowling or the self-centredness of Gordon Comstock. There are powerful arguments for and against this view. The case for may be illustrated by his apparent attitude towards manual workers.

The attitude to workers in the novel is revealing and at first sight contrasts strangely with Orwell's professed views in *The Road to Wigan Pier*. 'The 'proles' are depicted as an unthinking undertow, devoid of aspiration:

> In reality very little was known about the proles. It was not necessary to know much. So long as they continued to work and breed, their other activities were without importance. Left to themselves, like cattle turned loose upon the plains of Argentina, they had reverted to a style of life that appeared to be natural to them, a sort of ancestral pattern. They were born, they grew up in the gutters, they went to work at twelve, they passed through a brief blossoming period of beauty and sexual desire, they married at twenty, they were middle-aged at thirty, they died, for the most part at sixty. Heavy physical work, the care of home and children, petty quarrels with neighbours, films, football, beer, and above all, gambling, fil-led up the horizon of their minds. To keep them in control was not difficult.

The patronising tone of such passages, the comparison with 'cat-tle' and apparent indifference to the fate of manual workers, has led some critics to read into the book Orwell's final renunciation of socialism and his disillusionment with the common man. Two points need to be made here. Firstly, it must not be assumed that the 'I' of *The Road to Wigan Pier* is necessarily the same as the narrator of *Nineteen Eighty-Four*. It is at least arguable that in his fiction he tended to assume an invented personality which, whilst adopting many of his own idiosyncracies, has an indi-viduality of its own. Thus the relationship between Orwell him-self and his narrators may not be as straightforward as it appears. Secondly, the language of the passage in question needs to be read with care. Notice the use of such phrases as 'It was not necessary to know much' and 'To keep them in control was not difficult'. There is an element of irony here which should warn the reader once again that the book is predominantly a *satire*: the assumptions and postures underlining the narrative are not necessarily to be interpreted literally but are satirical in intent. One of the writers who influenced Orwell most profoundly was

Swift, and it is not difficult to discern in the proles the influence of the Houyhnhnms of *Gulliver's Travels*.[95] On this reading, the despondent tone of the book is itself satirical.

Against this view, it has to be said that it is difficult to reconcile with what is known of Orwell's character, his circumstances and his literary history. To read his works in the order in which they were written is to be aware of a deepening sense of hopelessness: a growing sense of doubt concerning the human condition. In 1946 he had written: 'When one considers how things have gone since 1930 or thereabouts, it is not easy to believe in the survival of civilisation', and again a year later: 'The actual outlook, so far as I can calculate the probabilities, is very dark, and any serious thought should start out from that fact'.[96] All the evidence suggests that the pessimism of *Nineteen Eighty-Four* was intensified by his illness and loneliness during the travail of writing.

The fact is that during the closing years of his life his world began to disintegrate about him, in a manner oddly reminiscent of the final years of Edgar Allan Poe exactly a century before. In March 1945 his wife Eileen died suddenly and unexpectedly at the age of thirty-nine. This was followed in May 1946 by the death of his sister Marjorie at the age of forty-eight. From October 1947 onwards his own health visibly and rapidly declined to the point where he must have known that death was a real possibility. It is true that he now had an adopted son, Richard, to whom he was deeply attached, that his reputation as a writer was now greater than at any time in his life, and that he had abundant reasons for wishing to remain alive. Nevertheless the cumulative effect of the demise of his wife and sister and his own wretched health must have been considerable and inevitably affected the tone of the book. He confided to Fredric Warburg: 'I think it is a good idea but the execution would have been better if I had not written it under the influence of T.B.', whilst to Anthony Powell he wrote: 'it's a ghastly mess now, a good idea ruined, but of course I was seriously ill for 7 or 8 months of the time'.[97] The despondent tone of the book cannot wholly be attributed to his own ill-health however. Of at least equal importance is the fact that all around him Orwell saw his gloomiest forebodings being realised. The growth of Soviet power, the emergence of atomic weapons, the debasement of the English language, the insidious growth of totalitarian tendencies in

Europe and elsewhere, the increasing uniformity of civilisation: all these trends alarmed and depressed him. What he sought to do in *Nineteen Eighty-Four* was to write a parable which could be interpreted as a warning: this, he was saying in effect, is what could happen if these tendencies proceed unchecked. And it has to be remembered that the effort of finishing it whilst desperately ill almost certainly hastened his death. For his tenacity and courage in seeing the work through whilst almost literally on his death-bed we should be profoundly grateful.

It is important to bear in mind, however, that the book is a *novel* – Orwell insisted that the words 'a novel' had to appear on the title-page – and that, quite apart from its political connotations, it is as a *literary* achievement that it must finally be judged. To attempt a dispassionate assessment of *Nineteen Eighty-Four* one has to draw a distinction between its message as a political satire and its accomplishment as a work of art. Writing to a friend in 1933 apropos James Joyce's *Ulysses* he had commented:

> In the first place one has got to decide what a novel normally sets out to do. I should say that it sets out first (I am placing these in order of difficulty, the simplest first) to display or create character, secondly, to make a kind of pattern or design which any good story contains, and thirdly, if the novelist is up to it, to produce *good writing*, which can exist almost as it were in vacuo and independent of subject.[98]

Viewing it simply from his own criteria, then, it can be said that it is the finest and most cohesive novel he had written since *Burmese Days* fifteen years earlier. Apart from one or two structural imperfections – the interpolation of lengthy passages from Emmanuel Goldstein's book *The Theory and Practice of Oligarchical Collectivism*, for example, is a rather clumsy device which is not readily assimilated into the whole – the novel as a totality is admirably executed and possesses an assurance most of his previous fictions lack.

Whilst the characterisation is perhaps less confident than in some of the earlier novels the love affair between Winston Smith and Julia is convincingly handled and in the character of Julia herself Orwell created one of his most solid and attractive female protagonists. The book also contains a rich diversity of minor characters, most notably Winston's neighbours at Victory Mansions, Mr and Mrs Parsons. These are drawn with a lively pen and with that acute eye for detail which is one of his most unmistakeable traits: 'an overpowering smell of sweat, a sort of unconscious testimony to the strenuousness of his life, followed him about wherever he went, and even remained behind him after he had gone'. The *design* of the novel is one of his most unified conceptions. One has only to compare it with the novels of his apprenticeship years to recognise at once a marked advance in tautness and credibility (again, with the exception of *Burmese Days*: it is significant that his two must fully realised novels are precisely the ones which had the longest gestation). Although planned and written over a period of several years it is a remarkably integrated work, notable for its consistency of mood and style. His third criterion, good writing, is present at each stage of the narrative and impresses one afresh with each re-reading.

One thinks, for example, of Winston Smith reminiscing about his mother, of the Ministry of Truth, of the antique shop, of the lonely, introspective world of the hero, almost unbearable in its intensity. The whole of Part Two, portraying the development of the love affair from its initial idyllic consummation to the final betrayal by the Thought Police, is one of his most accomplished pieces of writing. Rarely did he convey so intensely his deep love of the English countryside, his delight in natural beauty and in the simple joy of human affection.[99] The red-armed woman who sings in a powerful contralto whilst pegging out washing symbolises for Winston the contentment and simplicity he longs for:

> Her voice floated upward with the sweet summer air, very tuneful, charged with a sort of happy melancholy. One had the feeling that she would have been perfectly content, if the June evening had been endless and the supply of clothes inexhaustible, to remain there for a thousand years, pegging out diapers and singing rubbish.

It is interesting that the woman is completely apathetic and uninterested in her surroundings, and is in this sense an explicit denial of Winston's reiterated statement that 'If there is hope it lies in the proles'. Yet he does not condemn her; indeed his attitude towards her is one of admiration – at one point he describes her as 'beautiful'. Clearly she represents for Orwell qualities which he found desirable: contentment, peace of mind, stolidity, happiness. Once again we are reminded of his heartfelt comment in *The Road to Wigan Pier*: 'In a working-class home . . . you breathe a warm, decent, deeply human atmosphere which it is not so easy to find elsewhere'. Perhaps the most poignant aspect of the book is the evidence it affords of his deep longing for the simple pleasures he had tasted briefly in his life and his passionate wish to withdraw from the noise, violence and artificiality of urban living.

From a literary standpoint, then, *Nineteen Eighty-Four* must be counted as one of Orwell's outstanding artistic achievements, a work which marks a watershed in the history of sociological literature and has given the word 'Orwellian' to the English language as a term denoting nightmare oppression and thought control.

Since its original publication in 1949 the book has aroused extraordinary interest, particularly in the English-speaking world, and has never been out of print. It has been filmed, dramatised, adapted for television and translated into many languages. The title itself is known to many thousands simply by hearsay, as a synonym for the regimentation and despotism of the monolithic state. Its influence as a warning of the erosion of individual freedom has been profound.

As a literary composition it is superior to those which inspired it since it possesses a cohesion and inner logic lacking in the dystopias of Wells, Zamyatin and Huxley.[100] Of the four novels Orwell's is by far the most fully realised and probably for this reason is the most widely known. Although flawed in a number of respects it represents an artistic achievement greater than that of *Animal Farm* since in describing the society of the future he had to create an entire imaginary world with a history, organisation and rationale of its own. In so doing he overcame many of the problems implicit in writing a didactic satire and brought into being a myth which continues to haunt our literature.

It is a vision which, once read, becomes part of the mental furniture of the reader. To absorb Orwell's nightmare, to ponder upon it and reflect on its implications for the human spirit is an essential part of our intellectual pilgrimage.

Part III

THE ESSAYS

The Essays

Orwell's career as an essayist began with the publication of 'A Farthing Newspaper' in 1928 and ended with 'Reflections on Gandhi' almost exactly twenty years later. He began as an unknown writer on the brink of poverty and ended as a literary figure known and respected throughout the English-speaking world and beyond. These twenty years saw the depression, massive unemployment, the rise of Hitler and Mussolini, the Spanish Civil War, the Second World War, post-war reconstruction and the dawn of the nuclear age. His themes embraced not only these momentous issues but hop-picking, boys' comics, seaside postcards, English cooking, precise directions for making a cup of tea, murders, and the mating habits of the toad. He wrote extensively on political, social and literary topics and was also a prolific book reviewer. In all he wrote some 100 essays, 70 book reviews and 72 contributions to 'As I Please' in *Tribune*. In the process his style matured from the diffident (but still recognisably Orwellian) tone of the early essays to the polished, self-assured, incisive manner which has made his name a hallmark for all that is finest in modern English letters.

During his lifetime he published four volumes of essays: *Inside the Whale* (1940), *The Lion and the Unicorn* (1941), *Critical Essays* (1946) and *The English People* (1947). There are also four posthumously published collections: *Shooting an Elephant* (1950), *England Your England* (1953), *Such, Such Were the Joys* (1953) and *The Collected Essays, Journalism and Letters* (1968). These will now be discussed in turn.

Inside the Whale and Other Essays consists of three extended essays written during 1939–40: 'Charles Dickens', 'Boys' Weeklies' and

187

'Inside the Whale', each of which reflects Orwell's fascination with the literary and intellectual background of his times. 'Charles Dickens', the longest of his essays, should be studied carefully by any reader interested in either Dickens or Orwell for it is a perceptive exercise in literary criticism in its own right and tells us much about Orwell's characteristic preoccupations. In an autobiographical note written in 1940[1] he described Dickens as one of the novelists 'I care most about and never grow tired of', and in discussing Dickens's work he sought at the same time to express his indebtedness to a writer who was an important formative influence on his own approach to literature.

The essay is significant for the insights it provides into Orwell's concerns and attitudes for in analysing Dickens's novels he reveals *inter alia* his own radicalism, his interest in the surfaces of life, his curiosity, his interest in social forces and his deep-rooted class consciousness. It is a sustained attempt to define Dickens's moral and philosophical attitudes and to identify the assumptions underlying the novels. In attempting this broad theme he transcends the boundaries of the conventional literary essay and embraces sociological and historical discussion. What interests Orwell throughout is Dickens's world-view:

> I have been discussing Dickens simply in terms of his "message", and almost ignoring his literary qualities. But every writer, especially every novelist, *has* a "message", whether he admits it or not, and the minutest details of his work are influenced by it. All art is propaganda. Neither Dickens himself nor the majority of Victorian novelists would have thought of denying this.

Central to the essay is Orwell's discussion of two philosophical positions: the revolutionary, who argues that there can be no lasting improvement in human affairs until *the system*, i.e., the basic structure of society, has been radically changed; and the moralist, who asserts that human nature must itself change before social improvements can be achieved. He demonstrates the intellectual weakness of the moralistic position as exemplified by Dickens whilst at the same time acknowledges his profound admiration for the warm humanitarian vision which animates the novels. Dickens's works continue to be read and enjoyed, he concludes, because they are inspired by a fundamental human decency and not by a political belief. Orwell is quick to perceive that Dickens was untypical of the novelists of his period in combining a radical critique of society with a nostalgic longing to return to the simplicity and picturesqueness of an earlier period. The combination of these two attitudes in one and the same person was also characteristic of Orwell himself. (It can surely be no accident that Orwell and Gissing, both of whom wrote fine essays on Dickens, shared a nostalgia for the past. Gissing was also a writer whose work Orwell greatly admired.[2]) This is one illustration of the manner in which the essay continually illuminates his own attitudes and beliefs. At one point he remarks:

> His radicalism is of the vaguest kind, and yet one always knows that it is there. That is the difference between being a moralist and a politician. He has no constructive suggestions, not even a clear grasp of the nature of the society he is attacking, only an emotional perception that something is wrong.

When writing this he must have been aware that much the same criticism could be made of his own novels, particularly *Keep the Aspidistra Flying*, and that he was by no means innocent himself of some of the charges he levels against Dickens, e.g., his failure to understand manual workers.

At the root of his discussion is an examination of how far a novel can convey a political idea and remain a work of art. 'The thing that drove Dickens forward into a form of art for which he was not really suited, and at the same time caused us to remember him, was simply the fact that he was a moralist, the consciousness of "having something to say".' The phrase 'a form of art for which he was not really suited' is interesting and once again has a direct relevance to himself. It is as if Orwell is aware that the novel of character in the English tradition was a medium outside his legitimate range and that in commenting upon Dickens's aims and motivations he is at the same time analysing his own purposes as a creative writer. In this sense the essay is, as it were, a mirror: implicit within it is a comparison of his own artistic intentions with those of Dickens and an illuminating commentary upon the rationale of twentieth-century literature.

Despite the highly questionable nature of some of Orwell's

critical judgements – e.g., 'Heep, of course, is playing a villain-
ous part, but even villains have sexual lives; it is the thought of
the "pure" Agnes in bed with a man who drops his aitches that
really revolts Dickens' – and the attribution to Dickens of traits
of which he was guilty himself – e.g., 'When he writes about
Coketown he manages to evoke, in just a few paragraphs, the
atmosphere of a Lancashire town as a slightly disgusted southern visitor would see it' – the essay as a whole is a masterly
appraisal of Dickens's strengths and weaknesses. Orwell is
acutely perceptive about Dickens's limitations as a novelist yet
at the same time is generous in his praise for the enduring elements in his work: his memorable characters, his love of detail,
his descriptive powers and, above all, the sheer vitality of his
invention.

'Charles Dickens' is an entirely characteristic essay which
bears upon it the stamp of Orwell's idiosyncratic approach.
There is the tendency to make sweeping generalisations unsup-
ported by evidence, e.g., 'All art is propaganda', 'His [Tolstoy's]
characters are struggling to make their souls, whereas Dickens's
are already finished and perfect'; the fascination with sociological and polemical discussion; the preoccupation with issues of
class and background; the continual presence of the stimulating
phrase, e.g., 'Any writer who is not utterly lifeless moves upon a
kind of parabola, and the downward curve is implied in the
upper one'. What attracted him to Dickens was that the Victorian novelist represented for him the qualities of a liberal
humanitarian which he so much admired: decency, honesty,
generosity, compassion. Because he admired Dickens so much
the essay is more balanced than his essays on Swift, Tolstoy,
Kipling or Wells and is for that reason one of his finest pieces of
literary criticism. It tells us much about Orwell that in 1939
when the war clouds were ominously gathering he chose to forget
his immediate concerns and write a long, discursive, humane
essay on a long-dead English novelist. He concluded his survey
with an attempt to visualise Dickens's face:

> It is the face of a man who is always fighting against some-
> thing, but who fights in the open and is not frightened, the face
> of a man who is *generously angry* – in other words, of a
> nineteenth-century liberal, a free intelligence, a type hated
> with equal hatred by all the smelly little orthodoxies which are
> now contending for our souls.

'Boys' Weeklies' belongs to a category of sociological discussion which came increasingly to fascinate Orwell and which subsequent writers, most notably Richard Hoggart in *The Uses of Literacy*, have made their own. It is an examination of boys' weekly papers from a sociological and literary standpoint, concentrating in particular on the stories featuring Billy Bunter and Greyfriars School. The significant aspect of the essay is not the analysis itself – much of which is highly critical and provoked a lengthy riposte from Frank Richards, the author of the Billy Bunter stories – but the fact that he felt that weekly comics were an interesting and appropriate subject for serious analysis:

> You never walk far through any poor quarter in any big town without coming upon a small newsagent's shop . . . Probably the contents of these shops is the best available indication of what the mass of the English people really feels and thinks. Certainly nothing half so revealing exists in documentary form.

This is the prelude to a detailed examination of *Magnet* and *Gem*. Throughout the discussion the question which fascinates Orwell is: what are the assumptions and values underlying the Greyfriars stories? The stories are analysed from the point of view of their language, their relation to real life at a public school, the literary influences upon them and the social and political attitudes implicit within them. Such an exercise had not been attempted before and here Orwell was breaking new ground. He was astute enough to see that the values implicit in the stories would be imbibed by those who read them and therefore devotes considerable attention to defining the mental outlook suggested by Greyfriars. It is an outlook, he suggests, utterly remote from the contemporary world. The mental atmosphere deduced from *Gem* and *Magnet* is that of the year 1910, a world in which 'nothing ever changes, and foreigners are funny'. This safe, secure, solid world in which Billy Bunter and his friends have their adventures (never growing any older) bears no relationship to life in a real public school and is totally removed from the problems of the real world. It is a make-believe world in which behaviour is determined by schoolboy ethics of right and wrong and where the predominant appeal is one of snobbishness.

Despite some rather wild generalisations (e.g., '*All* fiction from the novels in the mushroom libraries downwards is censored in the interests of the ruling class') 'Boys' Weeklies' remains an impressive piece of writing which pointed the direction in which much of his finest journalism was to follow. In arguing that one's boyhood reading was important and left an indelible impression on the mind he was drawing attention to a neglected field of sociological study and it is entirely characteristic of Orwell that he concentrates his discussion on *Gem* and *Magnet* 'because they are more interesting psychologically than the others' and because they had survived almost unchanged into the 1930s.

The intellectual curiosity which is such a distinctive feature of his work can be discerned in 'Boys' Weeklies', as in 'The Art of Donald McGill' and much of his journalism of the period. Always the questions which fascinate him are: What do boys read between the ages of ten and fifteen? At what age do they cease reading comics? Is readership of public school stories confined to one particular social class? Do children from poor backgrounds read boys' weeklies? Are comics also read by adults? This curiosity ranges from the minutiae of everyday living to fundamental questions of attitude and belief. There can also be discerned indications of that curious ambivalence which is present at many points in his novels and essays. He is, for example, highly critical of the Billy Bunter stories because they are set in an unchanging world of *c.* 1910 where 'The King is on his throne and the pound is worth a pound' and 'Everything is safe, solid and unquestionable' – yet this is precisely the world looked back upon with such nostalgia in *Coming Up For Air*. Again, he notes with apparent disapproval the fact that in the school stories sex as a topic is completely taboo and yet concludes his discussion with the comment that 'on its level the moral code of the English boys' papers is a decent one'.

'Boys' Weeklies' is then the work of a highly original and yet ambivalent mind, a man who was both fascinated and repelled by the sub-culture of weekly comics and attracted above all by the question of their influence on the adolescent. He appears to have been conscious of its inconsistencies for when he learned that Frank Richards had been invited to reply he wrote 'I look forward to this with some uneasiness, as I've no doubt made many mistakes . . .'.[3] Re-reading the essay today one is impressed afresh with Orwell's skill in assembling and ordering his material, his insight into the imaginative world of the schoolboy and his gift for presenting a discussion in which issues are examined from both a literary and a sociological standpoint. One can only applaud his courage and honesty in approaching such a large subject with his characteristic verve.

His passionate interest in and concern for literature, including the debate on 'commitment' which so exercised the writers of his generation, found renewed expression in 'Inside the Whale', a lengthy essay on which he worked during the autumn of 1939. The title owes its origin to his contention that there were two schools of thought in twentieth-century literature. On the one hand were those who, like Henry Miller, were 'inside the whale', i.e., indifferent to the world political crisis and sealed off from political affairs inside a womb-like cushioned space. Their attitude could be summarised as 'Give yourself over to the world-process, stop fighting against it or pretending that you control it; simply accept it, endure it, record it.' Contrasted to this were those – including, by definition, Orwell himself – who were or strived to be 'outside the whale', that is, actively involved in world affairs and committed both in writing and in personal activities to helping to change the direction of human advancement.

Much of the essay takes the form of a discursive commentary on the novels of Henry Miller, a writer who was considered at that time *outré* and therefore unfashionable to praise. His comments on Miller, particularly on *Tropic of Cancer*, are penetrating and intelligent. The quality in Miller's writing which Orwell finds most attractive is its sense of optimism and happiness, even when describing sordid or unpleasant events. He contrasts this atmosphere with the pessimism which was so characteristic of the novels and poetry of the inter-war years, concluding that 'On the whole the literary history of the 'thirties seems to justify the opinion that a writer does well to keep out of politics'.

In an angry passage he discusses the sheltered life led by the fashionable writers of the 1930s and contrasts this implicitly with his own experience:[4]

It is the same pattern all the time; public school, university, a few trips abroad, then London. Hunger, hardship, solitude, exile, war, prison, persecution, manual labour – hardly even words.

The point Orwell is making here is that the inexperience of life which was a feature of middle-class education meant that (for example) the excesses of the Stalin regime were condoned by many well-meaning intellectuals simply because they were incapable of grasping the reality of totalitarian government. There is a wider sense however in which the passage is peculiarly apposite to an examination of Orwell as a literary figure: that is that his unusual combination of experiences since leaving Eton – poverty in London and Paris, teaching in private schools, the bookshop, observing the life of the unemployed, Spain – had inevitably given him a difference of perspective compared with that of his contemporaries. This can be seen, for example, in his awareness of the passivity of ordinary people:

> For the ordinary man is also passive. Within a narrow circle (home life, and perhaps the trade union or local politics) he feels himself master of his fate, but against major events he is as helpless as against the elements. So far from endeavouring to influence the future, he simply lies down and lets things happen to him.

It was perceptive of Orwell to see that this passivity had exercised a profound influence on the literature of the present century: that the most memorable books about the 1914–18 war had been written 'not by propagandists but by *victims*'. This acknowledgement that the social and political forces which had shaped the twentieth-century crisis were beyond the comprehension of ordinary people and that all one could do in the circumstances was 'to endure' was, he felt, close to the attitude of Miller and in the sharpest contrast to the omniscience which was then fashionable in political writing.

His difference of perspective can also be seen in his assertion that every book, every work of art, has an implicit message: 'And no book is ever truly neutral. Some or other tendency is always discernible, in verse as much as in prose, even if it does no more than determine the form and the choice of imagery.' The discussion of Henry Miller leads on to an examination of the works of Housman, Lawrence and Joyce, but at each stage of the analysis his concern is with the writer's point of view, the underlying *attitude* which determines his themes and presentation of material. The writers of the inter-war years were characterised, he felt, by a pessimism of outlook, a 'tragic sense of life' which led them to seek escape from the concerns of the moment in remote lands or psychological problems having little or no bearing on the significant events of the period – the Russian Revolution, the rise of Nazism and Fascism, the Spanish Civil War. His own attitude, as he expressed it some years later in 'Why I Write' was that 'When I sit down to write a book, I do not say to myself, "I am going to produce a work of art". I write it because there is some lie that I want to expose, some fact to which I want to draw attention, and my initial concern is to get a hearing.' Implicitly, then, throughout 'Inside the Whale' Orwell is defining his own approach to literature by comparison with that of the novelists and poets of his generation. As the essay proceeds the reader becomes increasingly aware that Orwell is distancing himself from such writers as Auden and Connolly and allying himself with Miller, not because he is in agreement with Miller's attitudes but because he respects and understands the indifference to world affairs which lay behind such works as *Tropic of Cancer*. Orwell had met Miller whilst *en route* for Spain in 1936 and had become convinced that his indifference was fundamentally honest, borne of a profound belief that the individual was powerless to change the course of world events. It was this honesty, this absence of pose, which deeply appealed to the Englishman.

Above all his distinctive voice can be seen in his awareness that totalitarianism and intolerance were about to engulf Europe:

> What is quite obviously happening, war or no war, is the break-up of *laissez-faire* capitalism and of the liberal–Christian culture ... Almost certainly we are moving into an age of totalitarian dictatorships – an age in which freedom of thought will be at first a deadly sin and later on a meaningless abstraction. The autonomous individual is going to be stamped out of existence.

This presage of some of the major themes of *Nineteen Eighty-Four* is remarkable in a work written on the eve of the Second World War (war had been declared whilst the essay was in draft). As early as 1939 he had recognised that freedom of thought would become 'a meaningless abstraction', that the individual would be 'stamped out of existence', that liberalism as an idea and a political reality would perish over much of the earth. His experiences in Spain had convinced him that totalitarianism was now the most insidious menace facing mankind and that the implications of this fact upon literature and art would be far-reaching. 'Good novels,' he observed, 'are written by people who are *not frightened*.' There could be no literature of enduring value until the present conflict and its implicit threat to the free mind had passed. Until then the only option open to the creative writer was to endure, to record, to accept what happened to him without deluding himself that by his actions he could affect the shape of history.

Seen in the conspectus of his work as a whole *Inside the Whale* is a seminal book which concerns itself with many of Orwell's most fundamental preoccupations. To his friend Geoffrey Gorer he confided: 'I find this kind of semi-sociological literary criticism very interesting & I'd like to do a lot of other writers, but unfortunately there's no money in it. All Gollancz would give me in advance on the book was £20!'[5] Despite the limited appeal of the book it was favourably reviewed and earned for him a wide reputation as a critic. All three essays bear upon them the unmistakeable stamp of Orwell the iconoclast and man of ideas. The tendency to make sweeping judgements (e.g., 'Considered as a poem "Grantchester" is something worse than worthless') is as inseparable a part of his personality as his enthusiasm for Dickens and his striking use of metaphor. What lifts these essays above the level of journalism is their ability to stimulate thought, to suggest novel ways of approach, to probe beneath the surface of each argument to reveal the hitherto unsuspected considerations beneath. Orwell's approach throughout is individual and unconventional. The essay on Dickens is much more sociological and historical than the conventional literary analysis; that on 'Boys' Weeklies' begins as a review of weekly comics but soon extends into a discussion of language and social mores; the title essay, whilst ostensibly a discussion of Henry Miller and his approach to literature, is in reality a profoundly serious statement of his own intellectual position. At each stage of the discussion he raises social, cultural, literary or aesthetic arguments which reveal the wide range of his reading and compel the reader to re-examine the issues in question from unusual points of view. Here, then, in his first volume of collected essays, can be discerned those qualities which were to earn for him a world-wide reputation as a man of letters: clarity of language, vividness of analogy, penetrating analysis of problems and diversity of argument. Above all there is an ability to see through pretension and hypocrisy, a gift for weighing up an issue with fairness and sifting the essentials of a problem from the dross. It is indeed prose 'like a window pane'.

During the autumn of 1940 Orwell was at work on a lengthy polemical essay 'The Lion and the Unicorn: Socialism and the English Genius', which was published as a booklet in February 1941. This was the first volume in a series of booklets, the 'Searchlight Books', which were intended to discuss a range of wartime problems and offer possible solutions to them. The series was edited by Orwell and T. R. Fyvel and, although the original conception was not fully realised – of the projected seventeen titles ten only were published during 1941–3 – it was an imaginative scheme which contributed significantly to the wider discussion of some fundamental contemporary issues.

The Lion and the Unicorn' is a remarkable piece of writing in which Orwell ranges widely over the English character and attempts to define the prospects for radical social reform within its context. Part One, 'England Your England', is a brilliantly written summary of English national characteristics which was later reprinted separately and has become well known in its own right. The title is taken from W. E. Henley's poem 'For England's Sake':

> What have I done for you,
> England, my England?
> What is there I would not do,
> England, my own?

He begins with a careful definition of what it is that constitutes Englishness: a survey of those qualities and traits which distinguish England from other nations. He concludes that these may be summarised as dislike of abstract thought; privateness; gentleness; hatred of militarism; liking for anachronisms; respect for legality; patriotism; emotional unity. In these pages his own affection for England and English culture (including its weaknesses) is clearly evident and in a striking paragraph he conveys in a memorable series of images a microcosm of national life:

> The clatter of clogs in the Lancashire mill towns, the to-and-fro of the lorries on the Great North Road, the queues outside the Labour Exchanges, the rattle of pin-tables in the Soho pubs, the old maids biking to Holy Communion through the mists of the autumn morning – all these are not only fragments, but *characteristic* fragments, of the English scene . . . Yes, there *is* something distinctive and recognisable in English civilisation. It is a culture as individual as that of Spain. It is somehow bound up with solid breakfasts and gloomy Sundays, smoky towns and winding roads, green fields and red pillar-boxes. It has a flavour of its own.

Orwell is impressed above all with the sense that, in spite of its diversity and class-consciousness, England was still emotionally one nation; he is struck by 'the tendency of nearly all its inhabitants to feel alike and act together in moments of supreme crisis'. Whilst acknowledging this sense of identity he discerns two significant trends in twentieth-century social history: the decline of ability in the English ruling class and the enlargement of the middle class through the rise of a new stratum of technicians and artisans. As evidence of the decay of ability in those in positions of power he cites the foreign policy pursued by British governments in the 1930s: the refusal to perceive the reality of Nazism and Fascism and the ambivalent attitude of Britain towards the traumatic events in Spain. This decline in integrity and intellectual grasp had been accompanied by the blurring of the old 'class' divisions. A new, indeterminate social class of technicians, engineers and publicists was emerging and this would exercise a profound influence on the future.[6] The post-war world, he felt, would be vastly different from that of 1940, but 'England will still be England, an everlasting animal stretching into the future and the past, and, like all living things, having the power to change out of recognition and yet remain the same'.

In Part Two, 'Shopkeepers at War', Orwell states the case *against* private capitalism and *for* a socialist society. His indictment of capitalism – 'that is, an economic system in which land, factories, mines and transport are owned privately and operated solely for profit' – is essentially that it did not work and was wholly inappropriate in wartime conditions. It is characteristic of Orwell that he is not content simply to pose 'a socialist society' as an alternative to this but proceeds to define more precisely his own understanding of the phrase. Socialism for him, he insists, is not only the common ownership of the means of production but also 'approximate equality of incomes . . . political democracy, and abolition of all hereditary privilege, especially in education'. His conception of socialism at this time is therefore considerably more far-reaching than that advanced in *The Road to Wigan Pier*. Indeed, having urged (in another memorable phrase) that 'England is a family with the wrong members in control' he extends the argument to embrace an open advocacy of revolution:

> It is only by revolution that the native genius of the English people can be set free. Revolution does not mean red flags and street fighting, it means a fundamental shift of power . . . What is wanted is a conscious open revolt by ordinary people against inefficiency, class privilege and the rule of the old.

He perceives that the war effort will inevitably involve immense sacrifices for the British people but is convinced that these sacrifices will be borne, willingly and cheerfully, provided that they know what they are fighting for and are presented with realistic hopes of a better life after the war. Orwell's most earnest aspiration is that post-war England will be a more egalitarian and just society, a society in which gross inequalities of income and opportunity will have been eradicated. His essential thesis is that the war and revolution are inseparable – there was no prospect of establishing a socialist society without first defeating Hitler; conversely, Hitler could not be defeated without fundamental social and economic changes.

The discussion is continued in the third and final section, 'The English Revolution'. Here he argues the case for a popular socialist movement: the use of the word *movement* is deliberate, for he is advocating a current of thought, not simply a political party – a movement 'that actually has the mass of the people behind it'.

What is urgently needed, he argues, is a clear definition of war aims. These should include, in his view, the 'nationalisation of land, mines, railways, banks and major industries'; the limitation of incomes; reform of the educational system; immediate Dominion status for India; and the declaration of a formal alliance with countries overrun by the Fascist powers. A popular movement motivated by a statement of aims approximating to such a programme could achieve a fundamental shift in the direction of domestic and foreign policies. He recognises however that a government inspired by such policies 'will transform the nation from top to bottom, but it will still bear all over it the unmistakeable marks of our own civilisation', the peculiar, illogical civilisation which is quintessentially England.

'The Lion and the Unicorn' was well received and made a brief but significant impact upon the English intelligentsia. In a warm review in the *New Statesman* V. S. Pritchett compared Orwell with 'the two outstanding figures of our tradition of pamphleteering, Cobbett and Defoe', and praised his lucidity and outspokenness. It was one of a number of radical booklets published in the early war years including Wells's *The Commonsense of War and Peace* and Sir Richard Acland's *Unser Kampf* and, whilst much of the discussion has inevitably become obsolete with the passage of time, it remains an interesting and valiant attempt to stimulate thought on some crucial issues of the day. He seems to have seriously underestimated the strength of national unity as a factor overriding all other considerations. As George Woodcock expressed it: 'Few even among the Socialists agreed with him on the wisdom of attempting a total social transformation in the mid-career of a world war, and the majority of the people were interested mainly in staying alive and staying uninvaded'.[7] On the other hand it could be argued that the Labour victory of 1945 confirmed much of Orwell's analysis and his prescience in realising that social change would take a distinctively English form. In defining English characteristics and then advocating revolutionary changes *within their context* he was unquestionably breaking new ground and rehearsing themes and issues which continued to fascinate him during the remainder of his life. But perhaps its deepest significance lies in the evidence it affords of his profound emotional attachment towards England:

And above all, it is *your* civilisation, it is *you*. However much you hate it or laugh at it, you will never be happy away from it for any length of time. The suet puddings and the red pillarboxes have entered into your soul. Good or evil, it is yours,

you belong to it, and this side the grave you will never get
away from the marks that it has given you.

Reading this passage one can only speculate afresh regarding his
feelings on returning from Burma in August 1927 and from Paris
at the end of 1929. Undoubtedly his ability to see England from
the outside 'warts and all' and to write with loving detachment
of its strengths and foibles, was one of his most distinctive
achievements. Writing as one who had been brought up in a
comparatively sheltered English middle-class environment and
had twice, of his own volition, removed himself from it, he expressed in 'The Lion and the Unicorn' his deep affection for his
country and his understanding of its special attributes. It is
plainly the work of a writer who cared passionately for his native
land and believed with fervent intensity in the resilience and
adaptability of its people.

Critical Essays (published in the United States under the title
Dickens, Dali and Others) contains, in addition to 'Charles Dickens' and 'Boys' Weeklies', eight essays written during the years
1941–5. All are exercises in literary or sociological analysis. 'The
Art of Donald McGill' is a survey of comic seaside postcards, a
subject in which Orwell had a lifelong interest; 'Benefit of
Clergy' is a review of Salvador Dali's autobiography; and 'Raffles and Miss Blandish' is a review of James Hadley Chase's *No
Orchids for Miss Blandish* and a commentary on its underlying
assumptions. The remaining five are assessments of writers who
had each, in their various ways, influenced his own literary
development: Wells, Kipling, Yeats, Koestler and Wodehouse.
Of this material the most significant from the point of view of
Orwell's distinctive approach to life and literature are 'Wells,
Hitler and the World State' and 'Raffles and Miss Blandish'.

The writings of H. G. Wells exercised a profound influence on
Orwell as man and writer. As a schoolboy he had eagerly read
The Country of the Blind and *A Modern Utopia* and frequently acknowledged his indebtedness to Wells as a literary and intellectual force. 'Wells, Hitler and the World State' is a curious mixture of criticism and praise. It is ostensibly a review of Wells's
Guide to the New World, a collection of newspaper articles published in 1941, but soon widens into an assessment of Wells and
of his place in modern literature. He is generous in his praise:

But is it not a sort of parricide for a person of my age (thirty-eight) to find fault with H. G. Wells? Thinking people who were born about the beginning of this century are in some sense Wells's own creation . . . I doubt whether anyone who was writing books between 1900 and 1920, at any rate in the English language, influenced the young so much. The minds of all of us, and therefore the physical world, would be perceptibly different if Wells had never existed.

Orwell's central criticism is that Wells's nineteenth-century, English, middle-class background – remarkably similar to that of Dickens – meant that he was incapable of understanding the irrationality of such men as Hitler. Wells's advocacy of a Declaration of Human Rights and a federal world control of the air was academic until Hitler and his armed forces had been eliminated. This fundamental question, Orwell urged, had never been faced by Wells who continued to believe that man would behave in a rational manner. Although Orwell overstates his case somewhat – his indictment overlooks Wells's pessimistic writings such as *The Croquet Player* and *Mr. Blettsworthy on Rampole Island* – unquestionably there is some substance in his criticism. There is a tendency in Wells's novels to underestimate the immense power of evil in human affairs and Orwell is one of the very few critics to have drawn attention to this fact.

The essay is, however, rather more than a conventional exercise in literary criticism. Apart from its shrewd assessment of Wells's strengths and weaknesses as a creative writer it contains a moving account of his significance to those of Orwell's generation. It is not difficult to imagine, in the light of this, the impact of *The Country of the Blind* on the young Eric Blair when he and Cyril Connolly read it at St. Cyprian's in 1914 and the liberating effect it must have had on his intelligence (as late as 1941[8] he listed one of the stories in this collection, 'A Slip Under the Microscope', as one of his favourite short stories). 'Traditionalism, stupidity, snobbishness, patriotism, superstition and love of war seemed to be all on the same side,' he observes: 'there was need of someone who could state the opposite point of view.' Of deeper significance is his recognition that such forces as nationalism and militarism had proved to be far more powerful influences in the twentieth century than movements for world unity and were, moreover, not affected by reasoned argument. This acknowledgement of the growing power of irrational forces such as hatred, bigotry and intolerance is of fundamental importance to his intellectual development and was to play a decisive role in the conception of *Animal Farm* and *Nineteen Eighty-Four*. 'Creatures out of the Dark Ages have come marching into the present, and if they are ghosts they are at any rate ghosts which need a strong magic to lay them.' It is these same 'creatures out of the Dark Ages' – hatred, cruelty and violence – which found expression in the Two Minutes Hate and the torture chambers of the Ministry of Love.

'Raffles and Miss Blandish' owed its origin to Orwell's deep admiration for the novels of E. W. Hornung, an enthusiasm which had remained unchanged since his boyhood. Jacintha Buddicom, in her memoir *Eric and Us*, records: 'Eric was a great admirer of Hornung, Conan Doyle's brother-in-law. He thought it rather nice for Holmes and Raffles to be in the same family.' Throughout the essay he makes it plain that the appeal of the Raffles novels for him is the gentlemanly code of conduct on which they depend:

> Hornung was a very conscientious and on his level a very able writer. Anyone who cares for sheer efficiency must admire his work. However, the truly dramatic thing about Raffles, the thing that makes him a sort of byword even to this day . . . is the fact that he is *a gentleman*. Raffles is presented to us – and this is rubbed home in countless scraps of dialogue and casual remarks – not as an honest man who has gone astray, but as a public-school man who has gone astray.

Orwell then devotes several pages to an examination of Raffles's code of behaviour and a comparison of this with *No Orchids for Miss Blandish*. For him the difference between the two is a moral one. 'Raffles and Bunny, after all, are gentlemen, and such standards as they do have are not to be violated.' To Raffles friendship is sacred; he is chivalrous towards women; he will never abuse hospitality; he is deeply patriotic. Orwell also draws attention to the absence of sadism and violence in Hornung's stories: the novels, though convincing, are notable for their genteelism. There is little bloodshed and few corpses. He concludes that the Raffles novels were written at a time 'when people had standards', when not to play the game was simply not done, when there was a clearly understood and accepted dividing line between good and evil.

This gentlemanly tone is then contrasted with that of *No Orchids*. Orwell finds the sordidness and brutality of the latter utterly repugnant. In the completest contrast to Hornung's work, Chase's novel apparently accepts no standards:

> . . . it takes for granted the most complete corruption and self-seeking as the norm of human behaviour . . . such things as affection, friendship, good nature or even ordinary politeness simply do not enter. Nor, to any great extent, does normal sexuality. Ultimately only one motive is at work throughout the whole story: the pursuit of power.

The discussion is then widened to embrace a comparison of *No Orchids* with the crime novels of Edgar Wallace and William Faulkner. Orwell shrewdly detects that despite superficial similarities the mental atmosphere of Chase's novel is fundamentally different. What he finds so reprehensible about *No Orchids* and stories of its type is that for him they symbolised a new departure in escapist fiction: a departure from the essentially civilised, gentlemanly world of Sherlock Holmes and Raffles to a world of violence, cruelty, sadism and amorality. The distinction was a crucial one, having repercussions throughout literature. On the one hand was a society governed by an ethical code, in which crime was invariably punished and in which there was a sharp distinction between legality and illegality. On the other hand was a society in which there were no standards, in which might was always right and the prime motivation was an insatiable quest for power. It was the dichotomy between a world governed by *values* and one dominated by unprincipled brutality.

Orwell concludes his analysis with a discussion of the relationship between *No Orchids* and Fascism. In a striking passage which clearly anticipates the sadism of *Nineteen Eighty-Four* he summarises the attitudes which he felt were implicit in such fiction:

> It is a daydream appropriate to a totalitarian age. In his imagined world of gangsters Chase is presenting, as it were, a

distilled version of the modern political scene, in which such things as mass bombing of civilians, the use of hostages, torture to obtain confessions, secret prisons, execution without trial, floggings with rubber truncheons, drownings in cesspools, systematic falsification of records and statistics, treachery, bribery and quislingism are normal and morally neutral, even admirable when they are done in a large and bold way.

This list of features of modern warfare, almost all of which he had witnessed at first hand in Spain, was for him the world of *No Orchids* writ large. The frightening aspect for Orwell was that such books ministered to a power-instinct, to an unspoken lust for dominance regardless of social consequences. It was, he felt, no accident that *No Orchids* reached its greatest popularity at the time of the Battle of Britain and the blitz. Between the heroes of popular fiction in 1900 and 1940 there was an unbridgeable gulf. It was a gulf which he profoundly deplored. Whilst acknowledging that the reading of his boyhood was not free of snobbishness it represented an essentially moral culture whose passing would have the most insidious consequences for civilisation.

'Raffles and Miss Blandish' merits an important place in the canon since it encapsulates within its short compass a number of his most characteristic themes. Throughout there is an emphasis on morality: on a code of ethics or standards upon which civilised conduct should be based. Orwell was a profoundly *moral* writer. His concern for ethical standards in writing and in behaviour is implicit in his work as novelist, essayist and critic over a period of twenty years. Lionel Trilling described him epigrammatically as 'a virtuous man'.[9] The essay, however, is more than a plea for morality in literature. It goes beyond this to point out the relationship between the values inherent in one's reading and the attitudes of the reader: 'People worship power in the form in which they are able to understand it'. A generation which had imbibed novels of this calibre would be unlikely to question policies based upon duplicity and torture. Above all the essay provides powerful evidence of Orwell's deepening pessimism in the face of totalitarianism and warfare. In both this and 'Looking Back on the Spanish War' (written in the previous year) can be discerned the apprehension of a sensitive man, a man alarmed at the rise of Nazism, Fascism and Communism and powerless to do more than voice his protest at the insidious advance of falsehood and the denial of objective realities.

The English People, published in August 1947, was written considerably earlier. It was commissioned by Collins in 1943 for their 'Britain in Pictures' series and written in the Spring of 1944 following the completion of *Animal Farm* (in common with *Animal Farm* it was subject to a long delay in publication due to the wartime paper shortage). Superficially *The English People* covers much the same ground as *The Lion and the Unicorn* – a discussion of the English national character and an assessment of the probable future of the English people – and the apparent similarity between the two essays has meant that the later work has received comparatively scant attention from literary critics. It is in fact a much more balanced and carefully written essay than *The Lion and the Unicorn* and reveals interesting modifications of some of his views.

The opening section, 'England at First Glance', is an attempt to define English characteristics as they would appear to a foreign observer.

> It is worth trying for a moment to put oneself in the position of a foreign observer, new to England, but unprejudiced, and able because of his work to keep in touch with ordinary, useful, unspectacular people . . . Almost certainly he would find the salient characteristics of the English common people to be artistic insensibility, gentleness, respect for legality, suspicion of foreigners, sentimentality about animals, hypocrisy, exaggerated class distinctions, and an obsession with sport.

The discussion which is so brilliantly foreshadowed in this paragraph has a twofold significance. First, it should be acknowledged that in attempting to identify and examine the distinctive qualities of the English people he was exploring ground which had not been penetrated in this way before. It is not until Geoffrey Gorer's pioneering study *Exploring English Character* (1955) that we find a similar sociological approach to the problem of delineating English culture. Orwell, with his intellectual curiosity, his ability to see his native country from outside, his freedom from xenophobia and freshness of outlook was uniquely qualified to attempt such an assessment. The capacity to look dispassionately at one's own country, to assess its strengths and weaknesses and identify its peculiarities must be exceedingly rare. In *The English People* he demonstrated once again his gift for presenting sociological discussion in a readable and popular form. Continually one is aware of his fascination with the rich diversity of national and regional life, his ability to grasp the essentials of a complex reality, his unrivalled forte for the memorable phrase and the penetrating simile. Always he is curious to learn why things are as they are. Why, for example, had England 'produced poets and scientists rather than philosophers, theologians, or pure theorists of any description'? Why did a manual worker wear a cloth cap whereas a non-manual worker wore one only for golf or shooting? What is the English attitude towards temperance and sexual morality? Orwell's curiosity ranges over the whole field of life, work and recreation and embraces the smallest details of daily living. The result is an essay which combines sociological commentary with an invigorating and highly individual freshness of approach.

Second, his distinctive voice is discernible at each stage of the analysis. In his essay on Dickens he had described a phrase of Dickens's as being 'as individual as a fingerprint'. The same comment could well be applied to Orwell himself. In the passage quoted above, for example, there occurs the phrase 'and able because of his work to keep in touch with ordinary, useful, unspectacular people': a characteristic touch from the author of *The Road to Wigan Pier*. (Notice also the use of the phrase 'Almost certainly': a very common Orwellian device.) Throughout the discussion he is at pains to point out that 'the real England is not the England of the guide-books', that the visitor has to probe beneath outward appearances to find the reality of English life and that not all English traits are praiseworthy. It is his unusual ability to draw attention to the less attractive features of the national persona as well as the more commendable, and to discuss both with equal dispassionateness, which makes Orwell such a fascinating guide. He dwells on the 'gentle-mannered, undemonstrative, law-abiding English of today', but also enlarges on our apparent indifference to ugliness, our conservative eating habits, our irrationality and class jealousy. Again and again the reader is struck by his honesty: by his commendable power of impartial discussion and his gift for summarising complex nuances in simple, lucid, polished prose. As an example of this one has only to turn to the final sentence of the introductory section:

> And he [the imaginary observer] might end by deciding that a profound, almost unconscious patriotism and an inability to think logically are the abiding features of the English character, traceable in English literature from Shakespeare onwards.

It would be difficult to better this sentence as a summation of the national character expressed in language of the utmost economy and precision. Rarely can the quintessence of Englishness have been expressed with such felicity.

Orwell follows this introduction with three sections concerned respectively with moral outlook, politics and class structure. In these he displays to the full his intense curiosity regarding beliefs and attitudes and an extraordinary faculty for identifying the essentials of a problem. Topics such as religious belief, attitudes to violence, puritanism, freedom of thought and political consciousness are discussed with frankness and a complete absence of rancour. At each stage of his analysis he presents both sides of the question and is careful to warn the reader against too facile an interpretation of the evidence. In his discussion of 'The English Class System' for example, after describing the broad social classes into which the population may be classified he adds cautiously: 'This roughly fits the facts, but one can draw no useful inference from it unless one takes account of the subdivisions within the various classes and realises how deeply the whole English outlook is coloured by romanticism and sheer snobbishness'. His fascination with the minutiae of class gradations is again abundantly evident and after noting the survival of the outward forms of feudalism – a hereditary aristocracy, the monarchy, the House of Lords – he discusses the increasing fluidity of class differences and foresees that 'the tendency of the working class and the middle class is evidently to merge'. Throughout these pages one is impressed anew with Orwell's unobtrusive skill as an essayist. Behind the deceptive simplicity of his style there is evident a compassionate intelligence borne of wide reading and shrewd observation. It is, however, not a conventional intelligence but one with a highly idiosyncratic (and decidedly un-Etonian) approach: that of a man who is intensely absorbed by matters of belief and emotion and is concerned above all else to present a balanced appraisal of his subject whilst not losing sight of the essentially quixotic nature of the English character. Even such an apparently simple statement as 'They have the virtues and the vices of an old-fashioned people' contains within it a wealth of truth and yet is expressed with the conciseness of an aphorism. *The English People*, in fact, bears all the hallmarks of a work which has been most carefully thought out and revised.

There follows an engrossing section on 'The English Language' in which he displays all that fascination with linguistics which came to the fore in 'Politics and the English Language' (1946) and the Appendix on 'The Principles of Newspeak' in *Nineteen Eighty-Four*. His discussion of English vocabulary and grammar is marked by a quiet erudition and an acute awareness of the subtleties of language. In a passage which strikingly anticipates some of the finest writing of his last years he observes:

> To write or even to speak English is not a science but an art. There are no reliable rules: there is only the general principle that concrete words are better than abstract ones, and that the shortest way of saying anything is always the best . . . Whoever writes English is involved in a struggle that never lets up even for a sentence.

A new line of argument is opened up by his observation that '"Educated" English has grown anaemic because for long past it has not been reinvigorated from below' and his perceptive comment that those who are in daily contact with physical reality – factory workers, miners, engineers, soldiers – are those likeliest to use simple concrete language. The vitality of English as a written and spoken tongue depended upon its continual reinvigoration through metaphors and words based firmly on everyday realities. He concludes with the vivid statement: 'Language ought to be the joint creation of poets and manual workers, and in modern England it is difficult for these two classes to meet'.

In a final section, 'The Future of the English People,' Orwell looks ahead to the probable shape of English society in the post-war decades. Urging the need for 'a rising birthrate, more social equality, less centralisation and more respect for the intellect' he anticipates some of the recommendations of the

Beveridge Plan of 1944, *Full Employment in a Free Society*, which laid the foundations of the Welfare State. His practical proposals are an odd mixture of authoritarianism and social welfare. He advocates penal taxation so that childlessness becomes 'as unbearable an economic burden as a big family is now' but at the same time argues the case for less inequality of wealth and greater democracy in education. There is also a cogent advocacy of decentralisation including more autonomy for Scotland and Wales, generous endowment of provincial universities, the subsidising of provincial newspapers and wider teaching of local history and topography. This co-existence within Orwell of dictatorial and libertarian attitudes is an interesting example of that ambivalence which makes him so rewarding a writer to study in depth. He is capable within the same essay of a generalisation such as 'the centralised ownership of the press means in practice that unpopular opinions can only be printed in books or in newspapers with small circulations' and the most profound assessments of national traits.

At the end of his life Orwell prepared a statement for his literary executors indicating which of his works he preferred not to see reprinted. This list included both *The Lion and the Unicorn* and *The English People*.[10] His inclusion of them would seem to indicate his awareness of their limitations and his sense that with the passage of time some of his comments would inevitably 'date'. Of the two *The English People* seems the most likely to survive, if only because of its publication in the 'Britain in Pictures' series: a series now much sought after by collectors. To read it in its original form, alongside illustrations by Ardizzone, Lowry and Henry Lamb, is to realise afresh Orwell's unusual achievement and to acknowledge that in such essays he was attempting to define his own attitudes towards the land he loved so much. In doing so he placed on record a wealth of penetrating comment and appraised the English psyche with a fresh, humanitarian vision.

Shooting an Elephant, the collection on which he was working sporadically during the last year of his life, includes much of Orwell's very finest work. There are a number of essays which could only have come from his pen – 'Books versus Cigarettes', a careful examination of the cost of reading compared with that of smoking and entertainment; 'Good Bad Books' and 'Decline of the English Murder', two characteristic pieces which testify to his fascination with popular culture; and 'Some Thoughts on the Common Toad' and 'A Good Word for the Vicar of Bray', two delightful essays which reveal his abiding affection for the English countryside and a simple joy in the passing of the seasons. The collection contains four essays which seem destined to earn for him a permanent niche in English letters: 'A Hanging', 'Shooting an Elephant', 'How the Poor Die' and 'Politics and the English Language'. These will repay careful study by all who seek to understand Orwell and his distinctive contribution to the intellectual climate of our times.

It is significant that 'A Hanging' is the only example of his apprenticeship years as a writer – i.e., the only work originally published under the name Eric Blair – which Orwell considered worthy of preservation. It was published in the *Adelphi* in August 1931 and is markedly different in style from the rather pretentious book reviews he was contributing to the magazine at that time (the only other enduring piece of work from this period is his essay 'The Spike', published in April of the same year, which he later reshaped to form part of *Down and Out in Paris and London*). Immediately the reader commences 'A Hanging' he is arrested by the direct, individual, assured tone of the opening paragraph:

> It was in Burma, a sodden morning of the rains. A sickly light, like yellow tinfoil, was slanting over the high walls into the jail yard. We were waiting outside the condemned cells, a row of sheds fronted with double bars, like small animal cages. Each cell measured about ten feet by ten and was quite bare within except for a plank bed and a pot for drinking water. In some of them, brown silent men were squatting at the inner bars, with their blankets draped round them. These were the condemned men, due to be hanged within the next week or two.

Already can be discerned here a number of those literary touches which were to become a hallmark of the mature Orwell. There is the vivid phrase: 'a sodden morning of the rains'; 'the condemned cells . . . like small animal cages'. There is the striking imagery: 'A sickly light, like yellow tinfoil . . .'. Observe also the characteristic preoccupation with detail: 'Each cell measured about ten feet by ten'. At the outset of his narrative he is concerned to set the scene for the reader with the utmost precision.

The incident described in 'A Hanging' – the execution of a nameless Indian and the realisation on the part of the narrator of the intrinsic wrongness of capital punishment – forms the framework for one of his most memorable and haunting essays. One is impressed, firstly, with its starkness. We are given no details of the prisoner's identity, nor of his offence, nor of his innocence or guilt. The narrator himself remains anonymous throughout: he is simply 'I', one of the officials who observe the hanging and drink together when it is over. The episode itself is told without preamble; it is simply related, as if it was a chapter from a volume of recollections of Burma. This very starkness adds immeasurably to its power: clearly the incident had made a deep impression on Orwell and each detail of it was etched permanently on his memory. Although 'A Hanging' is much closer in time to his Burmese experiences than the novel *Burmese Days* it must be borne in mind that even here he is looking back on an occurrence dating from five years previously. It seems clear therefore that the entire episode was one on which he had brooded long and deeply. The only way in which he could exorcise it from his mind was to commit it to paper and in doing so transfix indelibly each terrible detail of the execution and its impact on his consciousness.

From the moment that the hanging is set in motion – 'Eight o'clock struck and a bugle call, desolately thin in the wet air, floated from the distant barracks' – the story moves inexorably to its conclusion. The walk to the gallows, the pursuit of an escaped dog, the hangman and the gallows, the final prayer of the doomed man, the hanging, the relief of the onlookers: all are described in prose of astringent lucidity. The climax of the essay occurs not at the conclusion but at the instant of Orwell's realisation of the inhumanity of judicial death:

And once, in spite of the men who gripped him by each shoulder, he stepped slightly aside to avoid a puddle on the path. It is curious, but till that moment I had never realised what it means to destroy a healthy, conscious man. When I saw the prisoner step aside to avoid the puddle I saw the mystery, the unspeakable wrongness, of cutting a life short when it is in full tide.

Thus, an apparently trivial incident while on the way to the gallows acts as a catalyst, leading the narrator to meditate on the meaning of premature death. The prisoner, who at the beginning of the essay has been described in unsympathetic terms – he is a 'puny wisp' of a man with a comic moustache 'absurdly too big for his body' – becomes after the moment of realisation a fellow human being, united with the narrator in a common humanity:

> He and we were a party of men walking together, seeing, hearing, feeling, understanding the same world; and in two minutes, with a sudden snap, one of us would be gone – one mind less, one world less.

This shift from alienation to a recognition of kindred, from condescension to complete emotional identity, forms a powerful element within the structure of the essay and provides it with a convincing *raison d'être*. This ability to identify himself with the underdog, to achieve a sense of affinity with downtrodden or despised individuals, was to prove one of his greatest strengths as a novelist and critic.

Superficially 'A Hanging' and 'Shooting an Elephant' have much in common. Both describe incidents Orwell had witnessed in Burma, both are overtly critical of imperialism in practice, and both describe an apparently minor occurrence which serves as a watershed in the life of the narrator. The essays are however very different in spirit and intent. 'A Hanging' is the work of a tiro, and for all its brevity is unquestionably the result of a long process of polishing and revision. It is not, moreover, a conscious political document: Blair in 1931 was still feeling his way towards his mature political position and was still years away from the social awareness of *The Road to Wigan Pier*. 'Shooting an Elephant', by contrast, was written in 1936 when Orwell was an established writer with a clearly defined viewpoint: already by this time he had come to the view that everything he wrote was written 'directly or indirectly, *against* totalitarianism and *for* democratic Socialism, as I understand it'. It has therefore a much more deliberate didactic intention than the earlier piece. This is not to deny in any way its literary qualities, which are undeniable – the essay has been described as 'one of the master-pieces of the genre in this century'[11] – but to suggest that it needs to be approached with some caution. It should be treated as a literary recreation, as an artefact consciously shaped to point a moral, rather than as a piece of reportage.

The editor of the magazine *New Writing* wrote to Orwell in May 1936 inviting him to submit a contribution. He replied with a diffidence that was all too typical:

> I am writing a book at present & the only other thing I have in mind is a sketch (it would be about 2,000–3,000 words), describing the shooting of an elephant. It all came back to me very vividly the other day & I would like to write it, but it may be that it is quite out of your line.[12]

It seems incredible that one of the most celebrated essays of modern times was first mooted with such apparent casualness. Fortunately the editor replied that he would indeed be pleased to publish 'the sketch' and Orwell set to work.

In contrast to the consciously literary, dispassionate manner of 'A Hanging', the tone of 'Shooting an Elephant' is one of acute emotional involvement. The incident described took place at Moulmein in Lower Burma, where he was for a time sub-divisional police officer. Here, he declares, he was 'hated by large numbers of people – the only time in my life that I have been important enough for this to happen to me'. Before turning to the central episode of the essay the atmosphere of hatred is carefully described: the bitterness of anti-European feeling, the humiliations and insults to which Europeans were subject, the loathing Orwell felt for his job. As a uniformed agent of the occupying power he was an obvious target for petty indignities which he found 'perplexing and upsetting'. At the same time he was oppressed by feelings of guilt at the blatant injustices of the imperial regime; the floggings, executions and imprisonments convinced him of the evil of imperialism and of his own role within it. 'But,' he adds, 'I could get nothing into perspective. I was young and ill-educated and I had had to think out my problems in the utter silence that is imposed on every Englishman in the East.' (The use of the phrase 'ill-educated' in this context is curious and significant. Orwell must have been aware that having spent five years at Eton he had had the benefit of an education only available to a privileged minority. He may well have felt, however, that a public school education ill-fitted him for the harsh realities of service in remote outposts of empire.)

The crux of the story is then described. A tame elephant has escaped from its keeper and has run amok, causing much damage and killing livestock. As a police officer Orwell is requested to deal with the situation. On arriving at the locality in question he finds that the elephant has now calmed down and is browsing contentedly in a field. Since the animal now appears to be harmless he realises that, although he is armed with a rifle, it would be wrong to shoot it: the elephant has now recovered from its attack of madness and appears to be as harmless as a cow. However, a large crowd of Burmese has gathered round, confidently expecting the beast to be shot. At this moment he senses that, whether he wishes to or not, he will have to do what the crowd expects of him; failure to do so would result in intolerable humiliation.

> And suddenly I realised that I should have to shoot the elephant after all. The people expected it of me and I had got to do it; I could feel their two thousand wills pressing me forward, irresistibly. And it was at this moment, as I stood there with the rifle in my hands, that I first grasped the hollowness, the futility of the white man's dominion in the East. Here was I, the white man with his gun, standing in front of the unarmed native crowd – seemingly the leading actor of the piece; but in reality I was only an absurd puppet pushed to and fro by the will of those yellow faces behind. I perceived in this moment that when the white man turns tyrant it is his own freedom that he destroys.

The story thus becomes a powerful parable of the emptiness of imperial domination. Much against his will, for he feels that it would be murder to do so, he proceeds to shoot the elephant. The animal takes a long time to die even though he has aimed at the brain and heart. Its tortured gasping in its death agonies become intolerable and at last he can stand it no longer. He leaves the scene, abandoning the elephant to the natives who will strip the body for the meat and tusks.

Both 'A Hanging' and 'Shooting an Elephant' might well have found a place within the structure of *Burmese Days*, but some instinct persuaded Orwell to present them as separate essays rather than as incidents in a novel. Both gain significantly from this treatment. The two incidents stand out, sharp and clear, divorced from all extraneous matter. There remains indelibly impressed on the mind a series of unusually vivid impressions: the prisoner stepping aside to avoid the puddle; the impassioned praying of the doomed man; the terrible finality of the gallows; the excited, expectant crowd swarming around the policeman and the elephant; the lingering, painful, unbearable death of the stricken beast. The skill with which both incidents become the focal point of a parable is impressive in its dexterity. 'I perceived in this moment that when the white man turns tyrant it is his own freedom that he destroys . . . He wears a mask, and his face grows to fit it.' The power of his invective is more telling than any number of polemical tracts.

In March 1929 Orwell was for two weeks a patient in the Hôpital Cochin in Paris, desperately ill with pneumonia. This was an old-fashioned hospital maintained for the teaching of medical students and was at that time 'a stronghold of French medical obscurantism'.[13] His experiences during those two weeks were such that they were etched unforgettably on his memory and when he came to write about them in 1946 he could recollect in terrible detail each stage of his ordeal. No one has excelled him in the art of grim understatement:

> After the questioning came the bath – a compulsory routine for all newcomers, apparently, just as in prison or the workhouse. My clothes were taken away from me, and after I had sat shivering for some minutes in five inches of warm water I was given a linen nightshirt and a short blue flannel dressing-gown – no slippers, they had none big enough for me, they said – and led out into the open air . . . Someone stumbled in front of me with a lantern. The gravel path was frosty underfoot, and the wind whipped the nightshirt round my bare calves.

This scene forms the prelude to a series of nightmarish vignettes in which the antique practices of the hospital are described with Dickensian intensity. It is as if the reader is being conducted on a journey backwards through time. The cupping (the application of heated glasses to the body to draw out blood), the forcible subjection to a mustard poultice, the cramped ward with its rows of beds containing emaciated patients, the foul odours, the sense that each patient was a *specimen* and not a human being: all are described in a terse, emotionless prose reminiscent of *Down and Out in Paris and London*. Horror is piled relentlessly upon horror – patients dying like animals, corpses left exposed to view, the unspeakable atmosphere of death and decay – until the cumulative effect becomes almost unbearable. Long after 'How the Poor Die' has been read these impressions remain ingrained on the memory; the essay has the stark, inhuman quality of a short story by Edgar Allan Poe.

The significance of the essay lies precisely in this element of verisimilitude. 'How the Poor Die' is a moving and unforgettable document because it does not claim to be other than a factual account of an experience undergone by Orwell himself. There is no element of artificiality (as in the Etonian posing as a London tramp, or in the hop-picking scenes in *A Clergyman's Daughter*) but instead an attempt to describe as honestly as possible all that he saw and underwent. The essay gains immeasurably from this absence of pose. He was not pretending to be ill, nor pretending to be poor. He was admitted to the hospital as a pauper and was treated accordingly, suffering cruelty and indifference on the same terms as the other patients. As a result he is able to identify himself totally with the poor; he was one of them. It would not be too much to claim that his experience of hospitalisation was the turning point in the development of his unique literary style. However harrowing the experience at the time, the submerging of himself in identical conditions with others in like circumstances and the opportunity thus afforded of observing poverty *from the inside* proved to be a decisive step in the forging of his personality.

· 'Politics and the English Language', written for *Horizon* in April 1946, has justifiably become one of Orwell's most renowned essays. It was written when he was at the height of his powers and at a time when, with *Animal Farm* completed and *Nineteen Eighty-Four* at the planning stage, he was increasingly preoccupied with language and its repercussions on literature and politics. He is at pains to make clear at the outset that his concern stems not from linguistic theory or pedantic purism but from an essentially *moral* concern for the establishment of truth.

Modern English, especially written English, is full of bad habits which spread by imitation and which can be avoided if one is willing to take the necessary trouble. If one gets rid of these habits one can think more clearly, and to think clearly is a necessary first step towards political regeneration: so that the fight against bad English is not frivolous and is not the exclusive concern of professional writers.

He proceeds to examine five extracts from recently published books and pamphlets and analyses these for their faults; these faults are discussed at length under the headings 'dying metaphors', 'operators or verbal false limbs', 'pretentious diction', and 'meaningless words'. Throughout the discussion his concern is with the clarity and honesty of language, with 'language as an instrument for expressing and not for concealing or preventing thought'. He stresses that the careless use of language has an insidious effect since it corrupts thought by the introduction of meaningless phrases, clichés and platitudes which muffle clear statement. This concern with the capacity of language to express clear thought was Orwell's obsession: it had been his King Charles's Head since *Homage to Catalonia* (indeed its roots can be traced much earlier, in Gordon Comstock's preoccupation with language and his distaste for advertising slogans). What angered him was that in the twentieth century 'political speech and writing are largely the defence of the indefensible'. Imperialism, purges, nuclear weapons and political imprisonments could only be defended by phrases and sentences which were essentially bromides: statements designed to conceal rather than reveal the truth. In his view politicians had been responsible for much of the decay in the English language since political communication had to consist largely of euphemism, vagueness and subjective statement.

The process, Orwell concludes, is not irreversible. Through the application of a number of simple rules – the avoidance of hackneyed metaphors and similes, the avoidance of long words where short ones will suffice, the removal of unnecessary words, the shunning of passive words and foreign phrases – English could become once again a language of meaning and precision. This, he recognises, will 'demand a deep change of attitude in anyone who has grown used to writing in the style now fashionable'. It would demand an end to lazy habits of thought, a refusal to use worn-out phrases and a conscious determination to achieve the utmost clarity of statement.

This was to be his major preoccupation during the remainder of his life: a passionate concern for the use of English as an accurate and explicit instrument for the communication of ideas.

It underlies all his work from the war years onwards and was to find its final and most moving expression in *Nineteen Eighty-Four*.

Such, Such Were the Joys and *England Your England* are the American and English editions respectively of a second fine collection of posthumously published essays. The English edition differs from the former in that the long autobiographical essay 'Such, Such Were the Joys' is omitted: for legal reasons it was considered inadvisable to publish this in Britain at the time. The essay had its origins in an exchange of correspondence between Orwell and his old friend Cyril Connolly in 1938.

Writing to Connolly apropos the latter's *Enemies of Promise* Orwell commented:

> I wonder how you can write about St. Cyprian's. It's all like an awful nightmare to me, & sometimes I think I can still taste the porridge (out of those pewter bowls, do you remember?)[14]

The phrase 'awful nightmare' is revealing and indicates the deep impact which his preparatory school experiences made upon him. Following the publication of *Enemies of Promise* Connolly invited him to write his reminiscences of St Cyprian's for publication in the magazine *Horizon*. These reminiscences, which took the form of a novella-length essay, were not published until 1953 and did not appear in book form in Britain until 1968 with the publication of the *Collected Essays*. Orwell forwarded the manuscript to his publisher F. J. Warburg in May 1947 with a covering note: 'I am sending you separately a long autobiographical sketch ... I haven't actually sent it to Connolly or *Horizon*, because apart from being too long for a periodical I think it is really too libellous to print, and I am not disposed to change it, except perhaps the names.'[15]

The title is taken from 'The Echoing Green' one of Blake's *Songs of Innocence* with which he had been familiar since childhood:

Such, such were the joys
  When we all, girls and boys,
In our youth time were seen,
  On the Echoing Green.

The selection of this line for the title of his most painful and deeply-felt essay can only be ironical: far from being an evocation of childhood happiness it is a bitterly wrought indictment of childhood sufferings, a scathing account of mental and emotional repression in the years before 1914. In common with *Down and Out in Paris and London* and 'Shooting an Elephant' the essay needs to be approached with some caution as a fragment of autobiography. In deliberately casting the sketch in the form of an indictment, omitting all the happier aspects of his memories (apart from one beautifully written passage eulogising the joys of summer) he has created a powerful but highly selective document, a polemic which is so carefully fashioned and intensely conceived that it achieves the status of a work of art.

The essay is divided into six sections, each concerned with a different aspect of his childhood world: the effect is to view his memories from a number of different perspectives. The sections are concerned respectively with the violent punishment meted out to him for bed-wetting; the emphasis upon hereditary wealth and competitive examinations; the squalor and neglect which was a feature of some private schools; the prevailing sexual codes; the social and moral values inculcated by the school; and a comparison of his own schooling with that of the contemporary child. At the outset Orwell is careful to warn the reader of the distorting effects of memory (assuming that the essay was written in 1940 he was attempting to recall events that had occurred twenty-eight years previously).

> In general, one's memories of any period must necessarily weaken as one moves away from it . . . At twenty I could have written the history of my school days with an accuracy which would be quite impossible now. But it can also happen that one's memories grow sharper after a long lapse of time, because one is looking at the past with fresh eyes . . .

With candour and bitterness he describes the harsh regime of St. Cyprian's: the canings, the bullyings, the snobbishness, the petty humiliations, the discomfort, the acute unspoken misery which only childhood can know. What it can mean to a sensitive child to be removed from home at the age of eight and thrust into the uncongenial environment of a boarding school is vividly conveyed. At that age, Orwell asserts, he was in a state of sexual and worldly innocence; his years at St. Cyprian's were a painful introduction into a world of sexual repression, learning by rote, a code of 'get on or get out' and the heirarchy of wealth. His feeling that he was innately inferior and doomed to failure was reinforced by the prevailing code that strength and power mattered above all else: 'There were the strong, who deserved to win and always did win, and there were the weak, who deserved to lose and always did lose, everlastingly'. The emphasis on games, on the passing of examinations as an end in itself, on the social cachet of wealth, on the virtue of winning: all these were anathema to him. He did not question the prevailing values, however, since as a child he was too young and inexperienced to put other values in their place; he accepted his inferiority. (At one point he comments drily: 'The conviction that it was *not possible* for me to be a success went deep enough to influence my actions till far into adult life'. How far is this an accurate statement of his outlook as a young man and how far is it a rationalisation?) The technique employed is akin to that of 'How the Poor Die' – the relentless accumulation of detail upon detail to achieve an effect of unforgettable squalidness. The overwhelming impression is one of a boy who was a misfit: unbearably unhappy, realising to his chagrin that he had been accepted at reduced fees, unable to accommodate himself to a world in which physical prowess was the touchstone of achievement, a boy immersed in a lonely, introspective world of his own. The traumas of childhood, he adds, can be immense. The adults and bullies who seem to a child terrifying and all-powerful would seem from his mature perspective quite harmless: but to the child they assume monstrous, nightmarish proportions. 'Whoever writes about his childhood,' he concludes, 'must beware of exaggeration and self-pity. I do not claim that I was a martyr or that St. Cyprian's was a sort of Dotheboys Hall. But I should be falsifying my own memories if I did not record that they are largely memories of disgust.'

The question which has fascinated critics and biographers since Orwell's death is how far 'Such, Such Were the Joys' can be accepted as a literal statement of fact: how reliable is it as a recreation of his boyhood? The question is by no means easy to answer (and is not made any easier by his deceptively simple, direct style) but may most fruitfully be approached by separating its two aspects – the qualities of the essay as a literary composition and its reliability as a factual record of his schooling. From a purely literary standpoint 'Such, Such Were the Joys' must be accepted as one of Orwell's finest creations. Lucid, intelligent and fluent, it is a most carefully assembled piece of work and bears all the hallmarks of a closely revised text which has been long mulled over. The power of the writing is such that certain details remain in the mind long after the essay has been laid aside: the caning from the headmaster, the long walks on the Sussex downs, the earnest homily on the Temple of the Body, the tearful interrogations from the headmaster's wife. It is in this direction that the enduring value of the essay lies – as a memorable *interpretation* of schooling, a deliberately selective account of boyhood unhappiness written from the vantage point of adulthood. Its value as autobiography is more problematic. Memory is notoriously unreliable and before accepting the essay at its face value one has to place it in context alongside contemporary evidence: letters written at the time and the testimony of his friends and fellow pupils.[16] The evidence seen as a totality is not by any means a picture of unrelieved misery, although his account is confirmed in many of its particulars. The conclusion must be that he has carefully selected his material in order to present a case; the formulation of a dispassionate account of his school days was not his intention, since this would have involved the inclusion of episodes which did not minister to his overall design. In the last analysis it is therefore as a *literary* exercise that it must be judged and in these terms it has to be acknowledged as a wholly coherent and moving composition.

It is significant that Orwell concludes the essay with the reflection: 'Now, however, the place is out of my system for good. Its magic works no longer . . .' In forcing himself to dwell on painful childhood memories and to ponder episodes long consigned to neglected corners of the mind he succeeded in exorcising from his imagination a part of his life he had looked back upon with repugnance. In doing so he fashioned one of his most absorbing and personal essays.

'Such, Such Were the Joys' is one more instance of Orwell's technique of using his personal reminiscences as a basis for the presentation of radical ideas. 'All art,' he wrote elsewhere, 'is propaganda.' One may disagree with this statement while acknowledging that in the fusion of the two media he achieved a purposive and dynamic literary form.

The Collected Essays, Journalism and Letters published in four volumes in 1968 contains all the essays in the collections discussed above together with much of his journalism, his wartime diary, and a generous selection of his letters. It amounts in all to some 500 items and represents an impressive achievement for a man who was for much of his life in poor health and died at the age of 46. Of all this material – which embraces the whole range of his life, work and thought from 1920 to 1949 – the most enduring pieces (apart from those discussed in the previous pages) are his memorable essay 'Why I Write' and the numerous contributions he wrote for *Tribune* under the title 'As I Please'. Taken together these indicate the wide range of his interests, the depth of his concern for human betterment and the seriousness with which he approached his work. Above all they reveal the unshakeable moral stance which lay at the root of his art.

Between December 1943 and February 1945 Orwell contributed to *Tribune* a regular weekly column under the title 'As I Please' and continued this at irregular intervals thereafter until April 1947. In all he contributed 72 'As I Please' columns covering some 230 separate topics ranging from cosmetics to transport and from air raids to Christianity. The scope of the column embraced comments on the war effort, literary discussion, commentary on religious and philosophical ideas, discussion of current affairs, gardening, prominent people, and in fact any topic which took his fancy. Its catholicity must have been for him a large part of its appeal for it permitted him to comment on a diversity of issues without obliging him to confine his attention to politics or literature. The result is a fascinating exercise in a now unfashionable genre: the causerie. Tolerant, humane, stimulating and idiosyncratic, 'As I Please' was and is a major contribution to the art of the pot-pourri. The contributions illustrate the diversity of his reading and interests, his willingness to espouse unpopular causes and his gift for stimulating his readers with apposite and thought-provoking commentary:

That seems to be a fixed rule in London: whenever you do by some chance have a decent vista, block it up with the ugliest statue you can find.

The fact is that we live in a time when causes for rejoicing are not numerous. But I like praising things, when there is anything to praise, and I would like here to write a few lines . . . in praise of the Woolworth's Rose.

With no power to put my decrees into operation, but with as much authority as most of the exile 'governments' now sheltering in various parts of the world, I pronounce sentence of death on the following words and expressions: Achilles' heel, jackboot, hydra-headed, ride roughshod over, stab in the back, petty-bourgeois, stinking corpse, liquidate, iron heel, blood-stained oppressor, cynical betrayal, lackey, flunkey, mad dog, jackal, hyena, blood-bath.

With great enjoyment I have just been rereading *Trilby*, George du Maurier's justly popular novel, one of the finest specimens of that 'good bad' literature which the English-speaking peoples seem to have lost the secret of producing.

Two days ago, after a careful search in Hyde Park, I came on a hawthorn bush that was definitely in bud, and some birds, though not actually singing, were making noises like an orchestra tuning up. Spring is coming after all, and recent rumours that this was the beginning of another Ice Age were unfounded.[17]

The column gained him a wider readership than any of his books with the exception of *Animal Farm* and stimulated a lively correspondence. His readers were alternately amused, irritated, exasperated and enlightened by his wide-ranging comments; many were annoyed by his quirkiness, his refusal to respect the wartime convention that the Soviet Union was not to be criticised, and his frequent forays into apparently minor topics. Many more found the column essential reading and turned to his page before studying the remainder of the paper. In its unusual combination of earnestness and good humour, its liberality of subject matter, its evidence of diverse reading and an acute eye for neglected by-ways of knowledge 'As I Please' is a fascinating reflection of Orwell's personality and indicates many aspects of his complex make-up. George Gissing, in the preface to his *Private Papers of Henry Ryecroft*, wrote: 'But in this written gossip he revealed himself more intimately than in our conversation of the days gone by . . . Here he spoke to me without restraint, and, when I had read it all through, I knew the man better than before.' The same might be said of 'As I Please'. Freed from the conventions of the novel and the documentary, he was able to exploit to the full his formidable talents as raconteur, iconoclast and man of letters. Viewed in their entirety these short pieces are among the finest contributions to the English essay written in this century.

'Why I Write', written in 1946 and since frequently anthologised, is one of the very few essays in which Orwell discusses his own approach to literature. The editors of the *Collected Essays* have wisely placed it at the beginning of the collection since it is in a real sense a summary of his intellectual position and of the motives which led him to embark on a literary life.

After describing his early efforts to write poetry and short stories he makes the perceptive comment:

> . . . I do not think one can assess a writer's motives without knowing something of his early development. His subject-matter will be determined by the age he lives in – at least this is true in tumultuous, revolutionary ages like our own – but before he ever begins to write he will have acquired an emotional attitude from which he will never completely escape.

This emotional attitude, he acknowledged, was of crucial importance in the development of any writer and particularly so in his own case: 'if he escapes from his early influences altogether, he will have killed his impulse to write'.

The most interesting section of the essay to the student of his work is that in which Orwell examines his own motives as a writer. By temperament, he admits, he is a person in which egotism, aesthetic enthusiasm and historical impulse would normally outweigh political purpose. 'In a peaceful age I might have written ornate or merely descriptive books, and might have remained almost unaware of my political loyalties. As it is I have been forced into becoming a sort of pamphleteer.' The word *forced* in this connection tells us much concerning his attitudes; clearly he felt impelled by a powerful urge which he could not resist or ignore. The Spanish Civil War was the turning point, the catalyst which changed him from a littérateur uncertain of his motives and ideals to a politically committed writer with conscious aims and a vision of his ideal society. But the artistic purpose which shaped his work remained unchanged:

What I have most wanted to do throughout the past ten years is to make political writing into an art. My starting point is always a feeling of partisanship, a sense of injustice . . . But I could not do the work of writing a book, or even a long magazine article, if it were not also an aesthetic experience.

Again, Orwell deliberately uses the phrase 'I could not'; not 'I would not wish to' or 'I would find it difficult to', but *I could not*. It was simply not possible for him to write a book, however politically motivated, which was not also an artistic whole demanding the utmost attention to language. 'And yet it is also true,' he concludes, 'that one can write nothing readable unless one constantly struggles to efface one's own personality. Good prose is like a window pane.' For twenty years he had striven to make a permanent impression on English literature, to become a novelist and essayist in the manner of Swift. In doing so he had fashioned a distinctive prose style – simple, direct, and apparently effortless – recognised as Orwellian and sharpened to maturity in the writings of his final decade. What this had cost him in terms of health and happiness and sheer hard work can only be guessed at. Towards the end of the essay occurs the revealing passage: 'Writing a book is a horrible, exhausting struggle, like a long bout of some painful illness. One would never undertake such a thing if one were not driven on by some demon . . .'. Rarely can a writer have laid bare his innermost feelings with such honesty or expressed so tellingly the travail of literary effort.

For all these reasons 'Why I Write' occupies an important place in his work and forms a fitting conclusion to a discussion of Orwell as essayist. It was entirely characteristic of him that this essay, so finely and thoughtfully written, was prepared not for syndication in the major magazines but for *Gangrel*, a journal with a tiny circulation and which could have offered at best only a nominal payment. He was always willing to devote much of his energies on causes or publications in which he deeply believed.

As an essayist Orwell's achievement was very considerable. In volume, range and intellectual depth his essays are unrivalled in this century and reveal the extraordinary diversity of his reading and interests. Their subject matter is unusually catholic when one reflects that he was an essentially English writer from a solid Anglo-Indian background: the range of topics at his disposal is in itself a reminder that he was no ordinary writer. In these shorter pieces – so painstakingly written and so eloquent of the man – he combined the two great traditions of English letters. On the one hand there is the solid *belles-lettres* tradition of Hazlitt and Stevenson: the memorable, polished essay on life and literature and the passing scene. To this category belong such fine pieces as 'Some Thoughts on the Common Toad', 'A Good Word for the Vicar of Bray', 'Mark Twain' and 'Tobias Smollett'. These reflect his deep affection for the countryside, his pleasure in the simple joys of the open air and the world of literature. On the other hand there is the radical, questioning tradition of Defoe and Swift; to this category belong such characteristic essays as 'Looking Back on the Spanish War', 'The Prevention of Literature' and 'Writers and Leviathan'. In these he deployed to the full his passionate concern for human welfare, his concern for justice and the utmost freedom of thought and expression. There is a sense in which he not only made a significant contribution to those two strands but added a third mainstream of his own: that of the searching, incisive essay dealing with neglected aspects of daily living. Examples of this genre are 'A Nice Cup of Tea', 'Books vs. Cigarettes', 'Decline of the English Murder' and 'In Defence of English Cooking'. Here he displayed his fascination with the minutest details of everyday life and his gift for illuminating these with penetrating comment. No detail of living was too small to escape his notice; and to each topic, whether it was the cost of reading or the weightiest matters of international politics, he brought to bear the same critical intelligence.

When one considers the range of his essays, their consistent readability and overall literary qualities, one turns to Orwell with renewed respect. With the passage of time much of his political and wartime journalism will inevitably diminish in interest yet one has the firm impression that the bulk of his essays will continue to be read and enjoyed. In such pieces as 'A Hanging', 'Shooting an Elephant', 'Charles Dickens' and 'How the Poor Die' he made a lasting contribution to English literature and moreover enlarged the horizons of the English essay in a significant and dynamic way.

Part IV

KEY TO THE CHARACTERS AND LOCATIONS

Key to the Characters and Locations

This section consists of an alphabetically arranged dictionary of the characters and places having a significant role in the novels and non-fiction works. These are, in many cases, described in Orwell's own words.

The following abbreviations are used throughout:

Air	*Coming Up for Air*
Aspidistra	*Keep the Aspidistra Flying*
Burmese	*Burmese Days*
CEJL	*Collected Essays, Journalism and Letters*
Clergyman	*A Clergyman's Daughter*
Down and Out	*Down and Out in Paris and London*
Farm	*Animal Farm*
Homage	*Homage to Catalonia*
1984	*Nineteen Eighty-Four*
Wigan	*The Road to Wigan Pier*

BARCELONA. Orwell arrived in Barcelona in December 1936 and enlisted almost at once as a militiaman, fighting on the side of the Spanish Republic in the civil war. He returned to Barcelona on leave in April–May 1937 and witnessed the internecine street fighting there. He visited the city for the last time in June 1937 and from there he and his wife, pursued by the police, succeeded in escaping to France. Whilst in Barcelona Orwell stayed at the Hotel Continental and spent several days on guard duty on the roof of the Poliorama cinema (since renamed La Casamentera). *Homage*.

BENJAMIN. A donkey, 'the oldest animal on the farm, and the

worst tempered'. He is devoted to Boxer the cart-horse, and it
is Benjamin who alerts the animals to Boxer's fate when the
horse is being taken away to be slaughtered. When the animals overthrow the human beings and assume power for
themselves Benjamin remains sceptical of the revolution and
does not share the lofty expectations of the others. He expresses neither praise not criticism of the new regime, contenting
himself with the cryptic expression: 'Donkeys live a long time'.
Farm.

BORIS. A Russian waiter, lame from an arthritic leg, who has led
an adventurous life and looks back upon his soldiering days in
the First World War as a time of great happiness. He is 'a big,
soldierly man of about thirty-five, and had been good looking,
but since his illness he had grown immensely fat from lying in
bed'. He befriends Orwell in Paris and the two share many
experiences of poverty while seeking employment. Eventually
they are successful in finding employment in a restaurant,
Boris as a waiter and Orwell as a dishwasher. Boris cherishes
the ultimate ambition of owning his own restaurant and
becoming rich. *Down and Out*.

BOWLING, GEORGE. Born in 1893 in the Oxfordshire town of
Lower Binfield, the son of a seed-merchant, in middle-age
George looks back with nostalgia to the happy childhood he
spent in the golden years before 1914. After the First World
War he becomes an insurance salesman, eventually being
promoted to an Inspector. He marries the joyless Hilda Vincent and settles down to a humdrum married life in the suburbia of West Bletchley.

Nicknamed 'Fatty' or 'Tubby' because of his ample size,
George reflects that inside every fat man there is a thin man
trying to get out. Always a voracious reader, he is an imaginative man who resents the monotonous life in which he seems
trapped by his work and marriage. He determines to revisit
the scenes of his childhood in order to recapture the sense of
peace and security he knew as a boy. The visit to Lower
Binfield, however, spells complete disillusionment and he
returns to his unhappy home life, convinced that another
world war is imminent. *Air*.

BOWLING, HILDA (*née* VINCENT). The wife of George Bowling,
Hilda first meets him when she is aged twenty-four. She was
then 'a small, slim, rather timid girl, with dark hair, beautiful

movements, and – because of having very large eyes – a distinct resemblance to a hare'. She comes from an Anglo–Indian background and, despite the fact that this is an alien world to George, he is attracted to her and proposes marriage. The marriage is a failure from the outset, since George quickly realises that Hilda lacks 'any kind of joy in life, any kind of interest in things for their own sake'. She speedily degenerates into a carping, brooding wife who is endlessly worrying over money. She and George have two children, Billy and Lorna. When George goes away for a few days, ostensibly on business but in reality to revisit the scenes of his childhood, Hilda refuses to believe his explanation and accuses him of infidelity. *Air*.

BOWLING, MRS. Mother of George Bowling, she is 'a largish woman, a bit taller than Father, with hair a good deal fairer than his and a tendency to wear black dresses'. Hard-working and methodical about the home, she has little interest in or understanding of the world outside. Her favourite reading is *Hilda's Home Companion*, which she devours avidly each week. She is a skilful cook and housekeeper but leaves the running of the family business entirely to her husband. Following his death her own health deteriorates and she dies of cancer while her son George is serving in the First World War. *Air*.

BOWLING, JOE. Eldest son of Samuel Bowling and brother of George. An active, outdoor child, at the age of eight he joins a gang of boys known as 'the Black Hand' who are fond of fishing and bird-nesting. A misfit at school, Joe commences work in a bicycle shop but is incapable of steady effort. After years of loafing about he suddenly leaves home, apparently intending to emigrate to America, and is never heard of again. *Air*.

BOWLING, SAMUEL. Father of George Bowling. For many years he is a corn and seed merchant at 57 High Street, Lower Binfield, a market town in Oxfordshire. He is 'a small man, a sort of grey, quiet little man, always in shirtsleeves and white apron and always dusty-looking because of the meal. He had a round head, a blunt nose, a rather bushy moustache, spectacles, and butter-coloured hair.' An honest, conscientious man, he does his best to provide good service in an increasingly unfavourable economic climate but his business gradually declines and he becomes overwhelmed with financial worries.

When his eldest son leaves home without explanation he is heartbroken and eventually dies of pneumonia in 1915. His business is taken over by Sarazins, a large combine. *Air*.

BOXER. A large cart-horse, 'as strong as any two ordinary horses put together', widely respected on Manor Farm for his loyalty and capacity for hard physical work. He is not of high intelligence but makes an impressive contribution to the labour of the farm by his tremendous strength and willingness to shoulder more than his share of the burden. When the animals rebel against the humans and seize power for themselves Boxer supports the new regime and works for it with great tenacity, always ready to work even harder and trusting implicitly in the altruism of the ruling pigs. Shortly before he is due for retirement he collapses, having worn himself out with the drudgery over a period of many years. To the dismay of the other animals he is taken away to be slaughtered; his friends try to warn him of his fate but it is too late. The pigs allay their fears by asserting that Boxer had died in hospital whilst receiving treatment. *Farm*.

BOZO. A pavement artist who has a pitch on the Embankment near Waterloo Bridge, the son of a bankrupt bookseller. He is 'a small, dark, hook-nosed man, with curly hair growing low on his head'. His manner of talking is 'Cockneyfied and yet very lucid and expressive'. As an artist he specialises in cartoons of a political or sporting nature and looks down on the other screevers (pavement artists) on the Embankment, since he uses painters' colours and not blackboard chalks. He formerly lived in Paris as a house-painter and returned to England after injuring his foot in an accident. He has neither fear nor self-pity and accepts his way of life philosophically. Orwell finds him interesting and describes him as 'a very exceptional man'. *Down and Out*.

BROOKER, MR. An unemployed miner and former publican, he and his invalid wife are the owners of a tripe shop and of dingy lodgings. He is 'a dark, small-boned, sour, Irish-looking man, and astonishly dirty'. As his wife is bed-ridden he spends his time attending to the shop, preparing meals for the lodgers, and, very grudgingly, seeing to the household chores. He has permanently soiled hands and leaves a black thumb-print on slices of bread and butter passed to the lodgers. He hates his life and laments the fact that the shop does not pay and that he cannot attract respectable commercial gentlemen as lodgers. Orwell reflects that Mr Brooker 'was one of those people who can chew their grievances like a cud'. *Wigan*.

BROOKER, MRS. Landlady and owner of a tripe and pea shop in Wigan. She had 'a big, pale yellow, anxious face', and lay 'permanently ill, festooned in grimy blankets'. The real cause of her illness is not known: over-eating is suspected. She dates events by the long intervals between deliveries of frozen tripe. She seldom rises from her sofa in the kitchen and is too immobile to do anything except eat enormous meals. Mrs Brooker's self-pitying talk and the slatternliness of her lodgings eventually drive Orwell away. 'It was not only the dirt,' he reflects, 'the smells, and the vile food, but the feeling of stagnant meaningless decay, of having got down into some subterranean place where people go creeping round and round, just like blackbeetles, in an endless muddle of slovened jobs and mean grievances.' *Wigan*.

CHARRINGTON. The proprietor of an antique and junk-shop, 'a man of perhaps sixty, frail and bowed, with a long, benevolent nose, and mild eyes distorted by thick spectacles'. Winston Smith purchases an album of cream-laid paper from him and this is the beginning of a friendship between them. Later Charrington sells Winston a paperweight and offers the use of the room above the shop for his assignations with his girlfriend, Julia. The frail, aged appearance is however a disguise; Charrington is in reality a member of the Thought Police and he ensures that Winston and Julia are arrested. *1984*.

CLINTOCK [Wateringbury]. A village in Kent, the location of Cairn's farm. Dorothy Hare and her companion Nobby spend several weeks at the farm hop-picking. When the hop-picking season comes to an end Dorothy returns to London from Clintock by train. *Clergyman*.

CLOVER. A large cart-horse, 'a stout motherly mare approaching middle life' and companion to Boxer. Neither she nor Boxer possess high intelligence but both loyally accept the leadership of the pigs and absorb their teachings. As the pigs' regime, under the rule of Napoleon, becomes increasingly ruthless and dictatorial Clover becomes disillusioned. It is she who questions the pigs' walking on their hind legs and observes that ultimately they are indistinguishable from human beings. Although she cannot express her feelings coherently and continues to obey orders she senses that the revolution has failed to achieve the high expectations held out in the early days of the animals' victory. *Farm*.

COMSTOCK, ANGELA. Aunt of Gordon Comstock. She is an aged spinster, a 'poor, shrivelled, parchment-yellow, skin-and-bone' woman who lives alone in a small semi-detached house in Highgate, living off the proceeds of a tiny annuity. Since middle life she has been an inveterate reader of novels but is always twenty years behind current tastes in fiction. *Aspidistra*.

COMSTOCK, GORDON. Son of John Comstock, a chartered accountant, and the last male descendant of the Comstock family. He feels that the Comstocks are 'a peculiarly dull, shabby, dead-alive, ineffectual family. They lacked vitality to an extent that was surprising.' He forsakes his post with the New Albion Publicity Company in order to work as a bookshop assistant, as he feels that only by opting out of commercial life can he express his contempt for 'the money-god'. Gordon has literary ambitions and struggles half-heartedly to write a long poem, *London Pleasures*. He is dismissed from his post in the bookshop because of drunken behaviour and accepts even lower-paid work as custodian of a decrepit lending library. For a time he sinks into a twilight world on the fringe of poverty but his life is transformed when his girl friend, Rosemary, becomes pregnant by him. He decides to renounce his life of poverty, marry Rosemary, and return to his former post in an advertising agency. He is determined that his new home will be adorned with an aspidistra, the symbol of respectability. *Aspidistra*.

COMSTOCK, JULIA. Sister of Gordon Comstock. She is 'a self-effacing, home-keeping, ironing, darning, and mending kind of girl, a natural spinster-soul. Even at sixteen she had "old maid" written all over her.' She idolises her brother and throughout her life makes sacrifices on his behalf. Julia finds employment in a teashop at Earl's Court, where she works long hours in return for low pay. Gordon pities her lonely existence yet begs money from her periodically. Julia subsides into 'the typical submerged life of the penniless unmarried woman; she accepted it, hardly realising that her destiny could ever have been different'. *Aspidistra*.

COMSTOCK, WALTER. Uncle of Gordon Comstock. He has business connections 'in a small way' and lives in a cheap boarding-house in Holland Park. He is a fat, bronchitic man with a pompous face; 'when you looked at him, you found it totally impossible to believe that he had ever been young'. It is Uncle Walter who is responsible for Gordon's first opportunity in life by providing him with the introduction which leads to his first post. Walter's hobby is the study and diagnosis of the numerous diseases from which he imagines he is suffering. *Aspidistra*.

COOKSON, GEORGE. Proprietor of a confectionery and tobacconist's shop in Lower Binfield, he is 'a small stoutish chap, in shirt-sleeves, with a bald head and a big gingery-coloured soup-strainer moustache'. He is married to Elsie Waters, the former lover of George Bowling. *Air*.

CREEVY, MRS. Principal of Ringwood House Academy for Girls. She was 'a woman somewhere in her forties, lean, hard, and angular, with abrupt decided movements that indicated a strong will and probably a vicious temper'. A mean, ruthless and avaricious woman, she engages Dorothy Hare as a schoolmistress but disapproves of her teaching methods, insisting that handwriting and arithmetic alone are of supreme importance. She is obsessed with the collection of the pupils' fees to the exclusion of all other considerations. After two terms at Ringwood House school Dorothy is dismissed by Mrs Creevy without warning. *Clergyman*.

EASTASIA. *See* OCEANIA.

EDBURY [Finsbury]. Orwell and his mate Paddy Jaques walk from Romton [*Romford*] to Edbury, getting lost on the way 'among the desolate north London slums'. They spend a night at the casual ward there. *Down and Out*.

ELLIS. Manager of a company in Kyauktada and a prominent member of the Club. He is 'a tiny wiry-haired fellow with a pale, sharp featured face and restless movements'. When Flory proposes that a non-European should be admitted as a member of the Club Ellis violently opposes the suggestion. In a fit of anger he attacks a group of Burmese schoolboys whom he accuses of insolence; one of the boys is blinded and the incident provokes an attempted assault on the Club. *Burmese*.

EURASIA. *See* OCEANIA.

FLAXMAN. A travelling representative for the Queen of Sheba Toilet Requisites Company and a fellow-lodger with Gordon Comstock at 31 Willowbed Road, NW. A stout, good-humoured man, Flaxman lives in lodgings as he and his wife are temporarily estranged. He attempts to befriend Gordon but Gordon resists his advances on the grounds of poverty. *Aspidistra*.

FLORY, JOHN. A teak extractor stationed at Kyauktada in Upper Burma. He is 'a man of about thirty-five, of middle height, not ill made. He had very black, stiff hair growing low on his head, and a cropped black moustache, and his skin, naturally sallow, was discoloured by the sun . . . The first thing that one noticed in Flory was a hideous birthmark stretching in a ragged crescent down his left cheek, from the eye to the corner of the mouth.' He has lived in Burma since the age of nineteen and become acclimatised to the country and its way of life whilst being profoundly disillusioned with 'pukka sahib' values which he sees in evidence all around him. Years of drinking and womanising, combined with the damp tropical climate have aged him prematurely until he reaches a stage when he is weary and disgusted with his own existence. He is, however, a man of some sensitivity and intelligence and when an English girl, Elizabeth Lackersteen, arrives in Kyauktada he proposes marriage to her and dispenses with his Burmese mistress. The latter denounces him whilst he and Elizabeth are attending a church service. Alone and rejected, unable to face the pointlessness of his life, Flory commits suicide by shooting himself through the heart.

The character resembles Orwell himself not so much in physical appearance as in attitudes and ideas. 'Time passed, and each year Flory found himself less at home in the world of the sahibs, more liable to get into trouble when he talked seriously on any subject whatever. So he had learned to live inwardly, secretly, in books and secret thoughts that could not be uttered.' *Burmese*.

FREDERICK. A neighbour of Mr Jones of Manor Farm, 'a tough, shrewd man, perpetually involved in lawsuits and with a name for driving hard bargains'. After the rebellion on Manor Farm Frederick joins forces with Jones in an attack on the animals (the Battle of the Cowshed) but is ignominiously defeated. Years later, when the animals' regime has become successfully established, he trades with Napoleon but swindles him by paying in counterfeit money. In the Battle of the Windmill Frederick and his men destroy the windmill which has been so laboriously built by the animals. *Farm*.

GOLDSTEIN, EMMANUEL. The Enemy of the People, a traitor upon whom all crimes against the Party are blamed. He has 'a lean Jewish face, with a great fuzzy aureole of white hair and a small goatee beard – a clever face, and yet somehow inherently despicable, with a kind of senile silliness in the long thin nose, near the end of which a pair of spectacles was perched'. Goldstein was formerly one of the leading figures in the Party but had fallen into disgrace because of his alleged counterrevolutionary activities. He escapes from Oceania and writes a subversive book, *The Theory and Practice of Oligarchical Collectivism*, which circulates in secret among those critical of the Party. (The character is apparently based upon that of Trotsky, and his book upon Trotsky's *The Revolution Betrayed*). *1984*.

GRIMMETT, MR. A grocer in Lower Binfield, 'a fine, upstanding, white-whiskered old chap'. He is a Liberal, strongly opposed to trade unions, and active in the Baptist Chapel. A keen businessman, he employs George Bowling as an errand-boy, promoting him to an assistant after six months. During the First World War he becomes intensely patriotic and serves as a member of the local tribunal which considers applications from conscientious objectors. *Air*.

HAMPSTEAD. From October 1934 to January 1936 Orwell worked as a part-time assistant in a secondhand bookshop in Hampstead (Booklovers' Corner, 1 South End Road). From October 1934 to March 1935 he lived at 3 Warwick Mansions, Pond Street, Hampstead and from March–July 1935 at 77 Parliament Hill, Hampstead.

An exaggerated picture of the bookshop is presented in Chapter One of *Aspidistra* and a more accurate account in 'Bookshop Memories' (*CEJL*, Volume 1, 89).

HARE, CHARLES. The Rector of St Athelstan's Church, Knype Hill, Suffolk. He has 'thick, white hair' and a 'pale, fine, none too amiable face'. The younger son of the younger son of a baronet, he is in a state of permanent exasperation due to his poverty and the demands of his post. He cannot afford to employ a curate, and after the death of his wife he leaves much of the work of the parish to his daughter Dorothy whom he starves of money. *Clergyman*.

HARE, DOROTHY. Daughter of the Reverend Charles Hare. She is twenty-eight, with a 'thin, blonde, unremarkable kind of face' and an 'expression of almost childish earnestness in her eyes'. For years Dorothy serves her father and the parish as unpaid curate but one day loses her memory due to overwork and an attempted seduction. She finds herself in London, wandering and penniless, and falls in with a group of down and outs who are on their way to Kent for the hop-picking. She joins forces with them and spends several weeks working on a farm. Eventually she returns to London and finds employment as a teacher at a private school. When she is dismissed from this post Mr Warburton, a former acquaintance from Knype Hill, proposes marriage but she declines the offer. She returns to her home at the rectory and resolves to pick up the threads of her former life. *Clergyman*.

HARE, SIR THOMAS. Cousin of Dorothy Hare. He was 'a widower, a good-hearted, chuckle-headed man of about sixty-five, with an obtuse rosy face and curling moustaches'. Well-meaning but absent minded, he is approached by Dorothy's father following her disappearance with a request that he should attempt to trace Dorothy and find her employment in London. Through the agency of his butler, Blyth, he succeeds in locating her and is instrumental in finding her a post as a school-mistress. *Clergyman*.

HAYES. Orwell lived in Hayes from April 1932 to August 1933 whilst teaching at a private school for boys [The Hawthorns, Church Road]. There is a brief description of Hayes as 'Southbridge' in Chapter Four of *Clergyman*, but the school described in that novel is not intended to be a portrait of The Hawthorns. *See also* SOUTHBRIDGE.

HENLEY-ON-THAMES. During the years 1907–17 the Blair family lived in a number of houses in and around Henley: Nutshell, Western Road, Henley (1907–12); Roselawn, Shiplake (1912–15); and 36 St. Mark's Road, Henley (1915–17). In later years Orwell remembered his childhood there with affection and the district is fictionalised in *Air* as 'Lower Binfield'. 'I suppose Lower Binfield was just like any other market town of about two thousand inhabitants. It was in Oxfordshire . . . about five miles from the Thames. It lay in a bit of a valley, with a low ripple of hills between itself and the Thames, and higher hills behind. On top of the hills there were woods in sort of dim blue masses among which you could see a great white house with a colonnade.' *Air*. (For reminiscences of Orwell at Henley see Buddicom, Jacintha: *Eric and Us*, London, Leslie Frewin, 1974.)

JONES, MR. Owner of the Manor Farm, near Willingdon. The animals are discontented with their lot and, inspired by the teachings of the prize boar, Major, resolve to overthrow him. Whilst he is in a drunken stupor the animals on his farm take advantage of his sleepiness and drive him and his men away. Some months later Jones and his neighbours from the adjoining farms attempt to regain possession by force but are repulsed due to the skilful defensive tactics of the animals. At first the new regime, led by the pigs, works well but as disillusionment among the animals becomes increasingly prevalent they are continually told: 'Surely, comrades, there is no one among you who wants to see Jones come back?' With the passage of time there comes a day when recollections of Jones's rule have faded to the point that the cattle are uncertain whether it was as harsh as the pigs suggest. *Farm*.

JULIA. A young woman employed in the Fiction Department of the Ministry of Truth, 'a bold-looking girl of about twenty-seven, with thick dark hair, a freckled face, and swift, athletic movements'. Outwardly a loyal member of the Party, in private she detests orthodoxy and seeks to rebel against it. She falls in love with Winston Smith, who is employed in the Records Department of the same Ministry. Winston mistrusts her at first but soon comes to return her affection. They embark on a clandestine affair; their meetings have to be arranged with elaborate secrecy since their relationship is a crime against the state. They commence assignations in a room above an antique shop, the proprietor of which, unknown to them, is a member of the Thought Police. After a brief, idyllic friendship they are betrayed into the hands of the Police, arrested and tortured. During their torture they each implicate one another. After their release they meet again but no longer feel any emotional attraction. *1984*.

KNYPE HILL [Southwold]. A town of two thousand inhabitants in Suffolk. 'The two pivots, or foci, about which the social life of the town moved were the Knype Hill Conservative Club . . . and Ye Olde Tea Shoppe, a little farther down the High Street, the principal rendezvous of the Knype Hill ladies.' The town is divided by the High Street, running east and west.

The southern section is ancient and predominantly agricul-
tural; the northern side is modern and industrial. *See also*
SOUTHWOLD. *Clergyman*.

KOPP, GEORGES. The Belgian commander of the POUM militia
in which Orwell served during the Spanish Civil War. He and
Orwell become firm friends, Orwell being deeply impressed
with his courage and coolness at times of crisis. When the
POUM is suppressed, Kopp is imprisoned without trial and
Orwell attempts in vain to intercede on his behalf, even
though by doing so he is risking his own life. *Homage*.

KYAUKTADA [Katha]. A small town in Upper Burma, the scene
of the events described in *Burmese*. 'Kyauktada was a fairly
typical Upper Burma town, that had not changed greatly
between the days of Marco Polo and 1910, and might have
slept in the Middle Ages for a century more if it had not
proved a convenient spot for a railway terminus.' The description of the town and its surrounding countryside is based upon
that of Katha, north of Mandalay, where Orwell was
stationed in the spring of 1927.

KYIN, U PO. The sub-divisional magistrate of Kyauktada. He is 'a
man of fifty, so fat that for years he had not risen from his
chair without help, and yet shapely and even beautiful in his
grossness . . . His face was vast, yellow and quite unwrinkled,
and his eyes were tawny.' Totally unprincipled and devious,
for many years he leads a life of corruption, bribery and
intrigue. His overriding ambition is to be elected as a member
of the Club, a goal he eventually achieves after many setbacks.
Before his retirement he is promoted to the rank of Deputy
Commissioner but dies of apoplexy shortly after being honoured at a durbar. (In the first English edition of 1935 the
character is named 'U Po Sing', but is named 'U Po Kyin' in
the original edition published in the United States in 1934 and
in all English editions after 1944.) *Burmese*.

LACKERSTEEN, ELIZABETH. A young orphaned English girl, the
daughter of a tea-broker, who arrives in Kyauktada in Upper
Burma as guests of her uncle and aunt. 'Her face was oval,
with delicate, regular features; not beautiful, perhaps, but it
seemed so there, in Burma, where all Englishwomen are yellow and thin.' Brought up in Paris in an artistic menage, she
develops a mistrust of culture and book learning and a liking
for an active, outdoor life. When she is menaced by water-

buffaloes Flory comes to her rescue and she is for a time attracted by his manliness. She is, however, repelled by many of his attitudes and by his physical ugliness. When she learns that he has kept a Burmese mistress she abandons Flory in favour of the dashing Lieutenant Verrall; this flirtation comes to an abrupt end when Verrall leaves the district without warning. For a brief period she is reconciled to Flory but finally rejects him when he is publicly denounced by his former mistress. Eventually Elizabeth marries Mr Macgregor, the Deputy Commissioner, and settles down to 'the position for which Nature had designed her from the first, that of a burra memsahib', i.e., a married European lady. *Burmese*.

LACKERSTEEN, MR. The manager of a timber firm at Kyauktada. He is 'a florid, fine-looking, slightly bloated man of forty . . . He had a beefy, ingenuous face, with a toothbrush moustache'. He has a weakness for alcohol and women and his one obsession is to devise methods of indulging these appetites without being observed by his domineering wife. *Burmese*.

LACKERSTEEN, MRS. Aunt of Elizabeth Lackersteen and wife of the manager of a timber firm. She is 'handsome in a contourless, elongated way, like a fashion plate. She had a sighing, discontented voice.' She governs her husband 'by the only possible method, namely, by never letting him out of her sight for more than an hour or two.' When Elizabeth's mother dies she invites her niece to stay with her at Kyauktada as her guest, confident that Elizabeth will experience no difficulty in meeting an eligible gentleman in Burma. *Burmese*.

LONDON. Orwell lived at various addresses in London for much of his working life: 10 Portobello Road, Notting Hill, autumn 1927–spring 1928; 2 Windsor Street, Paddington, October–November 1931; 3 Warwick Mansions, Pond Street, Hampstead, October 1934–February 1935; 77 Parliament Hill, Hampstead, March–July 1935; 50, Lawford Road, Kentish Town, August 1935–January 1936; 18 Dorset Chambers, Chagford Street, Regents Park, May 1940–March 1941; 111 Langford Court, Abbey Road, St. Johns Wood, April 1941–summer 1942; 10a Mortimer Crescent, Maida Vale, summer 1942–June 1944; 27b Canonbury Square, Islington, October 1944–December 1948.

Much of the action of *Down and Out* takes place in and around London (see especially Chapters 24–38).

Dorothy Hare returns to consciousness after her attack of amnesia to find herself wandering on the New Kent Road. She travels to Kent to work as a hop-picker, and after returning to London occupies dingy lodgings in Wellings Court, off Lambeth Cut. After leaving this address she spends ten days living as a tramp, spending the nights in Trafalgar Square, before obtaining a post as a schoolmistress in a London suburb. *Clergyman*.

Gordon Comstock lives in lodgings at Willowbed Road, NW, whilst working as an assistant at McKechnie's bookshop. Later he occupies a furnished bed-sitting room 'in a filthy alley parallel to Lambeth Cut' whilst looking after the twopenny library at Mr Cheeseman's bookshop in Lambeth. *Aspidistra*.

George Bowling lives at 191 Ellesmere Road, West Bletchley, one of those identical streets which 'fester all over the inner-outer suburbs'. Prior to his marriage he lodges in a boarding-house in Ealing. *Air*.

Much of the story of *1984* takes place in and around London. The central character, Winston Smith, lives in a decaying block of flats, Victory Mansions, built in 1930. On his walks he explores neglected corners of the city, observing the drab landscape of crumbling buildings and bombed sites.

LOVEGROVE, SID. Younger son of a saddler and leader of a gang of boys known as 'the Black Hand'. He and his friends share many boyhood adventures with George Bowling and accompany him on fishing expeditions. He joins the army during the First World War and is killed in action on the Somme. *Air*.

LOWER BINFIELD. *See* HENLEY-ON-THAMES.

LOWER BINFIELD. A town in Kent, near Ide Hill [possibly Sevenoaks] where Orwell and his mate Paddy spend the night in a casual ward. They walk to Lower Binfield from Cromley [Bromley]. Not to be confused with previous entry. *Down and Out*.

MAJOR. A prize boar owned by Mr Jones of the Manor Farm. He is 'a majestic-looking pig, with a wise and benevolent appearance in spite of the fact that his tushes [tusks] had never been cut'. Shortly before his death Major summons the other animals together and imparts to them his conviction that the human race must be overthrown before the animals can enjoy the fruits of their labours. He instils into them the message that 'Weak or strong, clever or simple, we are all brothers. No animal must ever kill any other animal. All animals are equal.' Major's vision of a world without human beings acts as the spur to the animals in ousting Mr Jones. Later the pigs elaborate his teachings into a complete system of thought, known as Animalism. In death he is revered and his skull becomes an object of veneration. *Farm*.

MAY, MA HLA. The Burmese mistress of John Flory. She has a 'queer, youthful face, with its high cheekbones, stretched eyelids and short, shapely lips . . . She was like a doll, with her oval, still face the colour of new copper, and her narrow eyes; an outlandish doll and yet a grotesquely beautiful one.' Flory has a relationship with her for some years but abruptly abandons her when an English girl, Elizabeth Lackersteen, enters his life. Incited by the scheming U Po Kyin, Ma Hla May demands money from Flory and humiliates him by denouncing him in public whilst he is attending a church service. After Flory's suicide she enters a brothel in Mandalay, looking back on her past life with bitterness. *Burmese*.

MACGREGOR, MR. Deputy Commissioner of Kyauktada and secretary of the Club. He is 'a large, heavy man, rather past forty, with a kindly, puggy face, wearing gold-rimmed spectacles. His bulky shoulders, and a trick he had of thrusting his head forward, reminded one curiously of a turtle – the Burmans, in fact, nicknamed him "the tortoise".' Macgregor is a good-hearted man who seeks to administer the town and the Club with fairness. After Flory's death he proposes marriage to Elizabeth Lackersteen and is accepted gladly. *Burmese*.

McKECHNIE, MR. The 'rather dilapidated' proprietor of a second-hand bookshop in London. He is 'a sleepy, benign old Scotchman with a red nose and a white beard stained by snuff'; he seldom enters the shop but drowses by the gas-fire in the room above, immersed in calf-bound copies of the classics. A teetotaller and a nonconformist, he employs Gordon Comstock as an assistant but dismisses him when Gordon is found guilty of being drunk and disorderly. *Aspidistra*.

MINNS, MISS. A spinster who befriends Hilda Bowling, she is 'a tall thin woman of about thirty-eight, with black patent-leather hair and a very *good*, trusting kind of face'. Out of loneliness she makes friends with Hilda and Mrs Wheeler, and the three of them set out to 'develop their minds' by joining in turn a wide assortment of movements and societies. George Bowling is convinced that her father was a clergyman who 'sat on her pretty heavily while he lived'. *Air.*

MOLLIE. The 'foolish, pretty white mare who drew Mr. Jones's trap'. She is vain and cowardly, having been pampered by Jones. When the other animals eject the human beings from the farm she is unsympathetic with the aims of the rebellion, as she was more comfortable under the old regime than under the new one. Mollie avoids work as much as possible and seeks an opportunity to leave Animal Farm and return to the indulgent life she had known. Finally she is tempted away by sugar and ribbons, deserts her companions and finds happiness working for a publican. She is seen by the pigeons 'between the shafts of a smart dogcart'. *Farm.*

MOSES. A tame raven kept on Manor Farm. He was 'Mr. Jones's especial pet, a spy and a tale-bearer, but he was also a clever talker'. He claims to know of the existence of a paradise called Sugarcandy Mountain to which animals go when they die. Moses is disliked by the other animals since he does not work and tells tales. He disappears from the farm after the rebellion and does not return until some years later. He is tolerated by the ruling pigs though they declare that his stories are lies; many of the animals now believe in his descriptions of a better world elsewhere. *Farm.*

NAPOLEON. A young boar who rapidly assumes the leadership of Animal Farm. He is 'a large, rather fierce-looking Berkshire boar, the only Berkshire on the farm, not much of a talker, but with a reputation for getting his own way'. After the rebellion in which Mr Jones is overthrown he and another pig, Snowball, are pre-eminent among the animals. Rivalry between them intensifies until at length Snowball is expelled from the farm, leaving Napoleon in unchallenged command. Napoleon gradually becomes more and more dictatorial and at the same time adopts human characteristics such as living in the farmhouse, drinking alcohol and walking on two legs. At last, when he and the other pigs have established a tyranny over all the other animals, it becomes impossible to detect the difference between pigs and men. *Farm.*

NOBBY. A down and out whom Dorothy Hare encounters in London whilst on his way to Kent for the hop-picking. He was 'about twenty-six, squat, nimble, and powerful, with a snub nose, a clear pink skin and huge lips as coarse as sausages, exposing strong yellow teeth'. He and his companions Flo and Charlie befriend Dorothy and journey to Kent together. Despite his poverty he is a cheerful man, for 'he had that happy temperament that is incapable of taking its own reverses very seriously'. He is drawn to Dorothy by her loneliness and protects her during the weeks she spends on the farm but eventually he is arrested for stealing apples. *Clergyman*.

O'BRIEN. A member of the Inner Party, 'a large, burly man with a thick neck and a coarse, humorous, brutal face. In spite of his formidable appearance he had a certain charm of manner.' Winston Smith befriends him, mistrusting him yet attracted by O'Brien's intelligence and urbanity. Winston assumes that O'Brien is a member of the Brotherhood, an underground movement dedicated to the overthrow of the Party. Whilst encouraging this belief, he is in fact a fanatical supporter of the ruling regime. Winston is eventually arrested and tortured by O'Brien in the cells of the Ministry of Love. O'Brien believes that reality exists 'only in the mind of the Party, which is collective and immortal. Whatever the Party holds to be truth, *is* truth.' *1984*.

OCEANIA. One of the three great super-states in the year 1984, perpetually at war with Eurasia or Eastasia or both. Oceania comprises the Americas, the Atlantic islands including the British Isles, Australasia, and the southern portion of Africa. Eurasia comprises the whole of the northern part of Europe and Asia; Eastasia comprises China, Japan, Manchuria, Mongolia and Tibet. Fighting between the super-states, in one combination or another, has been continuous since 1960. The wars are not fought for ideological reasons but for the possession of the disputed territories lying between their frontiers, a source of cheap and abundant labour power. The supreme power throughout Oceania is 'the Party' which rules through the agency of four omnipresent Ministries. *1984*.

PADDY. An Irish tramp who befriends Orwell during his 'down and out' experiences. 'He was a tallish man, aged about thirty-five, with fair hair going grizzled and watery blue eyes. His features were good, but his cheeks had lanked and had that greyish, dirty in the grain look that comes of a bread and margarine diet.' He has been unemployed for two years and, although ashamed of the life, he has acquired the habits and philosophy of the tramp. He is ignorant and self-pitying but is generous by nature; he shares what little food he has with Orwell and the two of them are mates for two weeks during their wanderings around London casual wards. Eventually they part company and Paddy sets out for Portsmouth in search of work. Orwell believes that Paddy was 'a typical tramp and there are tens of thousands in England like him'. *Down and Out*.

PARIS. Orwell lived in Paris from the spring of 1928 to the end of 1929, lodging at 6 Rue du Pot de Fer in the fifth *arrondissement*. The area figures in *Down and Out* as the 'Rue de Coq d'Or'.

  Paris is the setting of Chapters 1–23 of *Down and Out* and also of the essay 'How the Poor Die'. Elizabeth Lackersteen in *Burmese* lives for some years in Paris when her mother has a studio in the Montparnasse quarter.

PARSONS. A tenant at Victory Mansions and neighbour of Winston Smith. He is 'a tubby, middle-sized man with fair hair and a froglike face. At thirty-five he was already putting on rolls of fat at neck and waistline, but his movements were brisk and boyish.' He constantly exudes a smell of sweat and is addicted to wearing shorts. He is employed in a subordinate post at the Ministry of Truth but, unlike Winston, his attitude is one of unquestioning loyalty to the Party. His children are zealous members of a patriotic youth organisation, the Spies, and his daughter ultimately betrays him to the Thought Police for talking in his sleep. *1984*.

PARSONS, MRS. Wife of Parsons, a fellow-employee of Winston Smith at the Ministry of Truth. She is a careworn woman of about thirty but looks much older. 'One had the impression that there was dust in the creases of her face.' Her dingy, untidy flat in Victory Mansions has a smell of boiled cabbage and perspiration and she lives in constant terror of her boisterous children, fanatical supporters of the Party. *1984*.

PENNYFIELDS [Limehouse Causeway]. The scene of Orwell's first experience of staying in a lodging-house. The experience is described in detail in Chapter 25 of *Down and Out* and also in Chapter 9 of *Wigan Pier*.

PILKINGTON. A neighbour of Mr Jones of Manor Farm, 'an easy-going gentleman farmer who spent most of his time in fishing or hunting according to the season'. He owns

Foxwood, a large, neglected farm notable for its worn-out pastures and overgrown woods and hedges. After the rebellion on Manor Farm Pilkington joins forces with Jones and another neighbour, Frederick, in an unsuccessful attack on the animals. With the passage of time relations between Pilkington and the animals become more friendly until at last they are allies. At a conference Pilkington proposes a toast to Animal Farm, expressing his pleasure that 'a long period of mistrust and misunderstanding had now come to an end'. *Farm*.

PITHER, MRS. The ailing and pious wife of a jobbing gardener. She led 'a dreary, wormlike life of shuffling to and fro, with a perpetual crick in her neck because the door lintels were too low for her, between the well, the sink, the fireplace, and the tiny plot of kitchen garden'. She suffers agonies with rheumatism but solaces herself against the trials of this world with thoughts of Heaven. Ultimately her rheumatism is cured by drinking angelica tea. *Clergyman*.

PORTEOUS. A retired public-school master and a bachelor, Porteous is a friend of George Bowling. He is 'rather a striking looking chap, very tall, with curly grey hair and a thin, dreamy kind of face that's a bit discoloured but might almost belong to a boy, though he must be nearly sixty'. He leads a cultured, bookish life immersed in poetry and Greek and Latin classics. Bowling enjoys his conversations with Porteous but one evening has an argument with him concerning Hitler. Porteous takes the view that Hitler is of no consequence and Bowling finally realises that 'a man really dies when his brain stops, when he loses the power to take in a new idea'. In this sense Porteous is already dead, a man incapable of change and resistant to new concepts. *Air*.

RAVELSTON, PHILIP. Editor of the monthly journal *Antichrist*. Ravelston is a wealthy man who befriends Gordon Comstock and does much to encourage his literary ambitions. 'He was very tall, with a lean, wide-shouldered body and the typical lounging grace of the upper-class youth.' He offers Gordon practical help and gifts of money which the latter feels unable to accept since such help cannot be repaid. When Gordon becomes involved in a drunken fracas Ravelston pays the fine on his behalf and provides him with accommodation until he can find alternative lodgings. Ravelston is the only friend who is present at Gordon's wedding. He 'had not merely a charm of manner, but also a kind of fundamental decency, a graceful attitude to life, which Gordon scarcely encountered elsewhere'. *Aspidistra*.

ROMTON [Romford]. The setting of Chapters 26 and 27 of *Down and Out*, in which Orwell and his mate Paddy spend the night in a spike (casual ward) and also take part in a religious service.

SEMPRILL, MRS. The town scandalmonger of Knype Hill and a source of much scurrilous gossip. 'She was a slender woman of forty, with a lank, sallow, distinguished face, which, with her glossy dark hair and air of settled melancholy, gave her something of the appearance of a Van Dyck portrait.' She sees Warburton embracing Dorothy Hare on the evening of Dorothy's disappearance from the town and spreads the rumour that the two have eloped together. Her career as a scandalmonger is brought to an end when she is sued for libel. *Clergyman*.

SMITH, KATHARINE. Wife of Winston Smith. She was 'a tall, fair-haired girl, very straight, with splendid movements. She had a bold, aquiline face, a face that one might have called noble until one discovered that there was as nearly as possible nothing behind it.' After their marriage Winston soon becomes disillusioned with her shallowness and lack of initiative and finds her submission to his sexual advances embarrassing. He nicknames her 'the human sound-track'. They agree to separate after fifteen months together. *1984*.

SMITH, WINSTON. A thirty-nine year old employee of the Ministry of Truth. He is described as 'a smallish, frail figure, the meagreness of his body merely emphasised by the blue overalls which were the uniform of the Party. His hair was very fair, his face naturally sanguine, his skin roughened by coarse soap and blunt razor blades and the cold of the winter that had just ended.' Although he is a member of the ruling Party, Winston becomes increasingly critical of the autocratic regime in Oceania and secretly dissents from many of its principles. At first his dissent takes the form of recording his private thoughts in a diary which he keeps hidden in his apartment. He continues with this practice even though he is aware that it is an offence punishable by death. At the Ministry he meets a girl employed in the Fiction Department,

Julia, who declares her love for him. Together they embark on a clandestine affair, fully realising that they are risking exposure and arrest by the secret police. Determined to express their rebellion in practical activity they attempt to join the Brotherhood, an underground movement dedicated to the overthrow of the Party. Unwittingly, however, they are betrayed into the hands of the Thought Police, arrested and tortured. After their release they meet again but no longer feel any affection for one another. Winston has lost his will to resist. 'He had won the victory over himself. He loved Big Brother.' *1984*.

SNOWBALL. A young boar who, acting at first in partnership with another boar, Napoleon, assumes the leadership of Animal Farm. He was 'a more vivacious pig than Napoleon, quicker in speech and more inventive, but was not considered to have the same depth of character'. The two pigs frequently disagree over policy and tactics, Napoleon arguing that the animals must arm themselves and defend the farm, Snowball arguing that they must not be content with a rebellion on one farm only but should foment revolution among animals on other farms. At length Napoleon succeeds in expelling Snowball by unleashing a pack of dogs on him. From this point onwards Snowball is blamed for the misfortunes which befall the farm. He is alleged to have agents acting as spies on his behalf and some of the animals confess to crimes allegedly instigated by him. *Farm*.

SOUTHBRIDGE [Hayes]. A 'repellent suburb ten or a dozen miles from London', the location of the Ringwood House Academy for Girls. Dorothy Hare is a teacher at Southbridge for a short time but is eventually dismissed from her post. She travels from Southbridge to London *en route* for Knype Hill. *See also* HAYES. *Clergyman*.

SOUTHWOLD. Orwell's parents lived at Southwold, Suffolk from December 1921 until 1942. The family lived first at 40 Stradbroke Road (1921–7); then at 3 Queen Street (1927–33); and finally at Montague House, 36 High Street (1933–42). Orwell lived with his parents intermittently from January 1930 to April 1932 and again from January to October 1934. The town is described in Chapter One of *Clergyman* as 'Knype Hill'. *See also* KNYPE HILL.

SQUEALER. A small fat pig, the best known of the male pigs on

Manor Farm. He has 'very round cheeks, twinkling eyes, nimble movements, and a shrill voice. He was a brilliant talker, and when he was arguing some difficult point he had a way of skipping from side to side and whisking his tail which was somehow very persuasive.' It is Squealer who, together with Snowball and Napoleon, elaborates Major's teachings into a complete system of thought which they term Animalism. After the rebellion, as Napoleon gathers more and more power into his own hands and the original principles of Animalism are gradually abandoned Squealer becomes Napoleon's mouthpiece, justifying his actions and glossing over the dilution of his ideals. *Farm.*

SYME. A specialist in Newspeak who befriends Winston Smith. He was a small man 'with dark hair and large, protuberant eyes, at once mournful and derisive, which seemed to search your face closely while he was speaking to you'. On political matters Syme is orthodox and zealously patriotic but on his special subject, the technicalities of language, he is learned and interesting. He is one of a team of experts engaged on the compilation of a Newspeak Dictionary, the aim of which is 'to narrow the range of thought'. Winston senses that Syme is too intellectual and bohemian and that sooner or later he will be vaporised (executed) by the Thought Police. *1984.*

TILBURY. Orwell arrived at Tilbury after his Parisian experiences and describes a hotel on the waterside whose flamboyant architecture astonishes his Rumanian fellow-travellers. *Down and Out.*

VERASWAMI, DR. An Indian doctor, the only real friend Flory has in Kyauktada. He is 'a small, black, plump man with fuzzy hair and round, credulous eyes . . . His voice was eager and bubbling, with a hissing of the s's.' Idealistic and cultured, the doctor has a high regard for English civilisation and its values. When Flory proposes him for membership of the Club, an exclusively English domain, Veraswami is deeply honoured but makes it clear that he would never presume to attend. The doctor is the subject of a campaign of vilification organised by the wily magistrate U Po Kyin, who regards him as a potential rival. After Flory's death Veraswami is left without an ally and is eventually demoted to the rank of Assistant Surgeon in another district. (In the first English edition of 1935 the character is named 'Dr. Murkhaswami', but is named 'Veraswami' in the original edition published in the United States in 1934 and in all English editions after 1944.) *Burmese*.

VERRALL. A lieutenant in the Burmese Military Police, the youngest son of a peer, who is stationed for a short time at Kyauktada. 'He was a youth of about twenty-five, lank but very straight, and manifestly a cavalry officer. He had one of those rabbit-like faces common among English soldiers. with pale blue eyes and a little triangle of fore-teeth visible between the lips;. yet hard, fearless and even brutal in a careless fashion.' He is obsessed with horses and polo, abhorring women and all social duties. While at Kyauktada he pointedly leads his own life, ignoring the English community, until he encounters Elizabeth Lackersteen. He embarks on a flirtation with her for some weeks; she feels confident that he will propose marriage but from his point of view she is merely an agreeable diversion. Their friendship is terminated abruptly when he leaves the district without warning. *Burmese*.

WALLINGTON. Orwell lived at The Stores, Wallington, Hertford-shire from April 1936 to May 1940 and retained it as a holiday cottage until 1947. Here he wrote *The Road to Wigan Pier*. He and his wife ran The Stores as a village shop and also tended a plot of land and reared hens and goats. He drew on his memories of Wallington in some of the 'Lower Binfield' reminiscences in *Air*; the village also figures as 'Willingdon' in *Farm*. (The Stores has since been renamed Monk's Fitchett.) For an account of the Orwell's life at Wallington see Stansky and Abrahams, *Orwell: The Transformation*, pp. 136–40, 162–8.

WARBURTON, MR. A painter residing in one of the new villas behind Knype Hill rectory. He was 'a fine, imposing-looking man, though entirely bald . . . and he carried himself with such a rakish air as to give the impression that his fairly sizeable belly was merely a kind of annexe to his chest'. He attempts to seduce Dorothy Hare on more than one occasion and finally proposes marriage to her. After a lengthy conversation together on a train she declines his offer despite his fore-cast that she will end her life as an impoverished spinster. *Clergyman*.

WATERINGBURY. A village in Kent, five miles SW of Maidstone. In September 1931 Orwell spent eighteen days hop-picking at Home Farm, sleeping on straw in a barn. The experience is described in his essay 'Hop-Picking' and in Chapter Two of

Clergyman, where the village figures as 'Clintock'.

WATERLOW, ROSEMARY. Girl friend (and eventually wife) of Gordon Comstock. The daughter of a country solicitor and one of fourteen children, she is a few months younger than Gordon. 'She was a strong, agile girl, with stiff black hair, a small triangular face, and very pronounced eyebrows. It was one of those small, peaky faces, full of character, which one sees in sixteenth-century portraits.' Gordon first makes her acquaintance at the advertising agency where they are both employed, he in the office and she in the studio. She has a kindly, magnanimous nature and adores Gordon despite his waywardness and lack of ambition. She and Gordon continue to be close friends after he has deliberately embarked on a life of poverty but rejects his advances when he attempts intercourse without a contraceptive. Later she relents and permits him to make love to her. Gordon decides to marry Rosemary when he learns that she is expecting his child, and resolves henceforth to lead a life of suburban respectability. *Aspidistra*.

WATERS, ELSIE. George Bowling first meets Elsie Waters in the vicar's Reading Circle in the year 1912. She is tall and pretty, 'with pale gold, heavy kind of hair which she wore somehow plaited and coiled round her head, and a delicate, curiously gentle face'. She is employed as an assistant at Lilywhite's the drapers and George befriends her. The two become lovers and for a time enjoy an idyllic romance but lose touch with one another when George enlists in the army in 1914. Twenty-four years later Bowling revisits the town in which he spent his childhood and encounters Elsie again, only to find that she has altered in appearance almost beyond recognition. She has become fat and slovenly and is married to a George Cookson, confectioner and tobacconist. Despite their former association she does not recognise Bowling at all; the deterioration in her appearance leads him to reflect on the sharp contrast between her present self and the lovely girl he had known. *Air*.

WHEELER, MRS. A widow who befriends Hilda Bowling, she is 'a faded little women and gives you a curious impression that she's the same colour all over, a kind of greyish dust-colour'. She has a passion for economising and 'making do' and takes an interest in all manner of societies and good causes, provided that the outlay is minimal. She becomes an enthusiastic supporter of the Left Book Club. *Air*.

WHYMPER. A solicitor living in Willingdon who agrees to act as an intermediary between Animal Farm and the neighbouring farmers. He is 'a sly-looking little man with side whiskers, a solicitor in a very small way of business, but sharp enough to have realised earlier than anyone else that Animal Farm would need a broker and that the commissions would be worth having'. Whymper conducts negotiations on behalf of the animals with the neighbouring farmers, Frederick and Pilkington, and is deceived by Napoleon into thinking that the farm is prosperous when in reality it has fallen on hard times. He arranges a number of trade agreements with other farmers, despite Major's original injunction: 'No animal must ever . . . touch money, or engage in trade'. *Farm*.

WIGAN. Orwell visited Wigan during February 1936 whilst gathering information on poverty, housing and unemployment amongst the Lancashire miners. He stayed in lodgings on Warrington Lane and on Darlington Road: the latter over a tripe shop (the 'Brookers'). His impressions of the town and its people are recorded in *CEJL* Volume 1, 74, and in *Wigan*, Chapters 1–7.

WILLINGDON. *See* WALLINGTON.

WISBEACH, MRS. The inquisitive landlady of 31 Willowbed Road, NW in which Gordon Comstock has a bed-sitting-room. She was 'one of those malignant respectable women who keep lodging-houses. Aged about forty-five, stout but active, with a pink, fine-featured, horribly observant face, beautiful grey hair, and a permanent grievance.' Gordon leads a furtive, squalid existence in her lodgings since he feels that he is always being watched and has no privacy. Her dining-room contains innumerable aspidistras. *Aspidistra*.

Appendix

1. FILM VERSIONS

The following outline contains details of the principal film versions of Orwell's novels.

Animal Farm (1955)
    Production company: Louis de Rochemont
    Written and produced by John Halas and Joy Batchelor
    Voices: Maurice Denham
    Running Time 75 minutes
    Filmed in Technicolour

    The first full-length animated cartoon to be produced by a British company, this is a straightforward and faithful adaptation of Orwell's satire.

1984 (1956)
    Made at Associated British Studios
    Released by Associated British-Pathé
    Executive Producer: N. Peter Rathvon
    Producer: John Croydon
    Director: Michael Anderson
    Photography: C. Pennington Richards
    Art Director: Terence Verity
    Editing: Bill Lewthwaite
    Screenplay: William P. Templeton and Ralph Bettinson
    Music: Malcolm Arnold
    The film starred Edmond O'Brien as Winston Smith and Jan Sterling as Julia. The supporting cast included Michael Redgrave, David Kossoff, Mervyn Johns and Donald Pleasence.

Running time 91 minutes
Filmed in black and white

This is a reasonably accurate version of *Nineteen Eighty-Four*,
but in adapting the rather complex narrative for the screen
much of the literary insight of the original story has been lost.

2. ORWELL'S METHOD OF COMPOSITION

When writing a novel Orwell's method of composition was to
prepare a complete first draft, which usually bore little resemblance to the final version. This rough draft was then thoroughly
and drastically revised, a process taking many months.

The process may be illustrated by comparing the opening
paragraph of *Nineteen Eighty-Four* in the first and final versions:

> It was a cold blowy day in April, and a million radios were
> striking thirteen. Winston Smith pushed open the glass door of
> Victory Mansions, turned to the right down the passage-way
> and pressed the button for the lift. Nothing happened. He had
> just pressed a second time when a door at the end of the
> passage opened letting out a smell of boiled greens and old rag
> mats, and the aged prole who acted as porter and caretaker
> thrust out a grey, seamed face sucking his teeth and watching
> Winston malignantly.
>
> (First Draft)
>
> It was a bright cold day in April, and the clocks were striking
> thirteen. Winston Smith, his chin nuzzled into his breast in an
> effort to escape the vile wind, slipped quickly through the glass
> doors of Victory Mansions, though not quickly enough to pre-
> vent a swirl of gritty dust from entering along with him. The
> hallway smelt of boiled cabbage and old rag mats.
>
> (Final Version)

The final version, with which readers will be most familiar,
clearly represents a considerable improvement on the rough
draft. The difference between the two versions is not so much
one of style as of language; the final text embodies a marked
tautening of narrative in addition to such literary touches as the
substitution of 'a bright cold day' for 'a cold blowy day', and so

on. But in transforming the draft into the published version
Orwell has not simply made minor textual amendments but
fundamental revisions: this is the essence of his creative method.

It is interesting to contrast Orwell's method of composition
with that employed by Wells and Dickens. Wells's method has
been described as 'largely quantitative rather than qualitative
. . . the typical Wells draft manuscript is a relatively unmolested
central text with insertions in the form of balloons crowding the
margins'. (Harris Wilson in the Appendix to *The Wealth of Mr.
Waddy* by H. G. Wells.) Dickens employed a similar method,
frequently altering words and phrases but rarely making *fundamental* alterations to his first draft.

The reader interested in pursuing these comparisons further is
referred to the following sources:

Orwell
Bernard Crick, *George Orwell: A Life* (especially the final
  chapter and Appendix A)
George Orwell, *The Collected Essays, Journalism and Letters*

Wells
H. G. Wells, *The Wealth of Mr. Waddy* Edited by Harry Wilson
  (Southern Illinois University Press, 1969)
H. G. Wells, *The History of Mr. Polly* Edited by Gordon N. Ray
  (Houghton Mifflin Company, 1960)

Dickens
John Butt and Kathleen Tillotson, *Dickens at Work* (Methuen,
  1957)
Michael Patrick Hearn, *The Annotated Christmas Carol* (Clark-
  son N. Potter, 1976)

References

The following abbreviations are used throughout:

CEJL	*Collected Essays, Journalism and Letters*
Crick	Crick, Bernard, *George Orwell*
CUA	*Coming Up For Air*
DOPL	*Down and Out in Paris and London*
HTC	*Homage to Catalonia*
KAF	*Keep the Aspidistra Flying*
RWP	*The Road to Wigan Pier*
Woodcock	Woodcock, George, *The Crystal Spirit*

The reference numbers for *CEJL* are *item*, not page, numbers.

PART I

1. Woodcock, 11.
2. 'A Good Word for the Vicar of Bray': *CEJL* 4, 44.
3. Stansky and Abrahams, *The Unknown Orwell*, 40.
4. 'Such, Such Were the Joys', III.
5. Leslie Frewin, London, 1974.
6. Op. cit., 37–8.
7. Stansky and Abrahams, op. cit., 73.
8. *Observer*, 1 August 1948 (not included in *CEJL*).
9. Cf. his essay 'Good Bad Books', *CEJL* 4, 6.
10. *RWP*, Chapter 7.
11. The verses are quoted in full in Crick, pp. 99–100.
12. *CEJL* 2, 7.
13. *RWP*, Chapter 9.
14. *CEJL* 1, 33.
15. *CEJL* 1, 23.
16. *CEJL* 2, 6.
17. Stansky and Abrahams, op. cit., 254.
18. *CEJL* 1, 20.

19. *CEJL* 1, 56.
20. 'Why I Write': *CEJL* 1, 1.
21. 'The Limit to Pessimism', *CEJL* 1, 167.
22. Wartime Diary, 9 August 1940.
23. Wartime Diary, 16 August 1940.
24. Crick, 287.
25. See his diary entry for 20 June 1940: 'Thinking always of my islands in the Hebrides, which I suppose I shall never possess nor even see'.
26. *CEJL* 4, 162.
27. Warburg, F. J., *All Authors are Equal*, 120.
28. Wilson, Edmund, 'Dickens: The Two Scrooges' in *The Wound and the Bow* (Methuen, London, 1961).
29. Wells, H. G., *Tono-Bungay*, Book 1, Chapter 1.
30. *CEJL* 4, 167.
31. *HTC*, Chapter 1.
32. Potts, Paul: *Dante Called You Beatrice* (Eyre & Spottiswoode, London, 1961).
33. Heppenstall, Rayner: *Four Absentees* (Barrie and Rockliff, London, 1960).
34. 'Why I Write'.
35. Crick, xiii.
36. Burgess, Anthony: *1985* (Hutchinson, London, 1978).
37. 'George Gissing', *CEJL* 4, 119.
38. 'Why I Write'.
39. *CEJL* 1, 52.
40. See his essays 'Charles Dickens', 'George Gissing' and 'Wells, Hitler and the World State'.
41. *CEJL* 4, 56.
42. *CEJL* 1, 84.
43. Crick, 325.
44. *CEJL* 1, 62.
45. For a detailed study of the Bildungsroman as a literary form see J. H. Buckley: *Season of Youth: The Bildungsroman from Dickens to Golding* (Harvard University Press, 1974).
46. *CEJL* 1, 146, Cf. Crick, 262–3.
47. *CEJL* 4, 115.
48. 'Looking Back on the Spanish War'.
49. 'George Gissing'.
50. Rees, Richard: *George Orwell*, 140.
51. 'Why I Write'.
52. Woodcock, 243.
53. *English Conservatism Adrift: The Twentieth Century*, 336.
54. *CEJL* 1, 3.
55. *CEJL* 1, 7.
56. *HTC*, Chapter 12.
57. Quoted in Miriam Gross (ed.), *The World of George Orwell* (Weidenfeld & Nicolson, London, 1971).
58. Wells, *The Island of Doctor Moreau*, Chapter 16.
59. 'Politics versus Literature', *CEJL* 4, 57.
60. V. S. Pritchett, *New Statesman*, 28 January 1950.

PART II

1. Stansky and Abrahams, *The Unknown Orwell*, 224–5.
2. Ibid., 247.
3. Ibid., 223.
4. Orwell, *RWP*, Chapter 9.
5. Stansky and Abrahams, *The Unknown Orwell*, 200.
6. *CEJL* 4, 115.
7. Stansky and Abrahams, *The Unknown Orwell*, 194–5.
8. *CEJL* 1, 18.
9. Woodcock, 271.
10. *CEJL* 1, 20.
11. *CEJL* 1, 59.
12. *CEJL* 1, 84.
13. Cf. his essays 'A Hanging' and 'Shooting an Elephant', and Chapter 9 of *The Road to Wigan Pier*.
14. *Burmese Days*, Chapter 5.
15. *CEJL* 4, 86.
16. Hollis, Christopher, *George Orwell*, 37.
17. Buddicom, Jacintha, *Eric And Us* (Leslie Frewin, 1974), 38–9, 150.
18. *CEJL* 1, 55.
19. *CEJL* 1, 58.
20. *CEJL* 1, 60.
21. Cf. the character 'Ginger' in the essay 'Hop-Picking'.
22. *CEJL* 1, 60. Cf. the description of the 'High Cross Preparatory School' in H. G. Wells's novel *Joan and Peter* (1918).
23. Hollis, Christopher, *George Orwell*, 62.
24. *CEJL* 3, 24.
25. *CEJL* 4, 56.
26. *CEJL* 1, 62.
27. Ibid.
28. *CEJL* 1, 72.
29. Cf. *KAF*, Chapter 3: ' "Gordon", "Colin", "Malcolm", "Donald" – these are the gifts of Scotland to the world, along with golf, whisky, porridge, and the works of Barrie and Stevenson.'
30. Woodcock, 119.
31. Stansky and Abrahams, *Orwell: The Transformation*, 117.
32. Gissing, George, *The Private Papers of Henry Ryecroft*, 'Spring', VIII.
33. Rees, Richard, *George Orwell*, 36.
34. *CEJL* 1, 74.
35. Preface to the first edition of *RWP*.
36. Cf. *The Road to Wigan Pier Diary*, 15–21 February.
37. In *Inside the Whale and Other Essays*.
38. Cf. 'Some Thoughts on the Common Toad', *CEJL* 4, 40.
39. Jenni Calder, *Chronicles of Conscience: A Study of George Orwell and Arthur Koestler*.
40. *DOPL*, Chapter 25; *HTC*, Chapter 1.
41. Cf. H. G. Wells, *Experiment in Autobiography*, Chapter 3 §2: 'So much for

the Hitlerite stage of my development, when I was a . . . pasty-faced little English Nazi.'
42. Cf. Stansky and Abrahams, *The Unknown Orwell*, Part Four.
43. *RWP*, Part One, 1.
44. 'Why I Write'.
45. Tom Hopkinson, *George Orwell*; Laurence Brander, *George Orwell*.
46. Woodcock, 126.
47. *HTC*, Chapter 8.
48. Ibid.
49. Ibid.
50. 'Why I Write'.
51. Woodcock, 134.
52. *HTC*, Chapter 8.
53. 'Looking Back on the Spanish War', *CEJL* 2, 41.
54. *HTC*, Chapter 8.
55. Wells, H. G., *Tono-Bungay*, Book 1, Chapter 1, §3.
56. *CEJL* 1, 128.
57. *CEJL* 1, 144.
58. Wells, H. G., *The War of the Worlds*, Book 2, Chapter 7.
59. *CEJL*, Volume 4, 115.
60. Wells, H. G., *The World of William Clissold*, 'A Note Before the Title-Page'.
61. For Orwell's own views on distancing see his letter to T. R. Fyvel on the subject, *CEJL*, 4, 153.
62. *CUA*, Part Two, 3.
63. Ibid., Part Two, 7.
64. *CEJL* 2, 7.
65. *CEJL* 3, 5.
66. *CEJL* 4, 115.
67. *CUA*, Part Two, 4.
68. *CEJL* 2, 7.
69. *CEJL* 4, 115.
70. *CEJL* 1, 159.
71. 'Why I Write'.
72. *CEJL* 3, 110.
73. Brander, Laurence, *George Orwell* (Longmans, 1954), 170.
74. Warburg, Fredric, *All Authors Are Equal* (Hutchinson, 1973), 58.
75. *CEJL* 4, 29.
76. 17 December 1947, Berg Collection, New York Public Library.
77. Richard Adams's *Watership Down* (1972), an allegory in which rabbits are cast in the leading roles, has enjoyed a similar critical and popular acclaim.
78. *CEJL* 4, 86.
79. Cf. H. G. Wells, *The Island of Doctor Moreau*, Chapter 15: '. . . each preserved the quality of its particular species: the human mark distorted but did not hide the leopard, the ox, or the sow, or other animal or animals, from which the creature had been moulded . . . every now and then the beast would flash out upon me beyond doubt or denial'.
80. Buddicom, Jacintha, *Eric and Us* (Leslie Frewin, 1974), 148.

81. 'Why I Write'.
82. Greenblatt, Stephen J., 'Orwell as Satirist'. Included in *George Orwell: A Collection of Critical Essays* (Prentice-Hall, 1974).
83. *CEJL* 4, 85.
84. Quoted by Michael Glenny in the Introduction to the Penguin edition of *We* (1972).
85. *CEJL* 2, 11.
86. Cf. especially Chapter 20 of *When the Sleeper Wakes*, 'In the City Ways'. The revised edition of 1910, *The Sleeper Awakes*, is considerably abridged.
87. *CEJL* 4, 158.
88. Thomas, Edward M., *Orwell*, 83.
89. *CEJL* 4, 158.
90. *CEJL* 4, 131.
91. *CEJL* 3, 64.
92. *CEJL* 4, 159.
93. 'George Orwell' in *Principles and Persuasions*, 150–9.
94. *CEJL* 4, 46.
95. For Orwell's indebtedness to Swift see his essay 'Politics versus Literature', *CEJL* 4, 57.
96. *CEJL* 4, 64 and 4, 88. Cf. Zwerdling, Alex, *Orwell and the Left* (Yale University Press, 1974) 104: 'the conflict between optimism and pessimism is evident throughout Orwell's career, and his fundamentally pessimistic cast of mind was constantly at war with his socialism'.
97. Orwell to Warburg, *CEJL* 4, 125; Orwell to Powell, *CEJL* 4, 128.
98. *CEJL* 1, 49.
99. It is interesting to compare Part Two, 2 with *KAF*, Chapter 7.
100. For a discussion of the relationship between the four novels see Steinhoff, William, *The Road to 1984* (Weidenfeld & Nicolson, 1975) passim. The influence of Zamyatin on Orwell is discussed in Deutscher, Isaac, '1984 – The Mysticism of Cruelty' in Williams (ed.), *George Orwell: A Collection of Critical Essays* and in Woodcock, 167–72.

PART III

1. *CEJL* 2, 7.
2. Cf. Orwell's essay 'George Gissing', *CEJL* 4, 119.
3. *CEJL* 1, 165.
4. Cf. Gissing's comments in *The Private Papers of Henry Ryecroft*, Autumn, XXI: 'Many biographical sketches have I read . . . but never one in which there was a hint of stern struggle, of the pinched stomach and frozen fingers. I surmise that the path of "literature" is being made too easy.'
5. *CEJL* 1, 165.
6. Cf. H. G. Wells, *Anticipations* (1900), Chapter 3: 'Developing Social Elements', for an interesting forecast of the emergence of this new class.
7. Woodcock, 205.
8. *New Statesman*, 25 January 1941.
9. 'George Orwell and the Politics of Truth', included in Raymond Williams (ed.), *George Orwell*.

10. See Crick, 402.
11. Stansky and Abrahams, *The Unknown Orwell*, 166.
12. *CEJL* 1, 79.
13. Woodcock, 96.
14. *CEJL* 1, 135.
15. *CEJL* 4, 85.
16. Cf. Buddicom, Jacintha, *Eric and Us*, Chapter 5, 'Were Such the Joys?'
17. These quotations are taken from 'As I Please' articles reprinted in *CEJL* as follows: 3, 12; 3, 16; 3, 27; 4, 65; 4, 81.

Select Bibliography

THE WORKS OF GEORGE ORWELL

Orwell's works are available in a uniform edition published by
Secker & Warburg, London. The following titles are available:

Animal Farm
Burmese Days
A Clergyman's Daughter
*Collected Essays**
Coming Up For Air
Down and Out in Paris and London
Homage to Catalonia
Keep the Aspidistra Flying
*The Lion and the Unicorn**
Nineteen Eighty-Four
The Road to Wigan Pier

The same titles, with the exception of those marked with an
asterisk, are also published by Penguin Books.

Two collections of essays, *Inside the Whale and Other Essays*, and
Decline of the English Murder and Other Essays, are available in
editions published by Penguin Books.

Collected Essays is also available in a paperback edition published by Secker & Warburg, London.

The Orwell Reader: fiction, essays and reportage by George Orwell
(Harcourt Brace, New York, 1956) edited by Richard Rovere,
contains a representative selection of the various facets of his
work.

LETTERS

The Collected Essays, Journalism and Letters of George Orwell. Edited by Sonia Orwell and Ian Angus. (Secker & Warburg, London, 1968, and Penguin Books, 1970.)

Volume 1: An Age Like This, 1920–1940
Volume 2: My Country Right or Left, 1940–1943
Volume 3: As I Please, 1943–1945
Volume 4: In Front of Your Nose, 1945–1950

This collection makes no claim to be definitive, but it does include a generous selection of the letters written by Orwell at various stages of his life. The editors make it clear that they 'have not set out to make an academic monument because neither his work nor his personality lends itself to such treatment and the period he lived in is too recent for any real history to have been written of it'.

BIBLIOGRAPHY

'George Orwell: A Selected Bibliography' by Zoltang Zeke and William White in *Bulletin of Bibliography* XXIII (Boston, Mass., May 1961).

'Orwelliana: A Checklist' by Zoltang Zeke and William White in *Bulletin of Bibliography* XXIII (Boston, Mass., September 1961 and January 1962).

'George Orwell: A Bibliography' by J. Meyers in *Bulletin of Bibliography* XXXI (Boston, Mass., July 1974).

BIOGRAPHY

Eric And Us: A Remembrance of George Orwell, by Jacintha Buddicom (Leslie Frewin, London, 1974). This is a sympathetic account of Orwell's boyhood and in particular of his friendship with the Buddicom family during the years 1914–22. It is particularly valuable for its insight into the Blair family background at Henley and Shiplake and for the evidence it offers of Orwell's early literary ambitions. There is much interesting material on his boyhood reading and on the literary influences which helped to shape his distinctive style and approach. The volume also contains three early poems and a number of hitherto unpublished letters.

The Unknown Orwell, by Peter Stansky and William Abrahams (Constable, London, 1972). This is a scholarly study of the first thirty years of Orwell's life, from his birth in 1903 to the publication of *Down and. Out in Paris and London* in 1933. The book owes its origin to a remark by Sir Richard Rees (a close friend of Orwell's) who observed: 'if you want to understand Orwell, you have to understand Blair'. The authors have painstakingly researched his school days at St Cyprian's and at Eton, his years in Burma, and the laborious literary apprenticeship he underwent in Paris and London before the publication of his first book.

As a study of the process through which Eric Blair became George Orwell the book is unlikely to be superseded. It is indispensable not only for its account of Orwell's life and times but also for its insight into his complex and reticent personality. The writers were assisted in their task by Orwell's sister and by friends who knew him in the years before he became a successful writer.

Orwell: The Transformation, by Peter Stansky and William Abrahams (Constable, London, 1979). Continuing at the point where *The Unknown Orwell* leaves off, this is a detailed study of Orwell's life during the period 1933–6, years in which 'a self-absorbed minor novelist with little or no interest in politics became an important writer with a view and a mission and a message'. It is particularly valuable for its account of his friendships during this crucial period and for the sensitive portrayal of his wife and her influence on his career. The book contains a full account of the background to the writing of *The Road to Wigan Pier* and *Homage to Catalonia* and of the decisive impact of the Spanish Civil War upon his attitudes and concerns as a writer.

George Orwell: A Life, by Bernard Crick (Secker & Warburg, London, 1980). This is the first full biography of Orwell and the first to have unlimited rights of quotation from his published and unpublished work. It does not claim in any sense to be an 'official' biography, nor does it claim to be definitive.

Bernard Crick has achieved an extremely readable and straightforward account of Orwell's life and times which includes generous extracts from his letters and from interviews with those who knew him. He deliberately eschews the English biographical tradition with its 'fine writing, balanced appraisal and psychological insight' and concentrates instead on presenting the story of 'how his books and essays came to be written and of how they were published'. The result is a fascinating and erudite biography which illuminates Orwell's own writings and helps the reader to understand the complexities of his life and friendships. The book is copiously annotated and has an excellent critical introduction which summarises his achievement.

Orwell requested in his will that no biography of him should be written. It was inevitable, however, that one would be attempted and it is to be hoped that Crick's will not be the last. Orwell still awaits his Boswell.

CRITICISM

Tom Hopkinson, *George Orwell* (Longman, London, 1953, latest revision 1977, 'Writers and Their Work' series). This is a concise introduction to Orwell and his work written by a distinguished editor and novelist. Not all readers will agree with some of the author's critical judgements (e.g., '*The Road to Wigan Pier* is Orwell's worst book') but as an introduction the study is useful and succinct. There is an excellent bibliography of books by and about Orwell.

John Atkins, *George Orwell: A Literary Study* (Calder & Boyars, London, 1954, revised edition, 1971). The author, a personal friend of Orwell, has here attempted a critical study of Orwell's *ideas*, tracing the main developments in his thinking and attitudes at each stage in his career. The book is of considerable interest not only because of Atkins's personal recollections but also because of the extensive quotations from Orwell's unreprinted journalism. Despite its apparent lack of organisation and the absence of an index, this is an indispensable study of Orwell from an intellectual rather than a literary standpoint. The revised edition includes a detailed additional section summarising Orwell's achievement and his influence on the world of ideas since his death.

Christopher Hollis, *A Study of George Orwell: The Man and his Works* (Hollis and Carter, London, 1956). This is a perceptive and stimulating study of Orwell's life and works written from a Roman Catholic standpoint. The author was a contemporary of Orwell's at Eton and is therefore able to write of his school days with an intimate knowledge. The chapters appraising the principal books and essays contain much shrewd criticism and, whilst later scholarship – in particular the researches of Stansky and Abrahams – has superseded his biographical account in a number of important respects, the book still has much to offer as a comprehensive portrait of Orwell as man and writer.

Sir Richard Rees, *George Orwell: Fugitive from the Camp of Victory* (Secker & Warburg, London, 1961). The author of this study was editor of *Adelphi* from 1930 to 1936 and met Orwell as a young contributor. Whilst the book aims to be an introductory outline only, it has the inestimable advantage of having been written by one who knew Orwell and worked closely with him. The study is particularly valuable for its insight into Orwell's fundamental attitudes and beliefs and for its sensitive understanding of the forces which helped to mould his distinctive outlook.

Edward M. Thomas, *Orwell* (Oliver and Boyd, Edinburgh and London, 1965, 'Writers and Critics' series). The author of this study, whilst providing an overview of Orwell's life and achievement, concentrates in particular on Orwell as polemicist and essayist. In doing so Mr Thomas demonstrates the unity between the themes which dominated his life and the literary forms he chose to use at the height of his powers. The author argues that Orwell's essays possess considerable literary merit and that in these he made a permanent contribution to English letters.

B. T. Oxley, *George Orwell* (Evans Brothers, London, 1967, 'Literature in Perspective' series). This is a concise introduction to Orwell's principal writings and basic attitudes and a useful attempt to place him in context against the background of the political and intellectual trends of his time. The author demonstrates that throughout his literary career Orwell was deeply concerned with the careful use of language and with the position of the writer in an age of intellectual ferment. It should be read alongside the study by E. M. Thomas as an introduction to the main elements in Orwell's work and a summary of his contribution to modern thought.

George Woodcock, *The Crystal Spirit: A Study of George Orwell* (Jonathan Cape, London, 1967). *The Crystal Spirit* is now acknowledged as the definitive critical work on Orwell and it is unlikely to be superseded as a study of the writer in all his aspects. The author, a critic and poet who worked closely with Orwell during the last decade of his life, examines his contribution as a man, a novelist, a patriot, and a stylist. The book is especially valuable as a study of the diverse, even contradictory elements which together made up Orwell's personality: 'gregarious but shy, gentle yet angry, quixotic yet a spartan moralist'. The sections which summarise the novels, non-fiction and essays are notable for their clarity and acute understanding, whilst the entire work is suffused with sympathetic insight. *The Crystal Spirit* is indispensable as an appraisal of Orwell's strengths and weaknesses and his unique place in twentieth-century literature.

Jenni Calder, *Chronicles of Conscience: A Study of George Orwell and Arthur Koestler* (Secker & Warburg, London, 1968). This is a stimulating and erudite study of Orwell which traces both his contemporary influence and his continuing impact on twentieth-century political thought. The author demonstrates that although the social and intellectual climate in which *Animal Farm* and *Nineteen Eighty-Four* were written is now vastly different, these and Orwell's other writings continue to have relevance for our times. The study brings together social, political and literary criticism to demonstrate the enduring qualities in Orwell's work and his influence upon his contemporaries. The author reveals a shrewd grasp of her subject and of the issues which dominated his life and times.

Robert A. Lee, *Orwell's Fiction* (University of Notre Dame Press, Indiana, 1969). The author of this study argues that Orwell's fiction has been consistently underrated and that his novels merit critical attention *as novels* rather than as political tracts. He examines each work of fiction through a process of detailed textual analysis, demonstrating their coherence and validity within the context of his literary career. Dr Lee's thesis throughout is that the novels must first be approached from a literary standpoint before their symbolic, social or political significance can be fully understood. There is an excellent scholarly apparatus including detailed references and a comprehensive bibliography of primary and secondary sources.

Raymond Williams, *Orwell* (Fontana/Collins, London, 1971, 'Fontana Modern Masters' series). This is an admirably succinct introduction to Orwell and his works which concentrates on the ideas and political beliefs underlying his writings. The author argues that Orwell was responsible for 'a remarkable enlargement of our literature – one that reveals fundamental questions about the identity of the writer in relation to himself, his society, and the literary forms he uses'. Williams is particularly stimulating on the changes which took place in Orwell's political attitudes as a result of the Spanish Civil War and the manner in which this shift in opinion manifests itself in *Animal Farm* and *Nineteen Eighty-Four*. Though some readers may find Williams's polemical approach too abrasive, this study is essential to a full understanding of Orwell as an ideological writer.

Miriam Gross (editor), *The World of George Orwell* (Weidenfeld & Nicolson, London, 1971). This is a collection of essays by many different writers which aims to discuss Orwell 'both in terms of what he means today and as a man whose achievement needs to be set in the context of his own period'. The essays cover the main aspects of his life from his childhood to the writing of *Nineteen Eighty-Four* and the book as a whole does succeed in presenting a composite portrait of Orwell in his strengths and weaknesses. One of its most valuable features is the excellent selection of contemporary photographs which help to place Orwell in the context of his life and times.

Raymond Williams (editor), *George Orwell: A Collection of Critical Essays* (Prentice-Hall, New Jersey, 1974, 'Twentieth Century Views' series). This anthology of scholarly essays on various aspects of Orwell's work is an excellent contribution to Orwell studies. The contributions range over many aspects of his life and achievement including his stature as a novelist, observation and imagination, the politics of truth, polemics, satire, and post-war prophecy. In his introduction the editor provides an overview of Orwell and of critical responses to his work.

Alex Zwerdling, *Orwell and the Left* (Yale University Press, New Haven and London, 1974). The theme of this excellent critical study is the evolution of Orwell's political ideas from the beginnings of his literary career to *Nineteen Eighty-Four*. The author demonstrates that his experiments in a variety of genres – realistic novel, documentary, essay, allegory and science-fiction – were all attempts to 'make political writing into an art', and illuminates the close links between Orwell's writings and his political ideals. Zwerdling's analysis of the major works and essays is stimulating and original. The study is particularly valuable for its insight into the development of Orwell's ideological thought and for the skilful way in which he is placed in context against the background of the English political tradition.

Jeffrey Meyers, *A Reader's Guide to George Orwell* (Thames and Hudson, London, 1975). This is an excellently written and produced guide to Orwell's works, tracing in chronological order the developments in his work and thought. The author's approach is thorough and scholarly and there is a comprehensive bibliography of critical books and articles. Strongly recommended.

Jeffrey Meyers (editor), *Orwell: The Critical Heritage* (Routledge & Kegan Paul, London, 1975). This is a collection of contemporary criticism of Orwell's fiction, ranging from *Down and Out in Paris and London* to the *Collected Essays, Journalism and Letters*.

Christopher Small, *The Road to Miniluv: George Orwell, the State, and God* (Victor Gollancz, London, 1975). In this illuminating study the author asserts that 'although Orwell's novels are in many essentials very much the same, they exhibit a clear sequence, as linked parts of a continuous movement, or journey'. In common with Christopher Hollis, Small argues that his major works had their origins in his religious conflicts. His analysis concentrates in particular on *Animal Farm* and *Nineteen Eighty-Four* but also ranges widely over the whole field of Orwell's writings. It is possible to disagree totally with many of Small's critical judgements whilst being simultaneously enriched by the abundant insights his study contains.

Burgess, Anthony, *1985* (Hutchinson, London, 1978). In this detailed and brilliantly written critique of *Nineteen Eighty-Four* the author challenges many of the intellectual assumptions on which the novel is based. He demonstrates that the type of society postulated by Orwell is inherently improbable and concludes that 'As a projection of a possible future, Orwell's vision has a purely fragmentary validity'. This is a stimulating and thought-provoking essay which should be widely read.

CRITICAL ARTICLES

Richard Hoggart, 'George Orwell and *The Road to Wigan Pier*' in *Critical Quarterly* VII (1965) 72–85. Also reprinted in Hoggart, Richard: *Speaking to Each Other*, Volume Two (Penguin Books, London, 1973).

Paul Potts, 'Don Quixote on a Bicycle: In Memoriam, George Orwell, 1903–1950' in *London Magazine* IV (March 1957) 39–47.

Anthony Powell, 'George Orwell: A Memoir' in *Atlantic Monthly* CCXX (October 1967) 62–8.

John Wain, 'George Orwell' in *Essays on Literature and Ideas* (Macmillan: London, 1963).

Anthony West, 'George Orwell' in *Principles and Persuasions* (Eyre & Spottiswoode: London, 1958).

ADDITIONAL RECOMMENDATIONS

Malcolm Bradbury, *The Social Context of Modern English Literature* (Basil Blackwell, 1971).

Cyril Connolly, *Enemies of Promise* (Routledge & Kegan Paul, 1938, and Penguin Books, 1961).

Rayner Heppenstall, *Four Absentees* (Barrie and Rockliff, 1960).

Paul Potts, *Dante Called You Beatrice* (Eyre & Spottiswoode, 1961).

William Steinhoff, *The Road to 1984* (Weidenfeld & Nicolson, 1975).

Julian Symons, *The Angry Thirties* (Eyre Methuen, 1976).

Fredric Warburg, *All Authors Are Equal* (Hutchinson, 1973).

Index